FROM FLOOD TO FALLEN KINGDOMS

FSC
www.fsc.org
MIX
Paperi vastuul-
lisista lähteistä
Paper from
responsible sources
FSC® C105338

From Flood to Fallen Kingdoms

A Biblical-Creationist History
of the Ancient Near East

New Short Introduction

By

Jarno Moilanen Th.M.

Fourth edition

From Flood to Fallen Kingdoms
A Biblical-Creationist History of the Ancient Near East: New Short Introduction

4th edition

© 2025 Jarno Moilanen

Published by BoD · Books on Demand, Mannerheimintie 12 B, 00100 Helsinki, Finland
bod@bod.fi
Printed by Libri Plureos GmbH, Friedensallee 273, 22763 Hamburg, Germany

ISBN: 978-952-80-8491-4

CONTENTS

APPENDICES

CHART 1: MESOPOTAMIA AND SURROUNDING AREAS AFTER THE DISPERSAL AT BABEL C. 2215 B.C.
CHART 2: COMPARATIVE STRATIGRAPHY OF TELL ARPACHIYAH, NINEVEH AND TELL HASSUNA
CHART 3: PALESTINE FROM THE CONQUEST OF THE LAND BY THE ISRAELITES UNTIL ALEXANDER THE GREAT
CHART 4: KINGS OF ISIN, LARSA AND BABYLON C. 1600–1480 B.C.

INTRODUCTION

Everyone should understand the fact that ancient history cannot be observed. The events from long time ago are already gone and will never repeat themselves. Past times just do not exist anymore. Can we observe and experience, that is to say, really prove something that does not exist anymore? Of course we cannot. That is why we are totally dependent on trusting our own interpretations and the external authorities that we choose for ourselves.

Trusting, or believing, is a human limit above which no student of ancient history can rise. In other words, history can be grasped only through faith — to have a view of history means to have an unprovable belief of history, no matter how well-reasoned the view is. To reconstruct/interpret/imagine historical events inside a head is not the same thing as seeing to the past and proving it. Unfortunately, many people do not understand this, and they deceive themselves and others by continually claiming that their historical views are not beliefs but scientific facts that no reasonable person should deny.

But what should we believe then? History does not exist anymore for us, but it still does exist for the eternal God, the almighty Creator of the universe, who is above time. If we wish to get a good understanding of the ancient times, and especially the ancient times of the Near East, we must found our interpretations and views on His own testimonies which are recorded in the Holy Bible, the inspired and inerrant book of God who cannot lie. Being grounded in this solid starting point I have now written a brief introduction to the history of the ancient Near East that is in agreement with the biblical timeline according to which the world was created about 6,000 years ago. I have tried to draw up a clear narrative which begins with the creation of the world and the great flood of Noah and then flows through the post-flood centuries to the end of the Old Testament time. The biblical storyline serves as the main road of history along which, as the journey progresses, the most important archaeological and cultural periods are explained in a simple and understandable way and set in their right chronological places. I have made use of the best available scholarly literature, Christian as well as secular, and argued that ancient history and archaeology are not in conflict with the Bible as long as they are understood and dated correctly.

Perhaps not many nonbelievers will be immediately convinced, but I am sure that this book will strengthen the faith of numerous believing readers who take the Holy Scriptures seriously. They will also be surprised to see how well the first five post-flood centuries, from Ararat to Abraham, which until now have been in great darkness, can be elucidated through proper interpretation of biblical and archaeological evidence.

My work would not have been possible without the previous contributions of many great scholars from whom I have learnt a lot and whose works I often refer to. Many thanks to them, and great praise to God for leading me to the best sources. When I started my research many years ago, I had no idea that I would someday complete a book like this. I have been very blessed. But still many things need more investigation, and errors correction. I strongly believe, however, that the overall picture of the ancient Near Eastern history (from the biblical-creationist perspective) is already very secure.

Finally, as an important advice to the reader, I suggest that he or she will always keep the chronological charts, appended to the end of this book, at their fingertips while they are reading through the chapters. But without waiting any longer, let's now begin our journey on a road of history during which we will learn a lot of new things about the ancient Near East. Dear Lord, please give light to our way and lead us to the truth; thank You for leading us to the truth. Amen.

Your word *is* a lamp to my feet
And a light to my path.

Ps 119:105 NKJV

CHAPTER 1: FROM THE BEGINNING TO THE FLOOD

In the beginning God created the heavens and the earth, the whole existing world (Gen 1:1).[1] He created everything in six days approximately 6,000 years ago, or 4000 B.C.[2] The first man and woman, Adam and Eve, were created on the sixth day (Gen 1:26–27).[3]

The whole creation was very good (Gen 1:31), and the life of Adam and Eve was perfectly happy in the garden which God had planted for them (Gen 2:8). Death or any suffering did not exist yet. After a while, however, Adam and Eve ate from a tree which God had forbidden (Gen 2:16–17; 3:6, 11, 17). In this manner the first man and woman violated God's will, that is to say, they sinned for the first time. This tragic event is known as "the fall of man/humankind".

The sin broke the perfect relationship and friendship that had been between the human couple and God. As a result of the fall man (including both man and woman) became mortal (Gen 2:17; 3:16–19). Death and suffering became now the reality for animals too. Because of the sin the original perfect purity and goodness of mankind was corrupted. Since the fall all kinds of evil things, errors and sufferings have entered the world: hatred,

---

[1] "To the question whether God used preexistent material to create the universe or rather he created it 'out of nothing' (the early Jewish-Christian doctrine of *creatio ex nihilo*, first explicitly occurring in 2 Macc 7:28; and see Rom 4:17; Heb 11:3), it must be admitted that Gen 1 neither precludes nor defends the possibility, and we must look elsewhere for data to decide the issue. However, such a concept is not false to the intent of Gen 1. Indeed, had we an opportunity to pose the question to the author of this text, we may assume with Westermann [1994, 108] and others that he would 'certainly have decided in favor of *creatio ex nihilo*.'" Arnold 2009, 35, 36. — "Regardless of how one reads [Gen]1:1–3, there is no room in our author's cosmology for co-eternal matter with God when we consider the theology of the creation account in its totality [...] Verse 1 declares that God exists outside time and space; all that exists is dependent on his independent will." Mathews 1996, 139. See also Collins 2006, 50–55; Day 2013, 6–9; 2022, 1–13; Chambers 2020. On the question how to correctly understand the verse 1 and its relation to verses 2 and 3 (or 2–31) see Young 1959; 1964a, 48; 1964b, 1–14; Fruchtenbaum 2009, 27 (the description of Young's view). — "The creation was a free and voluntary act of God. Scripture explains: 'He does whatever He pleases' (Psalm 115:3). Has God created or is He still creating other worlds? Scripture has not revealed this to us, so such a question cannot be answered. The Bible speaks of the creation of the world in which we now live." Koehler 2006, 73. Almost certainly, in my view, our created universe is the only one there is.

[2] A more precise estimate is 4004 B.C. See Floyd Nolen Jones (2015), *The Chronology of the Old Testament*, ix, 26–29, and Chart 1 and Chart 6 in the CD-ROM; see also Sarfati 2003; Freeman 2008; Cosner 2013; Hardy & Carter 2014; Sexton 2015; 2018; Day 2013, 3, 4. Floyd Nolen Jones' chronology strongly supports Archbishop James Ussher's chronology which is presented in his classic 17th-century work *The Annals of the World* (new updated edition published in 2003). In this book I have adopted Jones' year numbers for the important persons and events of the Old Testament.

[3] On the scientific evidence for the existence of Adam and Eve see for example Jeanson & Tomkins 2016; Sanford 2018.

envy, theft, murder, idolatry, witchcraft, atheism, drunkenness, adultery, fornication, war, oppression, slavery, hunger, sickness, sorrow, depression, loneliness. Indeed, the world has changed a lot from the original good condition that was in the beginning.

After the fall Adam and Eve began to have children. At first their children had to marry with each other because there were no other people in the world.[4] During the following centuries the number of people increased substantially (Gen 4; 5). But as the number of people increased so increased also the amount of sin, and the earth was filled with corruption and violence (Gen 4:8, 23; 6:1–4, 11–12). Then God grieved greatly that he had created man and decided to destroy the land everywhere and to wipe off all its inhabitants, including animals (Gen 6:5–7, 13). Of all the living people only Noah, a righteous believing man who found grace before God (Gen 6:8–9; 7:1), and his family would get deliverance.

God told Noah to build a wooden ark, a kind of large covered boat approximately 450 feet (137 meters) long, 75 feet (23 meters) wide and 45 feet (14 meters) high, inside which Noah's family and selected animals could survive through the determined devastation, the great flood (Gen 6:14–21). Noah's family consisted of his wife, his three sons and their three wives, eight persons altogether. God also caused seven pairs from each ritually clean animal kind and a pair from each ritually unclean animal kind, males and females, to come to Noah and go inside the ark. These were all air-breathing, land-dwelling animals (including birds) which could not have survived over the flood by themselves. The total number of animals inside the ark was probably only a few thousand.[5]

---

[4] God gave the law forbidding intermarriage between close relatives only much later, at the time of Moses about 2,500 years after the creation of Adam and Eve. Even Abraham (about 2,100 years after the creation) was married to his half-sister, Sarah (Gen 20:12). In those early times the number of genetic defects was still very low, so there was no great danger of serious biological problems in the offspring of brother-sister unions, unless close inbreeding continued over many generations.

[5] See Jonathan D. Sarfati (2015), *The Genesis Account*, 516; Ken Ham & Bodie Hodge (2016), *A Flood of Evidence*, 209–217; Froman (ed.) 2016. How could Noah's family and all the animals inside the ark stay alive during and immediately after the flood? For a comprehensive study answering this and related questions see John Woodmorappe (1997), *Noah's Ark: A Feasibility Study*. See also Laura Welch (ed.) (2016), *Inside Noah's Ark: Why It Worked*.

The flood started (approximately) 1,656 years after the creation of the world or 2348 B.C. when Noah was 600 years old (Gen 7:6):[6]

> Now the flood was on the earth forty days. The waters increased and lifted up the ark, and it rose high above the earth. The waters prevailed and greatly increased on the earth, and the ark moved about on the surface of the waters. And the waters prevailed exceedingly on the earth, and all the high hills under the whole heaven were covered. The waters prevailed fifteen cubits upward, and the mountains were covered. And all flesh died that moved on the earth: birds and cattle and beasts and every creeping thing that creeps on the earth, and every man. All in whose nostrils *was* the breath of the spirit of life, all that *was* on the dry *land,* died. So He destroyed all living things which were on the face of the ground: both man and cattle, creeping thing and bird of the air. They were destroyed from the earth. Only Noah and those who *were* with him in the ark remained *alive.* And the waters prevailed on the earth one hundred and fifty days. (Gen 7:17–24 NKJV)

This worldwide cataclysm lasted a little more than a year (Gen 7:11; 8:14) and killed all the people save Noah and his family. It also totally devastated the then-existing land and completely changed the geography all around the world. An enormous amount of plant material and billions of dead aquatic and terrestrial animals (and people) were buried in water-carried mud and sand which formed thick and wide sedimentary deposits which then slowly hardened into rock during the centuries after the flood. When plants and animals were buried in those sediments the world over, huge numbers of them were fossilized or turned into fossil fuels (coal, oil and natural gas).[7]

Many powerful geological and physical processes took place during the days of the great flood. It was then that almost all of Earth's radioactive material was produced naturally inside the continental granite crust. There occurred also extremely fast decay among the new radioactive atoms which fissioned (broke into many parts) and produced their "daughter atoms". During the flood, when "all the fountains of the great deep" were

---

[6] See Jones 2015, ix, 278 and Chart 6 in the CD-ROM. — "According to the existing text [of the Book of Genesis], the Flood began in the year 1656 after the creation and ended in 1657." Cassuto 1961, 252. See also Sailhamer 2008, 111, 112; Hendel 2024, 254.

[7] For an exhaustive study of the chronology and historicity of the flood see Steven W. Boyd & Andrew A. Snelling (eds.) (2014), *Grappling with the Chronology of the Genesis Flood.* See also, for example, John Morris (2007), *The Young Earth*; Michael J. Oard & John K. Reed (eds.) (2009), *Rock Solid Answers*; Andrew A. Snelling (2014), *Earth's Catastrophic Past*; John K. Reed (2014), *Rocks Aren't Clocks*; Michael J. Oard & John K. Reed (2017), *How Noah's Flood Shaped Our Earth.*

open (Gen 7:11 NKJV), large amounts of those new radioactive as well as non-radioactive isotopes[8] were transferred by water and dirt from deep inside the crust up to the surface. Finally, they ended up inside the sedimentary layers of mud and sand which later hardened into rock. Volcanic rocks contain those same elements too because molten magma rises towards the surface of the earth through the granite crust and the sedimentary rocks.[9]

Scientists who believe that Earth is billions of years old think that they can determine the age of a rock[10] by first measuring the sample's parent-daughter (e.g. potassium-40 and argon-40) isotope ratio and then calculating (by applying the present-day decay rate) how much time has passed since the rock solidified from the molten state. But those same scientists must assume that (1) the decay rate has always been as extremely slow as observed today, (2) the amount of parent and daughter elements in the original, newly solidified sample can be known, and (3) no parent or daughter atoms were lost or added to the sample over time. None of these assumptions is provable by real scientific testing.[11]

Relative concentrations, or ratios, of parent and daughter atoms can be measured very accurately from samples of rock, but those ratios are not applicable to radiometric dating because the daughter atoms did not come from their radioactive parent atoms over millions and billions of years — in reality most of the parent and the daughter atoms came into being practically at the same time, during the flood, and then they were rationed inside the sedimentary and volcanic rocks more or less randomly. Thus, in the light of the real origin of Earth's radioactive isotopes and their daughter products, it is

---

[8] Isotopes are atoms of the same element with differing numbers of neutrons in their nuclei.

[9] See "The Origin of Earth's Radioactivity", a chapter in the continually updated online edition of Walt Brown's *In the Beginning: Compelling Evidence for Creation and the Flood*; creationscience.com/onlinebook/Radioactivity.html. The highly simplified description in the main text above is based on that chapter. Most creationist scientists do not endorse Brown's theory (that the formation of Earth's radioactive material and its fast decay occurred both during the flood), but I think he may very well be right.

[10] Usually only volcanic (igneous) rocks are dated, not sedimentary rocks for certain reasons.

[11] See also, for example, Don Batten et al. (2012), *The Creation Answers Book*, 73, 74.

totally pointless to try to determine ages of rocks through analyzing their elemental compositions.[12]

Radiocarbon (or carbon-14, or ^{14}C) has been used to determine ages of organic remains of once-living plants and animals (particularly at archaeological sites) which are thought to be under 100,000 years old. For many reasons, however, radiocarbon dating is very unreliable.[13]

Radiocarbon is formed in high altitudes of Earth's atmosphere where fast-moving free neutrons convert ordinary nitrogen (^{14}N) into carbon isotope ^{14}C. After ^{14}C has been formed it can combine with oxygen to give the carbon dioxide $^{14}CO_2$ which then is absorbed by plants from the air. ^{14}C atoms will get into animals when they eat those plants. People too will get radiocarbon into their body tissues when they eat plants and animals.

Eventually ^{14}C will convert back to ^{14}N. A half of an amount of ^{14}C in a sample of a once-living organism will convert into ^{14}N in approximately 5,730 years. This rate of decay is so fast that after about 100,000 years there should theoretically be no detectable ^{14}C left in any sample. That is why radiocarbon dating cannot give ages of millions of years as other radiometric dating methods claim to do, albeit those dating results are not true (see above). In fact, if a sample contains a detectable amount of ^{14}C (contamination excluded) it positively cannot be millions of years old.

The startling fact is that detectable amounts of radiocarbon have been found inside plant and animal fossils[14] and fossil fuels (coal, oil and natural gas) from all around the world and from all depths. Even diamonds have been found to contain small concentrations of ^{14}C, which is truly amazing if diamonds are really millions or even billions of years old as is popularly believed. Contamination cannot explain these findings away.[15]

---

[12] On radiometric dating methods and their many flaws see also John Woodmorappe (1999), *The Mythology of Modern Dating Methods*; Don DeYoung (2005), *Thousands…Not Billions*; Rupe & Sanford 2019, 269–305.
[13] See Batten et al. 2012, 67–73, 79, 80. But see also Michael A. Cremo & Richard L. Thompson (1998), *Forbidden Archeology*, 764–794.
[14] See for example Brian Thomas & Nelson Vance (2015), *Radiocarbon in Dinosaur and Other Fossils*.
[15] See DeYoung 2005, 48–62. See also Baumgardner 2005.

The small quantities of ^{14}C inside coal, oil and natural gas are even quite uniform throughout the rock deposits of the Earth. Starting with the typical assumptions of the radiocarbon dating (e.g. that the ratio of radiocarbon ^{14}C to ordinary carbon ^{12}C in Earth's biosphere has been relatively constant for tens of thousands of years) the small ^{14}C-contents of these materials can be calculated to ages between 44,000 and 57,000 years, which greatly contradicts what is normally believed about their ages, usually hundreds of millions of years. The uniform distribution of ^{14}C throughout the pre-flood vegetation and animals explains the uniform traces (and "ages") of ^{14}C found at present within fossil fuels and carbon containing rocks.[16]

The fossil materials inside the rock strata are not really 44,000–57,000 years old, however. The ratio of radiocarbon to ordinary carbon (the ^{14}C/^{12}C ratio) in the biosphere was just very low during the centuries before the flood, much lower than today. The great flood which buried the then-existing biomass in the sedimentary layers all around the world happened only about 4,350 years ago.

So, the ^{14}C/^{12}C ratio in the biosphere just before the flood can be roughly estimated from the sedimentary fossil materials. After the flood the ^{14}C/^{12}C ratio increased quite rapidly because more ^{14}C is formed in the atmosphere all the time but the quantity of ^{12}C in the biosphere was vastly reduced by the flood. Other factors like the amount of cosmic rays hitting Earth's atmosphere, the decrease of the strength of Earth's magnetic field, volcanic activity and burning of fossil fuels have also significantly affected the carbon ratio in the course of history.

When organic remains from the immediate post-flood decades and centuries (about 2350 B.C. forward) are radiocarbon dated they may show ages of even tens of thousands of years because the ^{14}C/^{12}C ratio was then generally still much lower than today. Therefore, when ages of archaeological sites of the post-flood centuries are estimated by the radiocarbon dating method the obtained ages are very easily thousands of years older than the real ages of those sites.

---

[16] DeYoung 2005, 58, 59.

However, there are still some important factors which can greatly affect the radiocarbon dating results. Firstly, not all plants take ^{14}C-containing carbon dioxide inside them at the same rate. In other words, plants have different levels of discrimination against ^{14}C. Secondly, the organic remains lying in the earth are not closed systems, so ^{14}C-atoms can leach into an object from outside or they can leak out of it, thus altering the ^{14}C/^{12}C ratio and the obtained age of the sample.[17] For these and other reasons the measured ages may differ a lot from those expected. In fact, "incorrect" dating results are very common, which makes the whole method highly problematic and unreliable, as Robert E. Lee writes:[18]

> The troubles of the radiocarbon dating method are undeniably deep and serious [...] Continuing use of the method depends on a "fix-it-as-we-go" approach, allowing for contamination here, fractionation there, and calibration whenever possible. <u>It should be no surprise, then, that fully half of the dates are rejected. The wonder is, surely, that the remaining half come to be accepted</u> [...] No matter how "useful" it is, though, the radiocarbon method is still not capable of yielding accurate and reliable results. There are <u>gross discrepancies</u>, the chronology is uneven and relative, and <u>the accepted dates are actually selected dates</u>.

In 1969 an international scientific symposium was held in Uppsala, Sweden, on the subject of "Radiocarbon Variations and Absolute Chronology". Torgny Säve-Söderbergh and Ingrid U. Olsson begin their chapter in the proceedings of the symposium with these words:[19]

> C 14 dating was being discussed at a symposium on the prehistory of the Nile Valley. A famous American colleague, Professor Brew, briefly summarized <u>a common attitude among archaeologists</u> towards it, as follows: <u>"If a C 14 date supports our theories, we put it in the main text. If it does not entirely contradict them, we put it in a foot-note. And if it is completely 'out of date', we just drop it."</u> Few archaeologists who have concerned themselves with absolute chronology are innocent of having sometimes applied this method, and many are still hesitant to accept C 14 dates without reservations.

---

[17] It is, however, impossible to know objectively whether a sample's ^{14}C/^{12}C ratio has indeed been changed this way. See Woodmorappe 1999, 41.

[18] Lee 1981, 9, 29. Underlining added. J. G. Ogden wrote in 1977: "It may come as a shock to some, but fewer than 50 percent of the radiocarbon dates from geological and archaeological samples in northeastern North America have been adopted as 'acceptable' by investigators." Ogden 1977, 173.

[19] Säve-Söderbergh & Olsson 1970, 35. Underlining added. See also Bowman 1990, 62.

There are plenty cases of those "out of date" results in scientific literature. For an example, three charred grains of wheat from trench 300, layer 6, of Nahal Oren cave, Israel, were radiocarbon dated. The layer 6, an "extremely hard, stony and brecciated" layer, was thought to be approximately 16,000 years old. However, the first grain was dated over 33,000 years old, but the second grain was dated only 2,940 years old. The third grain was dated 3,100 years old (charred material) and 6,650 years old (humic extract).[20] Surely these measured ages are not reliable. Some kind of change in the carbon ratios could have happened while the grains were lying in the earth, or else they had different $^{14}C/^{12}C$ ratios already when they were still fresh and unburied. Of course both could be true.[21] In any case, in reality those grains were most probably about the same age — in my view from the middle of the 22nd century B.C. (c. 200 years after the flood), approximately.

Sometimes radiocarbon dating can give very absurd results. For example, some modern mollusks have been dated up to 2,300 years old.[22] Some living snails, in turn, were dated even up to 27,000 years old.[23]

It is obvious that radiocarbon dating results are quite arbitrary and thus practically useless in determining the absolute or even the relative ages of ancient organic remains and archaeological sites. In reality the researchers just pick out the "fit" dates and explain away or simply dismiss the "unfit" ones.[24] Such is the dating game. All this is done (by the supposedly objective scientists) to validate the prevailing historical and archaeological views which are based on naturalistic and evolutionistic presuppositions. In contrast the historical view presented in this book is based on the biblical accounts and chronology which are allowed to guide also all archaeological interpretation. Radiometric dating methods are deliberately ignored.

---

[20] See Legge 1986.

[21] A change in carbon ratio through contamination can occur also when the sample is being collected and stored, and during the dating procedure itself.

[22] See Keith & Anderson 1963, 634–637.

[23] See Riggs 1984, 58–61.

[24] This is the truth not only of the radiocarbon dating but of all the other radiometric dating methods too. See for example Woodmorappe 1999; Rupe & Sanford 2019, 287–305.

I hope the following chapters will give a clear and sound Bible-centered survey of the ancient Near Eastern history, an overview which could be able to lift the reader's historical understanding to a new high level and to kindle his or her heart to appreciate and love the Holy Scriptures even more.[25]

---

[25] There exist many excellent scholarly and biblically faithful literary resources which together examine, explain and clarify all kinds of pertinent topics of the first chapters of the Bible (and consequently of the earliest times of the world). Some of those resources have already been named in the previous footnotes (e.g. Woodmorappe 1997, 1999; DeYoung 2005; Boyd & Snelling (eds.) 2014; Snelling 2014; Jones 2015; Sarfati 2015). Besides these see also, for example, Henry M. Morris (2002), *The Biblical Basis for Modern Science*; Terry Mortenson & Thane H. Ury (eds.) (2008), *Coming to Grips with Genesis*; Andrew S. Kulikovsky (2009), *Creation, Fall, Restoration*; Jonathan Sarfati (2011), *Refuting Compromise*; Henry M. Morris III et al. (2013), *Creation Basics and Beyond*; Jason Lisle (2015), *Understanding Genesis*; William VanDoodewaard (2015), *The Quest for the Historical Adam*; Henry M. Morris III (2016), *The Book of Beginnings*; Terry Mortenson (ed.) (2016), *Searching for Adam*; Nathaniel T. Jeanson (2017), *Replacing Darwin*; (2022), *Traced*. Still many other books will be mentioned later. For the beginners, however, I recommend John F. Ashton (2012), *Evolution Impossible*; Don Batten et al. (2012), *The Creation Answers Book*; Ken Ham (2012), *The Lie*; (2021), *Creation to Babel*; Carl Wieland (2013), *Stones and Bones*; Paul Garner (2015), *The New Creationism*; Ken Ham & Bodie Hodge (2016), *A Flood of Evidence*. See also *The New Answers Book*, volumes 1, 2, 3 and 4, by Ken Ham and others.

CHAPTER 2: AFTER THE FLOOD — A NEW BEGINNING

The flood had lasted 150 days when the water level began to "decline" (Gen 8:3).[26] This was caused by the rapid uplifting of the new continents from below the global sea. At the same time were formed the wide and deep basins of the present-day oceans.[27] On that same day the ark was floating above a region which was later known as "Ararat" (Gen 8:4) or "Urartu", located in modern eastern Turkey. There the ark finally rested when the floodwaters withdrew and the land dried.[28]

When the land was dry enough God told Noah to leave the ark (Gen 8:14–19). So, Noah, his family and all the animals which had stayed in the ark a little more than a year entered a new world. This new and strange world was rugged and barren, only little vegetation growing yet on the exposed soil. The climate was cool and wet, probably much different than before the flood. It took a while to get used to those unprecedented harsh conditions.

Fairly soon, however, the life of Noah's family became settled. They built their housings at some distance from the resting place of the ark. There they began to cultivate crops (Gen 9:20) which they found from the surroundings or which they had stored in the ark.[29] They probably kept some domestic animals too. After many years, when wild animals had already somewhat multiplied, they could start hunting.

---

[26] See also Hamilton 1990, 298–300; Gertz 2018, 266; Hendel 2024, 308, 322, 323; Boyd & Snelling (eds.) 2014, 201–212; B2000.

[27] Today about 70 percent of Earth's surface is still underwater. If, however, the topography of Earth were totally smooth everywhere the amount of water in the existent oceans would cover the whole planet to a depth of approximately 1.8 miles or three kilometers (Batten et al. 2012, 178). So, the flood waters have not vanished anywhere — they are in today's seas, lakes, rivers and glaciers.

[28] Many people have been looking for the remains of Noah's ark (see Nissen 2017). There exists an interesting though controversial large boat-shaped formation on a certain mountain next to the village of Üzengili, some 20 miles or 30 kilometers south of Mount Ararat in eastern Turkey (coordinates: 39° 26' 26.3" N 44° 14' 05.3" E). Many people believe that the formation is the ark or what is left of it. — "Many ark landing sites have been proposed over the years. One that has been rejected as a geological formation by most scholars in recent years is the Durupinar or Akyayla site in Turkey, near the Iran and Turkey border. That site consists of something akin to a boat-shaped feature that is readily recognizable (think of a football field-sized 'footprint' in the shape of a boat). The area contains several of these geological features and that is really all that it is." Ham & Hodge 2016, 267; see also Graves 2014, 111–114; Price & House 2017, 66. But see also Mary Nell Wyatt (2004), *The Boat-Shaped Object on Doomsday Mountain*; www.noahsarkscans.nz; Powell 2022, 320, 321.

[29] "There are, even today, large stands of wild wheat in Anatolia from which [...] one could gather enough grain with a flint sickle in three weeks to feed a family for a year." Scott 2017, 11.

God had commanded Noah and his sons to multiply in the earth (Gen 9:1, 7). Accordingly new members were born into Noah's family during the years after the flood. Finally, possibly after some decades, the group decided to leave the mountainous and challenging Ararat region and to go in search of a better place to live. They "journeyed from the east" (Gen 11:2 KJV)[30], that is to say, they "migrated westward" (ISV) from their initial habitation. Most probably they followed the river Murat which is the major headwater stream of the Euphrates. It starts near Mount Ararat and flows some 440 miles (700 kilometers) westward through the mountains of eastern Turkey.

After journeying alongside the rivers Murat and Euphrates and after all that mountainous terrain Noah and his extended family arrived finally at an edge of a wide and fertile plain. This plain lies approximately between the modern cities of Gaziantep and Diyarbakır in southeastern Turkey which is also the area where the two great Mesopotamian rivers, Euphrates and Tigris, originate. Perhaps that is the reason why this region was named "Shinar" (Gen 11:2) which probably meant originally "the two rivers".[31]

It was not necessary for the people to wander any farther from the extensive plain that they had just found in the land of Shinar. There they could easily grow and domesticate

---

[30] KJV's "from the east" is a correct translation of the Hebrew word מִקֶּדֶם (miqqedem) (BHS; BHQ-Gen) in this verse, not NIV's and many others' "eastward". LXX (and other old translations), RSV, NKJV, NJPS, NRSV, CEV, CJB, NABRE, LEB, MEV, ESV and CSB among many others also read "from the east"; so do also Skinner (1910, 225), von Rad (1981, 112), Sarna (1989, 81, 99), Hamilton (1990, 349, 352), Rosenberg (1993, 134, 136), Westermann (1994, 533), Ruppert (2003, 484, 497), Speiser (2007, 74), Bandstra (2008, 555), Schüle (2009, 161), Alter (2018), Fischer (2018, 597, 606), Carr (2021, 314). Another possible translation could be "they journeyed/wandered about *in the east*" (cp. GNB; REB; NIV margin; EHV; Cassuto 1964, 238; Wenham 1987, 233, 238; Goldingay 2020, 176, 187; Hendel 2024, 390, 392), in the sense of "on the eastern side (of the land of Israel), that is, in the countries of the east" (Cassuto 1964, 240). On translating miqqedem see also Day 2013, 170. — "These people migrate from Ararat in a westerly/south-westerly direction—the direction 'from the east' is from the perspective of someone in or near Canaan." Currid 2015, 242. In my view "from the east" is from the perspective of the plain of Shinar.

[31] On the meaning of the name "Shinar" see Anne Habermehl (2011), *Where in the World Is the Tower of Babel?*, 25, 26. Originally I got this important idea of the real location of the land of Shinar in southeastern Turkey from Mary Nell Wyatt, *The Tower of Babel*. See also Lennart Möller (2010), *The Exodus Case*, 26, 27. It is less probable, in my opinion, that the plain in question is situated a little further north, around the city of Malatya.

their crops and raise their animals. The area offered everything they would ever need, and the climate too was more pleasant there than in the mountainous land of Ararat.[32]

After Noah and his people had settled down in some place, probably in the vicinity of Euphrates, they continued to live together like before. As years and decades passed the number of people grew so that they became a large tribe. Wild animals had the capability to increase much faster so there was always more prey to hunt. Some persons became exceptionally skillful in this art. The most famous among the hunters during those days was Noah's great grandson Nimrod, "a champion hunter before the LORD"[33] (Gen 10:9). It can be speculated that he was not only very able to provide game animals for food but that he could also heroically protect his folks against ferocious predators and dangerous beasts like lions, wolves, bears, and even dinosaurs which were known in ancient times as dragons.[34]

---

[32] "While many scholars believe that plant domestication occurred within the Jordan Valley and adjacent regions, Lev-Yadun et al. (2000) propose, instead, that it is only in a small area near the upper reaches of the Tigris and Euphrates rivers in southeastern Turkey and northern Syria that the wild progenitors of the Neolithic founder crops all occur [...] Other scholars [...] propose multiple centers of domestication." Simmons 2007, 65, 66. Augusta McMahon (2005, 23) writes that "Accumulation of evidence for einkorn and emmer wheats points toward a southeastern Turkey or northern Syria origin for domestication". Domestication and consequent morphological changes in the cultivated wild plants may be achieved within just a few decades if specific harvesting techniques are used (see Hillman & Davies 1990; see also Sagona & Zimansky 2009, 67, 68; Willcox 2012, 167). In my view initial domestication of various plants and animals occurred probably quite soon after the flood by Noah and his descendants, first in the land of Ararat and later in the land of Shinar in southeastern Turkey. However, most domestication in the Near East happened still later, at different times in different places, after the dispersal at Babel (see more about this event in this and the next chapter). We do not know if there were, for example, domesticated pre-flood grains stored in the ark.

[33] Wenham 1987, 211, 223. The original meaning of Nimrod's name was probably "He who subdues the leopards" or "He who rules over the leopards", or something similar (from the roots *nmr* [leopard] and *rdd* [subdue] or *rdh* [rule]; see for example TWOT, 581, 833), reflecting his fame as a masterly hunter. Wall paintings depicting men hunting or taunting animals have been found amongst the archaeological remains of the Neolithic town of Çatalhöyük, located in south-central Turkey. Some of the men (maybe the elite hunters) are shown to wear leopard skin garments (see Sagona & Zimansky 2009, 90, 91). — "The name Nimrod is derived from Akkadian namru or nimru ('shining') [...] Nimru also means 'panther,' [...]" Scurlock 2009, 275. See also TDOT, 9:432–434; Hamilton 1990, 338; HALOT, 701; HAHAT, 820, 821. Wall paintings at Çatalhöyük "included themes that seemed identical to cave paintings in western Europe dated supposedly tens of thousands of years earlier. This can only mean that Catal Huyuk was thriving at the same time as the Ice Age Paleolithic hunter (Mellaart, 1967, p.22, 67) [...] Another remarkable fact is that nearby modern villagers still paint walls and doorways with ancient themes and patterns only rediscovered in excavations that began in 1961" (von Fange 1994, 85, 86). On Çatalhöyük see also Ian Hodder (2006), *The Leopard's Tale*.

[34] See Darek Isaacs (2010), *Dragons or Dinosaurs?*. See also Paul S. Taylor (1998), *The Great Dinosaur Mystery and the Bible*, William J. Gibbons & Kent Hovind (1999), *Claws Jaws and Dinosaurs*, Phillip O'Donnell (2006), *Dinosaurs: Dead or Alive?*, Dennis Swift (2006), *Secrets of the Ica Stones and Nazca Lines*, Duane T. Gish (2009), *Dinosaurs by Design*, Tim Clarey (2015), *Dinosaurs: Marvels of God's Design*, and Bodie Hodge (2023), *Dinosaurs, Dragons, and the Bible*.

The outside world might be scary but together in the village people had safety and fellowship. In order to firmly establish the common identity and to strengthen the communal harmony a shared decision was made to improve the settlement infrastructure and to build a monument which all could be proud of.[35] They spoke to one another:

> Come, let us build ourselves a city, and a tower whose top *is* in the heavens; let us make a name for ourselves, lest we be scattered abroad over the face of the whole earth. (Gen 11:4 NKJV)

People wanted to build their new town fine and durable. Therefore, they made hard-burnt clay bricks and had bitumen for mortar (Gen 11:3).[36] However, this new achievement of Noah's descendants did not please God:

> But the LORD came down to see the city and the tower which the sons of men had built. And the LORD said, "Indeed the people *are* one and they all have one language, and this is what they begin to do; now nothing that they propose to do will be withheld from them. (Gen 11:5, 6 NKJV)

God knew that those people's strong intimacy and unity would ultimately lead to great depravity and wickedness, as had happened before in the pre-flood world. That is why He decided to execute a preemptive action:

> Come, let Us go down and there confuse their language, that they may not understand one another's speech. (Gen 11:7 NKJV)

As a result of this miraculous intervention tens of new (proto-)languages were suddenly spoken by different groups of people.[37] This was a mighty shock and a clear sign from

---

[35] "The resultant monumental edifice would have been a great source of civic pride and would have fostered a spirit of unity." Sarna 1989, 83.

[36] Even in modern days there has existed a natural source of bitumen in Samsat which is situated just northeast of the Atatürk Dam in southeastern Turkey (Moorey 1999, 333). That source lies probably not immensely far from the location where the early people started to build the city and the tower. Of course, possibly, they could have got bitumen also from some other spots closer to the construction place. Besides bitumen various metals are also found in Turkey whose "mountainous terrain is literally studded with metalli-ferous sites, including copper, iron, lead, silver, and gold, especially in the northern and eastern regions [...] Combined with human ingenuity, this richness in ores also enabled the ancient Anatolian smiths, known for their technical sophistication and artistry, to play a leading role in metallurgy" (Sagona & Zimansky 2009, 200).

[37] See for example Bodie Hodge (2013), *Tower of Babel*, 65–74. Although I disagree with Hodge on the location of the land of Shinar and some other issues, the chapters in his book contain much valuable information.

God that they should not all live together anymore.[38] For the fear of God's additional punishments people gathered their closest family members and friends and quickly left the city and the area to stay somewhere else:[39]

> So the LORD scattered them abroad from there over the face of all the earth, and they ceased building the city. Therefore its name is called Babel, because there the LORD confused the language of all the earth; and from there the LORD scattered them abroad over the face of all the earth. (Gen 11:8, 9 NKJV)

In those early days people married generally at a young age and gave birth to lots of children rapidly. With an annual growth rate of almost five percent there could have been a population of 3,000–4,000 persons at the time of the dispersal, approximately 135 years after the flood or 2215 B.C.[40]

---

[38] In verses Gen 9:1, 7 God had commanded people to multiply in the earth. The three imperatives in verse 1, "Be fruitful and multiply and fill the earth" (ESV), are all meaning basically the same: multiplying/procreation (cp. Gen 1:22, 28; Ex 1:7, 12; see also Mathews 1996, 158, 400; Kaminski 2004, 11–14, 130–137, 143). Therefore, contrary to the very common explanation, the words "fill the earth" do not mean here that God had commanded people to spread out in groups to all over the world. In other words, before the confusion of languages there existed a command from God to multiply, but there was no specific order to scatter yet. Building the city and the tower (in order to stay together) was not an intentional rebellion against God. — "There has been a tendency in Old Testament scholarship to associate 'scattering' in the primaeval history with 'filling the earth' (Gen. 9.1) [...] It is worth underscoring, however, that God never commanded Noah's descendants to *scatter* [...] the Babelites are not disobeying the command to fill the earth when they say, 'otherwise we shall be scattered abroad'." Kaminski 2004, 28, 29. — "[...] the commands to fill the earth are set within the context of humanity being fruitful and multiplying, something which there is every reason to believe the people of Genesis 11 had been doing in view of their apparently large numbers so soon after the flood (Gen. 11.1)." Day 2013, 184.

[39] "Eventually, if not immediately, each family became a tribe and moved away from Babel to work out its own manner of life [...] The stronger and more industrious and intelligent tribes took and held the more favorable regions. With resulting greater resources, they soon became great nations. The weaker and less ambitious families were pushed further and further away from the great centers of civilization, being forced to colonize new regions altogether, before they could set about to establish their own particular culture." Henry M. Morris 2009, 274, 275. See also von Fange 1994, 177, 178.

[40] For example, $8 \times 1.046^{135} \approx 3500$ (8 initial people, annual growth rate 4.6 % for 135 years; of course, the growth rate was much higher right after the flood when the wives of Noah's sons began to have their first babies). This would have been almost as high growth rate as the Israelites had in Egypt at a much later date (see page 66 in this book; on biblical human population growth see also Carter & Hardy 2015). Also, according to Jonathan D. Sarfati (2015, 659) "there could have been over 3,000 people alive at the time" of the dispersal (but some 164 years after the flood, Sarfati's annual growth rate being just 3.7 %). The confusion of languages and the dispersal at Babel happened sometime during the lifetime of Noah's great-great-great-grandson Peleg, for "in his days was the earth divided" (Gen 10:25 KJV). This is the correct interpretation of these words (see for example Pierce 1999; Hodge 2013, 37–39; Sarfati 2015, 651–653, 655, 656). Peleg lived approximately 2247–2008 B.C. (Jones 2015, 278 and Chart 6 in the CD-ROM), but my opinion is that "the division of the earth" happened during the very early part of his life or more precisely when he was about 30 years old. Accordingly, I think that the Babel incident occurred around 2215 B.C. This date functions at least as a good working hypothesis.

It was possible for such a large number to live together in Babel because they practiced agriculture. People's diet consisted mainly of different kinds of grains, nuts, fruits, legumes and other vegetables. Besides these they got meat from domestic animals and hunted prey. However, when the population fled to the wilderness they had to survive almost solely by hunting and gathering. Consequently, it was no longer possible to keep together a very large party of people; otherwise, local resources would have become rapidly exhausted. Therefore, possibly, about a hundred small groups were formed soon, one usually incorporating only a few families.[41]

The confusion of tongues and the subsequent scattering in every direction from Babel did not merely cause a mental shock. People left their homes and livelihood and took only a low amount of personal property with them. Some were completely unfamiliar with the world outside the realm of Babel. Many knew nothing about hunting or living in the wilderness. Very many had never felt before so isolated and terrified. Nonetheless all those cast out bands had to try to survive and make it through this cultural catastrophe with the few possessions, skills and knowledge they happened now to own. For an unknown number of people, unfortunately, staying alive in this totally new situation was too much required.

Although all kinds of people, old and young, could have participated in building the city and the tower, normally different tasks, skills and expertise were not evenly distributed among the Babelites. This had been the case also with the antediluvian (i.e. pre-flood) people:

> Then Lamech took for himself two wives: the name of one *was* Adah, and the name of the second *was* Zillah. And Adah bore Jabal. He was the father of those who dwell in tents and have livestock. His brother's name *was* Jubal. He was the father of all those who play the harp and flute. And as for Zillah, she also bore Tubal-Cain, an instructor of every craftsman in bronze and iron. (Gen 4:19–22 NKJV)

Most of the people in Babel worked on farming and herding. Then there were a small number of professional hunters, carpenters, stone tool makers, tailors, possibly even

---

[41] "The nature of the food supply keeps hunter-gatherer groups small in size — normally under 50 persons — as larger concentrations rapidly exhaust local resources and cause members to disperse into smaller foraging units." Jordan & Cummings 2014, 9.

some metal smiths and artists. Further, it is possible that the most innovative and specialized individuals belonged so far only to a few family lines, as seems to have been the case also during the time before the flood (see Gen 4:19–22 above). So, when the scattering occurred, only some groups possessed right away the potential for a higher material and cultural output. The others had to make it with simpler goods and way of living a much longer time.

The people who fled to the wilderness and became hunter-gatherers had to exploit the resources they chanced to find. Caves offered excellent natural shelters but temporary huts could also be built of trees, rocks, branches and skins. To survive they also had to have necessary tools made out of stone, bone or wood.[42] Flint was especially useful and workable hard material to produce sharp flakes, blades, points, axes, scrapers, awls, all kinds of implements which were very much needed, for example, to kill and butcher animals for meat and hides. Fortunately for those people, making stone tools was not difficult. John J. Shea writes:[43]

> If one has not tried to make stone tools, one could delude oneself that it is difficult. It isn't [...]

People also learned fairly soon to use a variety of stone tool making techniques, according to their needs. Some support for this view can be found in the following quote, again from Shea:[44]

> Much of the "culture history" of the Stone Age reflects perceived differences in stone tool designs and production techniques. Using these variables to construct quasi-historical entities, such as stone tool industries or archaeological cultures, potentially underestimates <u>prehistoric toolmakers [sic] versatility and behavioral variability</u>. Ethnographic stone-tool-makers vary their production techniques widely in response to seasonal differences in demands for tools [...] and other factors, including shifts in their cultural landscape [...] Many modern-day flintknappers can shift between widely differing modes of stone tool production [...] Behavioral variability is a hallmark of hominin adaptation, particularly *Homo sapiens* adaptation [...] It is only logical to expect that such

---

[42] Metal tools became common only in much later times.
[43] John J. Shea (2013), *Stone Tools in the Paleolithic and Neolithic Near East*, 3.
[44] Shea 2013, 43. Underlining added. See also von Fange 1994, 6–8.

Those "earliest times" are usually thought to have begun more than two million years ago but in reality, they started just after the dispersal at Babel. It is true that significant changing can be noticed in the stone tool making techniques through the early hunter-gatherer archaeological "periods" (namely the Lower Palaeolithic, the Middle Palaeolithic, the Upper Palaeolithic and the Epipalaeolithic/Mesolithic) in the Near East and elsewhere, but the matter is not really that simple, as will be seen.

Focusing on the eastern Mediterranean Levant,[45] the earliest one of these Palaeolithic periods (and in theory stratigraphically the lowest), the Lower Palaeolithic, is characterized by lithic assemblages (i.e. sets of stone tools found in the same archaeological contexts) consisting typically of simple pebble cores and/or large cutting tools (LCTs, including the famous Acheulian hand-axes) together with associated retouched and unretouched flakes.[46] During the next phase, the Middle Palaeolithic, pebble cores and LCTs were still used albeit the number of LCTs decreased. Instead, this period saw an increase in preparing cores carefully to get points, blades and flakes of predetermined sizes and shapes. However, this more advanced mode of stone tool making, also called "the Levallois technique", was already known in the Lower Palaeolithic.[47]

The Upper Palaeolithic period, in turn, saw an emphasis on blade production, especially through the so-called prismatic blade core reduction. A shift also happened away from flake-based to blade-based retouched tools. The use of the Levallois technique was

---

[45] This area encompasses the Sinai Peninsula, Israel/Palestinian territories, Jordan, Lebanon, Syria and southeastern Turkey; sometimes even Cyprus is included.

[46] Shea 2013, 70–78. Core means a chunk of rock from which flakes, blades and points are detached in stone tool making process. Blade is a flake whose length is at least twice its width. Point is a triangular flake. Retouching means the modification of a piece of stone to make it a more effective tool, usually by removing a series of chips from the working edge.

[47] Shea 2013, 64, 75, 84, 114. — "None but a very few Lower or Middle Paleolithic tools required more than a few minutes knapping effort, or fabrication tools other than stones and bones readily at hand. Upper and Epipaleolithic tools were significantly more labor-intensive […] making reproductions of Neolithic stone tools, particularly groundstone tools, can consume hours, or even days, of focused labor." Shea 2013, 289.

greatly reduced, and large cutting tools disappeared completely.[48] However, prismatic blade cores are already present in Middle Palaeolithic and Lower Palaeolithic contexts.[49]

The stone tool production methods in the Epipalaeolithic period differed only a little from those of the previous Upper Palaeolithic. The emphasis was still on blade production. The microlithic technology, in other words the making of very small blades, points, geometric pieces and other tool types, became common during this time. Also carving and abrasion began to be used more often in stone tool production.[50] It is worth noting, however, that "micro-tools" existed even in the Middle and Lower Palaeolithic periods.[51]

Hereby it has become clear that stone tool technologies were quite diverse right from the beginning. Indeed, it is possible to find technologically advanced artifacts even amongst the (supposedly) earliest and crudest stone tool assemblages. On the other hand, some humans have continued to produce the simplest stone utensils until the present time.[52] So, in reality, there have always existed stone tools of various levels of sophistication.

Right after the dispersal at Babel most people were inexperienced stone tools makers, but it did not take a very long time to become accustomed to various production methods. They also learned fairly soon that tools of certain sizes and shapes were more useful than others in particular jobs. Now, to understand those times better, let's read what Shea writes about a technological shift from the Lower to the Middle Palaeolithic in the Levant:[53]

> It is unlikely that hominin tool users would long remain oblivious that tools of some particular shapes and sizes work better than others — either for use in particular tasks or as general-purpose tools. This recognition likely led to more stereotyped core reduction strategies and more consistently patterned choices about how the resulting flakes were used. Middle

---

[48] Shea 2013, 122, 157, 159.
[49] Shea 2013, 54, 93, 94.
[50] Shea 2013, 164, 166, 167, 183, 210–212.
[51] Shea 2013, 67, 68, 104, 112, 296. See also von Fange 1994, 90, 319; Jan Micha Burdukiewicz & Avraham Ronen (eds.) (2003), *Lower Palaeolithic Small Tools in Europe and the Levant*.
[52] See Cremo & Thompson 1998, 194–196, 208, 209. See also von Fange 1994, 11; Marvin L. Lubenow (2004), *Bones of Contention*, 131, 132 (the same information also in Lubenow 1994); Rupe & Sanford 2019, 241–244, 255–258, 261.
[53] Shea 2013, 300, 301.

<blockquote>

Paleolithic retouched artifact-types are generally viewed as more morphologically standardized than Lower Paleolithic types [...] one novel aspect of Middle Paleolithic core technology is repetitive patterns of core preparation and reduction seemingly aimed at recovering morphologically consistent flakes, blades, and points. A shift toward more standardized patterns of flake tool production during the Middle Paleolithic [...]

</blockquote>

Indeed, people who fled to the wilderness from Babel did certainly not "long remain oblivious that tools of some particular shapes and sizes work better than others", which recognition soon led to "more stereotyped core reduction strategies", that is to say, to "a shift toward more standardized patterns of flake tool production during the Middle Paleolithic". Accordingly, the Lower Palaeolithic period did not last a long time. In other words, the "particularly sharp"[54] transition from the Lower to the Middle Palaeolithic period in the Levant occurred quite soon after the new hunter-gatherer groups had started their novel way of living. In my opinion the initial "Lower Palaeolithic period" lasted generally in the Near East no more than two decades and possibly even less, and the whole time (the whole Palaeolithic period) during which people lived predominantly as mobile hunter-gatherers lasted only about 80 years. Then, in the beginning of the Neolithic period, they began to settle down in their new lands and to live increasingly on agriculture.

For many it may be difficult to believe that it took only a century or so for the whole Palaeolithic period in the Near East when the common teaching is that it lasted almost two million years. However, the biblical chronology does not allow much more time for the era of the hunter-gatherers. On the other hand, the conventional view is based on great errors, namely naturalistic worldview, evolutionary interpretation, and flawed dating methods. Properly understood the "Old Stone Age" fits very well into the historical framework of the Bible. Certainly, it is much more meaningful to see in the Palaeolithic archaeological record the struggle, success and rapid development and adaptation of the post-Babel populations over a relatively short period of time than a

---

54 Shea 2013, 313.

very sluggish progress of some wretched savages over incredibly long ages of hundreds of thousands of years.[55]

The global flood had utterly devastated the then-existing world, washing away all the antediluvian people and pulverizing their villages and towns. Lots of historical remains from that oldest civilization must still be left but they are now lying randomly inside the sedimentary rocks the world over, making their discovery very unlikely. Thus, the archaeological sites and findings all around the world represent almost without exception the settlements and operations of the post-flood, post-Babel humans.[56] Sometimes early hunter-gatherers, migrating to all parts of the world, became victims of major local and regional natural disasters which buried people, artifacts and animals under thick layers of earth which secular researchers may now erroneously date even tens of millions of years old.[57]

This chapter has concentrated on those people from Babel who became hunter-gatherers. The next chapter, in turn, will deal more with people groups who continued to be farmers very soon after the dispersal.

---

[55] "No doubt a great many of the evidences of the so-called Paleolithic and Neolithic cultures of early man, when rightly interpreted, are merely commentaries on the difficult struggle to survive by small tribes in the early centuries following the great Flood and their separation at Babel." Morris & Morris 1996, 314. See also von Fange 1994, 89; Garner 2015, 231, 232.

[56] See also Morris 2002, 425.

[57] See the chapters 2, 3, 4, 5, 6 and 11 in Cremo & Thompson 1998. See also von Fange 1994, 39–42, 47, 126; Batten et al. 2012, 196, 197; Brandt 2013. — "The events after the Flood in a very turbulent world shaped much of the physical world as well as the many cultures in it [...] Geologically, it was a time of a plastic, unstable, watery earth." Erich A. von Fange (1994), *Noah to Abram: The Turbulent Years*, 3, 23, 24.

CHAPTER 3: HUNTERS, FARMERS, AND NEW CIVILIZATIONS

When God confounded the languages and scattered the people in all directions the town of Babel and the fields around it were mostly abandoned. As there was no requirement for all to leave their homes many stayed and continued the old way of living, cultivating crops and keeping domestic animals like sheep, goats, pigs and cattle.[58] Nimrod, that much celebrated hunter-hero, became the chieftain of those people and the king of Babel and many other settlements which were later established in the land of Shinar:[59]

> And the beginning of his kingdom was Babel, Erech, Accad, and Calneh, in the land of Shinar. (Gen 10:10 NKJV)

At first the remnant population of Babel corresponded probably only to a moderate sized village. Later, when the number of the people increased and also many hunter-gatherers started to settle down, new villages were founded in the land of Shinar.[60] Over time some of those villages must have grown at least into small towns. It is very likely, however, that the remains of many of those places lying somewhere in southeastern Turkey have never been excavated. Surely, they have never been correctly identified as the villages and towns which were under the rule of Nimrod. Further, settlements that were situated by the river Euphrates are now possibly underwater due to the Atatürk Dam, built between 1981 and 1990.

Besides Nimrod's subjects in Shinar there was a fairly large number of other people who also maintained the ability and the will to continue as agriculturists. However, unlike the people who stayed in Babel, these other groups wanted or were forced to move far away. In search of a place where to start life anew they first wandered toward the east across the plains of Shinar until they were met by the river Tigris which they began to

---

[58] At the outset all these people did not necessarily speak the same language. The situation could be the same also in many other groups.

[59] Another possible scenario is that Babel became first totally abandoned and that people, including Nimrod, returned there only after many decades of total hunting-and-gathering lifestyle, in the beginning of the Neolithic period. The words "they ceased building the city" in Gen 11:8 (NKJV) may well indicate that Babel was temporarily uninhabited ("the city was left forsaken and in ruins", Cassuto 1964, 248).

[60] According to Antonio Sagona and Paul Zimansky (2009, 23, 24) the first permanent settlements in Anatolia/Turkey were founded by hunter-gatherers who lived in the southeastern part of the country.

follow southward. When they had travelled far enough and found good spots to stay, they decided to set up permanent camps and started to create a new future.

Noah's grandson Asshur (Gen 10:22) was the leader of one of the culturally more potential groups which left the plain in the land of Shinar. In modern northern Iraq, next to the river Tigris, he and his subjects established a small settlement that was to become one of the most famous cities in the ancient world:

> Out of that land went forth Asshur, and builded Nineveh, and the city Rehoboth, and Calah, And Resen between Nineveh and Calah: the same *is* a great city. (Gen 10:11, 12 KJV)[61]

Like Nineveh these other somewhat later places were also at first small villages only, but over the course of history they grew into cities and together with Nineveh formed a large metropolis (Jon 3:2, 3). Some other groups of people founded two additional historically important farming communities in the same general area. These ancient villages, whose remains are now called Tell Arpachiyah and Tell Hassuna, were most probably started at the same early date as Nineveh. Tell Arpachiyah is located approximately four miles (six kilometers) northeast of the modern city of Mosul within which the ruins of ancient Nineveh are lying. Tell Hassuna, in turn, is situated some 22 miles (35 kilometers) south of Mosul.

The original encampments were composed merely of tents and huts, but soon people began to construct better buildings whose walls were made of piled-up mud, lumps of clay, or sun-dried bricks. Some houses in Tell Hassuna, for example, were in many ways

---

[61] KJV's "Out of that land went forth Asshur, and builded Nineveh" is a correct translation of that part of Gen 10:11, not NKJV's and many others' "From that land he went to Assyria and built Nineveh". Nahum M. Sarna (1989, 74) writes that "Either Asshur or Nimrod could be the subject of the Hebrew verb *yatsa'*, 'went forth'". H. C. Leupold (2010, 229) notes that KJV's rendering is grammatically possible. See also Skinner 1910, 210, 211; NLTSB, 40 (the study note on Gen 10:11); Mathews 1996, 451; Ruppert 2003, 467; BHQ-Gen, 103*, 104*; Goldingay 2020, 175; Carr 2021, 292; Day 2022, 202; Hendel 2024, 369. Everett Fox (1983, 39), Gordon J. Wenham (1987, 211, 223, 224), Victor P. Hamilton (1990, 335, 339, 340), A. J. Rosenberg (1993, 130), Benno Jacob (2000, 283; 2007, 73), Ephraim A. Speiser (2007, 64, 67), Barry Bandstra (2008, 528, 532, 533), Zvi Grumet (2017, 103), Robert Alter (2018), Georg Fischer (2018, 542, 544, 548, 549, 568, 569), LXX (and other old translations; see Delitzsch 1888, 325; Dillmann 1897, 355; Skinner 1910, 210; Rösel 1994, 209; Gertz 2018, 296; LXX.B; LXX.D; Kraus & Karrer (eds.) 2011, 177; John William Wevers (1993, 134), Susan Brayford (2007, 59, 283), OSB, NETS and LES translate Gen 10:11a incorrectly), NJB, NJPS, CJB and CEB translate similarly to KJV. According to Josephus (JA, Book I:vi.4 (p. 71)) it was Asshur who founded Nineveh. See also Gill 1810, comments on Gen 10:11.

similar to those of modern-day northern Iraqi villages.[62] These people had worked with clay probably already in Babel so they did not have to come up with that skill from nothing.

Even though the Babelites had known how to make hard-burnt bricks for the construction of the city and the tower, it is not certain that they had produced baked clay vessels, that is, pottery too. However, the inhabitants of Nineveh, Tell Arpachiyah and Tell Hassuna began to mold out of clay many types of bowls, jars and plates almost immediately. Along with simple and coarse items they made also much finer burnished, incised and painted specimens, many of which were marvelous pieces of art.[63]

The most elegant and archaeologically most important early pottery styles from those three sites are the so-called "Hassuna ware"[64], "Samarra ware", and "Halaf ware".[65] Skillfully painted geometric patterns and stylized human, animal and plant motifs formed sophisticated and elaborate decorative designs on the surfaces of both the Samarran and Halafian ceramics. In fact, the Halaf pottery is generally considered "the most beautiful ever used in Mesopotamia".[66] The Hassuna ware was originally made, probably, both in Tell Hassuna and Nineveh. The Samarra ware and the Halaf ware, in turn, were probably developed in Nineveh and Tell Arpachiyah respectively; at least that is my view.[67]

Over the course of time these three pottery traditions were widely distributed as imports or local copies within the large area covering the upper half of modern Iraq and even beyond.[68] Samarran or Samarran-like ceramics have been found also in certain

---

[62] Georges Roux (1992), *Ancient Iraq*, 49. See also Oates & Oates 1976, 99; Redman 1978, 5 (Figure 1-3).
[63] "From the beginning, pottery vessels were more than containers. Different ways of treating their surface turned them into a medium for creating identities. An inexhaustible range of patterns and motifs could be incised or painted on vessels to represent membership and definition [...] shapes as well as decoration were subject to fashion and technological changes [...]" Nissen & Heine 2009, 12.
[64] It is often also referred to as the "Hassuna Standard ware".
[65] The Hassuna ware has got its name from Tell Hassuna. The Samarra ware is called so because it was first found in an ancient cemetery near the modern city of Samarra, some 156 miles or 250 kilometers southeast of Mosul. The Halaf ware has been named after Tell Halaf, a site in northeastern Syria.
[66] Roux 1992, 56. See also Bourke 2018, 51–53.
[67] See also Chart 2 at the end of this book.
[68] Ceramics belonging to the same underlying tradition could have, however, much stylistic variation depending on the time and place. The excavated pottery is usually in the form of sherds/fragments.

North Syrian and Southeast Turkish sites.[69] However, the overall distribution of the Halaf pottery — the most thriving and longest lasting of the three — was eventually by far the widest, extending "from the region of Aleppo to the Diyala valley, covering the whole of Jazirah and of future Assyria, and it was surrounded by a halo of peripheral areas where this pottery was copied or merely imported; these included the heart of eastern Anatolia, Cilicia and northern Syria up to the Mediterranean coast, the Harim basin [sic; the Hamrin basin] and parts of western Iran and Transcaucasia".[70] Although in their local occurrences the Hassunan, Samarran and Halafian potteries could be successive (as in Tell Hassuna) from the broad geographical perspective they were contemporary, beginning just about the same time.[71]

So, during the early decades after the confusion of languages and the dispersal at Babel, new civilizations began to take shape in certain areas. Some time (maybe even 30 to 50 years) after the establishment of Tell Arpachiyah, Nineveh, Tell Hassuna and probably many other places, the people living and increasing in northern Iraq continued to colonize new locations and to found new farming communities.[72] At the same time, however, most of the people were still living as hunter-gatherers. In my estimation it was not until some 80 years after the dispersal that a large number of mobile hunter groups started to settle down permanently next to fertile lands for a new agrarian lifestyle. This happened first all around the Near East and adjacent areas, and later also in other regions further away. Before that the early Mesopotamian farmers were living side by side with hunter-gatherers in their respective territories. Although it is possible

---

[69] Wares similar to the so-called "face-urns" of the Samarran pottery tradition from Tell Hassuna and other sites have been found in the deepest archaeological deposits of Troy in the northwestern coast of Turkey (Lloyd 1984, 78, 79), showing possibly how far early northern Iraqi ceramic styles could be transported.

[70] Roux 1992, 58, 59. Aleppo is a city in northwestern Syria. Diyala is a river in east-central Iraq, just northeast of the capital Baghdad. Roger Matthews (2000a, 137) writes that the Halaf ware was "the first widespread cultural horizon of prehistoric Mesopotamia". In my view, however, the Halaf ware shares this honor with the contemporary Ubaid ware of southern Mesopotamia, discussed more below. For a map of the extent of the Halaf culture see Roaf 1990, 49; Bryce & Birkett-Rees 2016, 37.

[71] See Mellaart 1975, 16, 143, 144; see also Roux 1992, 48, 49. Further, see Chart 2: Comparative Stratigraphy of Tell Arpachiyah, Nineveh and Tell Hassuna, at the end of this book.

[72] For example, Chagar Bazar and Tell Aqab in northeastern Syria, Yarim Tepe, Umm Dabaghiya, Tell es-Sawwan, Matarrah, Shimshara and Choga Mami in the upper half of Iraq. Note that these are the modern names of those sites. — "In Iraq alone, of the estimated 100,000 [archaeological] sites which probably exist, only around 10,000 have been discovered, and only a fraction of them have been excavated. New sites are discovered daily." Bourke 2018, 20.

that these people — still suffering socially from the mental shock caused by the Babel incident — normally tried to keep a distance between each others, there could be occasional encounters and closer cooperation like trading. However, hunters' contacts with farmers did not necessarily lead to any immediate changes in their material repertoires. Instead, cultural transformation could be slow, hunter-gatherers freely selecting what and in which order to adopt for themselves from farmers' goods and technologies, for example.[73]

Robert J. Braidwood writes about hunters coexisting with more culturally advanced people:[74]

> In archaeology we are still somewhat bound by late nineteenth-century classifications, bar diagrams, neo-Grecisms such as "mesolithic" and "neolithic" for period terminology, and so on. These tend to establish an image of quick and all-pervading change from one level to another. I think the evidence increasingly instructs us otherwise: that <u>different levels of complexity — hunting camp, village, city — integrated with one another in their development; that the hunter in effect was always there</u>; that in the early villages the proportion of food which was actually produced by agriculture, or the proportion of other bands in the cultural spectrum that responded to this subsistence pattern, was not at all bounded by a clear horizon.

Alfred J. Hoerth, after quoting the same above text by Braidwood, adds this remark: "It should be remembered, therefore, that while increasing complexity is encountered, there were always some nearby people living a simpler existence."[75] Indeed it is conceivable that many hunter-gatherers in the Near East chose to continue to live as such even after all others had changed their Palaeolithic subsistence to Neolithic one. Actually, there is nothing to wonder at that decision because living as hunter-gatherers

---

[73] See Jordan & Cummings 2014, 17; Cummings 2014.
[74] Braidwood 1960, 242. Underlining added. See also von Fange 1994, 9, 10, 30, 90; 2006, 174, 240. — "Most of the world's population in the epoch of the early states comprised nonstate hunters and gatherers." Scott 2017, 217.
[75] Hoerth 1998, 36.

can be easier than living as farmer-herders — at least hunters have to work much less.[76]

Benjamin R. Foster and Karen Polinger Foster write:[77]

> For almost its entire history, the human race subsisted by hunting game and gathering naturally occurring plants. This mode was <u>so successful and so undemanding as a way of life</u> that it ensured human survival for hundreds of thousands of years. To judge from present-day hunting cultures, <u>hunters need exercise their skill only two or three days out of seven to provide sufficient meat for their community</u>. They kill and collect only what they need to live, and do not reduce their resources for sport or entertainment.

However, agriculture brought some great benefits for the new sedentary peoples. Alan H. Simmons writes:[78]

> Food production conferred enormous advantages to farmers over hunter/gatherers living outside of farming homelands. One of these was that farming provides higher food yield per area; thus, food production can support higher populations. Another advantage is that most hunter/gatherers are mobile, but most farmers are sedentary and can accumulate stored food surpluses, which are necessary for subsequent development. A third advantage is that [...] farmers developed immunities to infectious diseases, whereas hunter/gatherers did not.

So, to make it clear, right from the beginning after the dispersal at Babel there lived in the Near East both transitory hunter-gatherers and — in increasing proportion — sedentary farmers. While hunter-gatherers were becoming agriculturists some already existing villages were growing larger and slowly evolving into towns. The emergence of towns and later on the first large cities was typical for southern Mesopotamia or the fertile alluvial plain in the lower half of Iraq, a very important region which I have hitherto left untreated.

---

[76] Price & Gebauer 1995, 4: "A number of studies have indicated that hunters and gatherers, even in very marginal environments, spend only a few hours a day obtaining enough food to eat; farming, on the other hand, is very labor intensive and much more time consuming." — "Contrary to earlier assumptions, hunters and gatherers – even today in the marginal refugia they inhabit – are nothing like the famished, one-day-away-from-starvation desperados of folklore. Hunters and gathers [sic] have, in fact, never looked so good – in terms of their diet, their health, and their leisure [...] We know that even contemporary hunter-gatherers, reduced to living in resource-poor environments, still spend only half their time in anything we might call subsistence labor." Scott 2017, 9, 10, 93.

[77] Benjamin R. Foster & Karen Polinger Foster (2009), *Civilizations of Ancient Iraq*, 8. Underlining added.

[78] Simmons 2007, 23. But see also Akkermans 2020, 54–56.

The truth is that not all groups settled down in northern Iraq, but many travelled farther south into the region later known as Sumer and Akkad/Babylonia. There they soon established villages and began to cultivate the land. One of the earliest of those settlements in southern Iraq was Tell el-Oueili (or Tell Awayli), founded probably just a little later than the first farming communities in northern Iraq and somewhat earlier than another important southern site, Eridu.[79] In the same manner as in the northern villages of Tell Arpachiyah, Nineveh and Tell Hassuna the people living in Tell el-Oueili, Eridu and so on began soon to produce their own pottery called in archaeological literature as the "Ubaid ware", named after the site of Al-Ubaid which lies near Eridu. The Ubaid pottery tradition has been divided into five successive phases, from the earliest Ubaid 0 to the latest Ubaid 4.[80] In this southern part of Mesopotamia where stone is rare many types of everyday utensils (including sickles and even axes and knives) were commonly made of baked clay.[81]

In southern Mesopotamia the early farming communities were founded along the river Euphrates and its branches.[82] Over time some of those villages grew larger than others and functioned as economic and ritual centers "from which were to spring later on all the main cities of ancient Sumer", cities like Eridu, Ur and Uruk.[83] It is possible that among the early southern Mesopotamian villages was also a settlement which later became the famous city called in Sumerian language as *Kadingirra* and in Akkadian language as *Babili* (plural *Babilim*). A much later form of the name of that city was *Babilani* which the Greeks transliterated as Βαβυλών, from which comes the English

---

[79] In actual fact Tell el-Oueili is generally regarded as "the oldest-known settlement on the southern Mesopotamian alluvium" (Peasnall 2002, 388; Akkermans 2020, 72; on the site see also Calvet 1987; Huot 1989; 1996), and according to an ancient Mesopotamian tradition Eridu was the first city on earth (Leick 2002, 1–3; on the site see also Safar et al. 1981).

[80] Ubaid 0 ceramics have been found in the deepest excavated levels of Tell el-Oueili; above the levels of Ubaid 0 pottery were found samples of Ubaid 1 pottery which is also called "Eridu ware". The pottery of the next phase, Ubaid 2, is known also as "Hajji Muhammad ware". The final phases Ubaid 3 and Ubaid 4, in turn, are called only as such. See for example Roux 1992, 60, 61. However, when in some literature (e.g. Mellaart 1975) the designations "Eridu ware" and "Hajji Muhammad ware" are regularly used for Ubaid 1 and Ubaid 2 potteries, Ubaid 3 and Ubaid 4 may be called "early Ubaid" and "late Ubaid" respectively.

[81] Roux 1992, 62.

[82] The river Tigris "seems to have played a relatively minor role in that region, either because its bed was dug too deep into the alluvium for simple canal irrigation or because it was surrounded — as indeed it is now — by extensive marshes" (Roux 1992, 6).

[83] Roux 1992, 65. In the large centers the hub of economic and ritual life was a temple, some of the earliest of which were built in Eridu.

Babylon. Contrary to the very common view this southern Mesopotamian city had in reality nothing to do with the town of Gen 10:10; 11:4–9, Babel. Even though the names of these two places look and sound very similar and are in fact written the same way (בָּבֶל bāḇel)[84] in the present (Masoretic) Hebrew Old Testament, they have different origins: *Kadingirra* and *Babili* both mean "gate of god" whereas Babel "is a play on the verb meaning *to confuse*" (NRSVue margin, Gen 11:9; see also REB; LES (LXX)).[85] The early phases of the city of Babylon are archaeologically very obscure but it is generally regarded by secular researchers as "not one of the oldest cities of Mesopotamia".[86]

During the Ubaid 1 pottery phase the southern Mesopotamian cultural influence extended to east-central Iraq and southwestern Iran (Khuzestan).[87] During the next phase the Ubaidian culture spread the first time outside Mesopotamia proper when Ubaid wares began to be present at settlements along the shores of the Persian Gulf.[88] However, it was not until the third phase that the Ubaid tradition really started to expand its influence — especially into the upper part of Iraq where it gradually and

---

[84] Transliteration made according to Pratico & Van Pelt 2007.

[85] See the discussion of the meanings of the names "Babel" and "Babylon" in Habermehl 2011, 30, 31. See also, for example, Hamilton 1990, 357; HALOT, 107, 108; HAHAT, 122; Beaulieu 2018, (40, 41,) 50, 51, 58. It is told in Gen 10:10 that besides Babel Nimrod ruled over Erech, Accad and Calneh in the land of Shinar which I have located in southeastern Turkey. There existed in ancient times two famous cities called Uruk (cp. Erech) and Akkad/Agade (cp. Accad) in southern Mesopotamia but those must have been different places despite the similarity of the names. There has not been identified yet any ancient city named Calneh on the alluvial plains of southern Iraq, but there seems to have been a place with a very similar name somewhere in northern Syria (see Hamilton 1990, 339; Habermehl 2011, 39–41; Day 2022, 178, 201; Hendel 2024, 369). It is most probable that there were many villages, towns and cities across the whole of Mesopotamia bearing same-sounding names. Possibly some places were named after famous pre-flood locations whose memory survived a long time after the flood. Even the present rivers Euphrates and Tigris were named after two great rivers which existed in the antediluvian world (see Sarfati 2015, 316–318).

[86] See Leick 2002, 248, 249. On the archaeology of early Babylon see Beaulieu 2018, 41, 119, 120. See also Walton 2009, 59, 65.

[87] Peasnall 2002, 372.

[88] "These 45 apparently intermittent settlements are spread from the southern border of Kuwait to Bahrain and Qatar; another has been found in Bushir peninsula (Iran). They seem to have been camps of fishermen using 'Ubaid 2, 3 or 4 pottery made in Mesopotamia and local flint tools." Roux 1992, 442. See also Oates 1983, 255; Peasnall 2002, 372; Akkermans 2020, 72. The very early southern Mesopotamians were able to travel by water; this is proven by the clay models of boats which have been found at Eridu and Ur. See also Roaf 1990, 122. The so-called marsh Arabs who live in the marshes in the far south of Iraq "still travel by a type of boat used in antiquity" and "live in reed houses still constructed in the same way as the reed houses of the Sumerian past" (Bahrani 2017, 36; see also Roaf 1990, 50, 51).

peacefully replaced the culture characterized by the late phase of the Halaf pottery tradition. Brian Peasnall writes:[89]

> Throughout the long period spanning the Ubaid Tradition, there appears to have been very little conflict. Even in those regions into which Ubaid culture spread during the late Ubaid, there appears to have been <u>a remarkable degree of coexistence between it and the indigenous Halaf culture</u>. The presence of a burnt layer between the Halaf and Ubaid occupations at a small number of northern sites may indicate some localized incidents of conflict. However, in most cases <u>the two cultural traditions seem to have existed side by side even in the same villages</u>. This expansion was probably the result of the replication of the political, social, and ideological structures from the south by indigenous Halaf elites rather than migration or conquest from the south.

To me the best explanation for the spreading of the Ubaid culture to the more northern parts of Iraq seems to be peaceful migrations of people from the south, triggered by a drought, a population explosion, internal conflicts, some combination of these, or something else.[90] It was also during this time that a number of Halafian villages were abandoned by their inhabitants who — in addition to some people from other villages — set out to search for new homelands where to settle down afresh. In my view it was not until this period that people from central and northern Iraq and northeastern Syria started moving farther to the west into northwestern Levant (more specifically northwestern Syria and southeastern Turkey), bringing with them among other things a mix of Halafian wares of early, middle and late phase styles[91] as well as Hassunan and

---

[89] Peasnall 2002, 376. Underlining added. See also Oates 1983, 254. — "The lack of rupture between the Halaf and Ubaid cultures excludes a conquest of northern and central Iraq by 'Ubaidians' coming from the south, and the most plausible hypotheses are a peaceful infiltration or the adoption by the 'Halafians' of the culture of another population after a long period of contact." Roux 1992, 59.

[90] See also Frangipane 2001, 321, 322; Carter & Philip 2010, 7; Gibson 2010, 88; Bourke 2018, 54; Akkermans 2020, 72.

[91] For a long time, on the basis of the pottery sequence observed at Tell Arpachiyah, the Halaf pottery tradition has been divided into the early, middle and late phases (see Perkins 1949, 16–21, 42; see also Curtis 1982, 33, 34; Watson 1983, 233; Gut 1995, 194, 216, 217, 221; Matthews 2000b, 87). However, according to Peter M. M. G. Akkermans and Glenn M. Schwartz (2003, 116), "recent fieldwork at sites such as Sabi Abyad demonstrates that the Arpachiyah framework is not necessarily applicable outside of northern Iraq". Tell Sabi Abyad is situated in the Balikh river valley in northern Syria. There, above the levels of the pre-Halafian occupation, "Samarran pots, either imported or locally imitated, occurred in small quantities [...] shortly before the first occurrence of ceramics in genuine early Halaf style" (Akkermans & Schwartz 2003, 116). Even though the Halaf ware of Sabi Abyad has been defined as "early", in reality it was, in my opinion, temporally very late (approximately Amuq C, see below in the main text). After the migration of people from the east many native northwestern Levantine Pottery Neolithic (see below in the main text) communities began to emulate the high-quality ceramics which were introduced to them by the newcomers. As a matter of fact, a local technological and stylistic

Samarran ceramics and the skills to produce them, and the tradition of the characteristic Halafian domed circular houses called *tholoi* which "must be the prehistoric ancestors of the beehive villages of northern Syria which have survived in this primitive agricultural country until recent times".[92] Some groups took the direction also towards the north (eastern Turkey and Transcaucasia), some towards the east (western Iran).

In my estimation the migration of Ubaidians to the north started approximately during the beginning of the second quarter of the 21st century (or after c. 2075 B.C.). Halafians started their relocation probably somewhat later. At that time in northwestern Levant there were already Neolithic settlements inhabited by indigenous populations who had forsaken their former hunting-and-gathering lifestyle over half a century earlier. When hunter-gatherers began to settle down, cultivate crops and build their hamlets and villages, they usually lived first without ceramic wares; this stage of cultural development is called the "Pre-Pottery Neolithic period" (PPN) which in the Levantine archaeology is commonly divided into two successive subperiods "Pre-Pottery Neolithic A" (PPNA) and "Pre-Pottery Neolithic B" (PPNB).[93] Early agricultural settlements where pottery is already massively present are classified as belonging to the "Pottery Neolithic period" (PN).[94]

---

development from coarser pre-Halaf ware into fine Halaf-like ware through a transitional phase of fine Samarra-like pottery may be seen at Sabi Abyad itself (see Nieuwenhuyse 2007; 2018) — a village situated in a northern Syrian area which was particularly exposed to external cultural influences from many directions, so that according to Roger Matthews (2000b, 99; see also Matthews 2002, 148) "we should be cautious in seeing an exclusively autochthonous Halaf development in this region". Furthermore, "Sites with an uninterrupted occupation spanning pre-Halaf into Halaf are extremely rare, only Sabi Abyad in the Balikh valley providing at all convincing evidence in this respect" (Matthews 2000b, 108). Tell el-Kerkh in western Syria and Tell Halula in northern Syria, for example, show ceramic development similar to that at Sabi Abyad (see Odaka 2003; 2017; Faura & Molist 2017).

[92] Mallowan 1977, 92. See also Roux 1992, 55, 56; von Fange 1994, 87. Tholoi is a plural form of tholos.

[93] Many scholars call the very late Pre-Pottery Neolithic period as the "Pre-Pottery Neolithic C" (PPNC).

[94] Note that the periodization from the Palaeolithic through the Pre-Pottery Neolithic to the Pottery Neolithic (PALEO-PPN-PN) is relevant almost exclusively to territories and regions which were populated after the dispersal at Babel by people who lived first as hunter-gatherers for decades before they became agriculturists. The early Iraqi settlements using the Hassunan, Samarran, Halafian and Ubaidian wares are sometimes termed as "Chalcolithic" (meaning "copper-stone" and abbreviated by me as "C") because in certain of those places metals like copper and lead were already used in small amounts. Usually, Chalcolithic cultures followed chronologically the Pottery Neolithic cultures which did not have yet any metals. However, the PN-settlements established throughout the Near East by former hunter-gatherers and their descendants were preceded for a period of time by many of the early C-classified sites of Iraq, sites like Tell Arpachiyah, Nineveh, Tell Hassuna and Eridu; in other words, these latter (culturally more advanced) places were established earlier than the previous (less advanced) places.

In many northwestern Levantine sites Halafian wares (of early, middle and late phase styles) and other artifacts (brought or made by the migrants, imitated by the locals or traded by merchants) succeeded — in various compositions — a native PN-phase (Amuq A–B).[95] Subsequently the Ubaidian culture — being then already in its last stage (Ubaid 4) — spread into Syria and beyond and succeeded the Halaf-influenced cultures (Amuq C) in many places.[96] This started to happen at the end of the 21st century B.C (Amuq D).

I have collectively named all the above-mentioned movements of Ubaidians (the third phase onwards) and Halafians as "Great Migration". It was also early in the 21st century B.C., during the time when the Pre-Pottery Neolithic B was prevalent along the Levantine shores of the Mediterranean Sea, that farmers moved to the island of Cyprus from the mainland, probably the nearby Syria.[97] Somewhat later, probably via Cyprus and the coast of southern Turkey, agriculture arrived with migrating Levantine peoples in Crete, the Aegean Islands and Greece.[98] Still somewhat later, in my view in the end of the 21st century and the beginning of the 20th century, agricultural settlements began to be established along the shores of the central and western Mediterranean and, finally, along the Atlantic coast of Portugal. At that time appeared also the first pottery to be made in those new communities, called the "Impressed ware" or "Cardial ware".[99]

While the coastal lands of southern Europe were being colonized during the 21st and 20th centuries B.C. by the maritime Neolithic peoples migrating from the east, the European hunter-gatherers, who lived at that time mostly in more northerly latitudes, were themselves slowly retreating further south. They were forced to do so because of the constantly deteriorating climate in eastern, central and western Europe, caused by the rapidly developing Ice Age.

---

[95] See Mellaart 1975, 145. The label "Amuq A–B" denotes the two phases of the Pottery Neolithic period in northwestern Syria and southeastern Turkey. The Amuq pottery sequence was first defined on the Amuq plain which is located in the Hatay region of southern Turkey, some 30 miles or 50 kilometers west of the city of Aleppo (Braidwood & Braidwood 1960).
[96] See Mellaart 1975, 168; Peasnall 2002, 372. For a map of the extent of the Ubaid culture see Roaf 1990, 53.
[97] See Clarke 2014, 190; Moore 2014, 463. See also Sharon 2014, 50. On the Neolithic Cyprus see also Simmons 2007, 229–262.
[98] See Moore 2014, 466, 468.
[99] See Moore 2014, 471.

Right after the flood the oceans were warm even in the polar regions, resulting in abundant moisture in the atmosphere. This together with year-round low temperatures over land at high latitudes and altitudes triggered the formation of giant ice sheets. The ice sheet in Europe spread from Scandinavia to England and northern Germany, reaching its maximum extent in just about 500 years. After the glacial maximum (which occurred possibly during the 19th century B.C.) the ice sheets began to melt and shrink in size at increasing speed. The Ice Age — the only ice age that has ever been — finally ended some 200 years later. "Thus", writes Michael J. Oard, "the total length of time for a post-flood ice age from beginning to end, is about 700 years".[100]

Possibly around the year 1800 B.C. hunter-gatherers started the recolonization of the more northerly parts of Europe from their refugia (areas of survival) in "Iberia and south-west France, the Carpathian Basin, the Italian and Balkan peninsulas, and the Russian Plain".[101] Some groups survived over the glacial maximum even in areas further north. In my opinion it was not until the 15th century B.C., possibly, that agriculture spread from the south to central and western Europe. During the next century farming was adopted also in southern Scandinavia where communities belonging to a late and advanced Mesolithic culture called "Ertebølle" then existed.

So, hunting-and-gathering as a way of subsistence persisted in most parts of Europe since the time right after the dispersal at Babel until the latter part of the second millennium B.C. At the same time in the Near East — during the seven centuries of the Ice Age and more — agriculture began to be practiced everywhere from early on, pottery began to be produced, metals began to be used; later on, cities were built, writing was invented, the first empires were established, royal dynasties rose and fell, great civilizations flourished. Henry M. Morris is very close to the truth when he writes:[102]

> At the same time that Neanderthal man was trying to survive near the ice cap in Europe, and Siberian tribes in Asia, the great civilizations of Egypt, Sumeria, and others were developing in the lower latitudes, where the ice

---

[100] Michael J. Oard (1990), *An Ice Age Caused by the Genesis Flood*, 116. For concise accounts of the origin and effects of the Ice Age see for example Oard & Oard 1993, 62–71; John Morris 2009; Batten et al. 2012, 201–212; Sarfati 2015, 587–590; Oard 2019, 59–63, 129.
[101] Pettitt 2014, 291.
[102] Morris 2002, 427. See also Batten et al. 2012, 205.

did not extend, but where there was much more rainfall and the climate was more pleasant.

I disagree with the above quote just a little; whereas Morris appears to think that the Neanderthals lived in harsh and cold conditions near the edge of the ice sheet during the mature phase of the Ice Age, in my view they lived in Europe (and in some parts of the Near East) in the 22nd century B.C., mostly during the Lower and Middle Palaeolithic periods, during the time when the European ice sheet was still in its early stage in northern Scandinavia and the climate in central and western Europe was still very temperate. Some support for this view can be found in archaeology: at least it would appear that "the types of artefacts used to make tailored, weather-resistant clothing and well-insulated artificial shelters [...] (for instance, needles and awls made of bone, antler, or ivory) only become common in the Upper Palaeolithic".[103] It was already at the beginning of the Upper Palaeolithic period in Europe that the Middle Palaeolithic Neanderthal man started to become extinct. Further, Steven L. Kuhn and Amy E. Clark talk about an interesting observation made of the material record of the Neanderthals:[104]

> Looking specifically at the material record of the Neanderthals, however, there are some interesting anomalies. One is the lack of obvious technological responses to environmental variation, whether across space or though [sic] glacial/interglacial cycles. The archaeological and ethnographic records show clearly that the complexity, diversity, and contents of tool-kits of recent foragers varied in predictable ways across environmental gradients. It is difficult to identify analogous patterned variation in the Middle Palaeolithic, despite the vast range of environments in which it occurs [...] This anomaly cannot simply be attributed to an innate inflexibility among the makers of Middle Palaeolithic technologies in Eurasia [...]

It was not the mainly Middle Palaeolithic Neanderthals who had to live through the "environmental variation" during the Ice Age but the Upper Palaeolithic peoples[105] who

---

[103] Zilhão 2014, 200.
[104] Kuhn & Clark 2014, 615.
[105] First the so-called Aurignacians, followed in time by the Gravettians, followed in turn by the Solutreans, Badegoulians and Epigravettians who lived in the southern refugia during the glacial maximum, followed then by the so-called Magdalenians who recolonized central and western Europe. See Pettitt 2014; Riede 2014.

began to succeed them in Europe possibly even before the middle of the 22nd century B.C., only some 50 years after the dispersal at Babel.

The Neanderthals — having somewhat brutish looks with low foreheads, very noticeable arching brow ridges, and robust bodies, for example — did not just all die out, however, but many of them bred and merged with the "normal-looking" (so-called "modern *Homo sapiens*") Upper Palaeolithic people who migrated to Europe from the east. That is not to say that there were not any "normal-looking" people living in Europe among the Neanderthals already during the Lower and Middle Palaeolithic periods. Despite their abnormal appearance Neanderthals (as well as their smaller version, namely the *Homo erectus* in Asia and Africa) were normal humans, descendants of Noah's three sons Shem, Ham and Japheth. The high variational potential of the pre-dispersal people's gene pool (together with environmental and social factors such as extreme isolation, inbreeding, and subsequent genetic degeneration) explains the morphological variation seen in the fossil record of the early post-Babel man,[106] as well as the origin of the human "races".[107]

By mentioning earlier things like cities, writing and empires (as well as by dealing with the European hunter-gatherers and the Ice Age) I have gone little bit ahead of the actual time period and subject of this chapter which is intended to clarify briefly the complex cultural and geographical developments in the Near East during the first two post-Babel centuries. The formation of the first great cities, the invention of writing, and the establishment of the first empires are, however, among other things discussed in greater detail in the next chapter where the text also starts to follow more closely the Bible's own narrative — from the days of patriarch Abraham onwards.

---

[106] On this fossil record of the post-Babel humans (namely *"Homo erectus"*, "early *Homo sapiens*", "Neanderthals", and "modern *Homo sapiens*") see Marvin L. Lubenow (2004), *Bones of Contention*. See also Jack Cuozzo (1998), *Buried Alive*; Christopher Rupe & John Sanford (2019), *Contested Bones*; Line 2020, 59, 60. — "A biblical framework sees Neandertals as post-Babel people who were among the first to emigrate into Europe." Sanders 2021, 56.
[107] See for example Batten et al. 2012, 221–234; Sarfati 2015, 668–673. See also Ken Ham & A. Charles Ware (2010), *One Race One Blood*, and Carl Wieland (2011), *One Human Family*.

CHAPTER 4: IN THE DAYS OF ABRAHAM, ISAAC AND JACOB

The end of the southern Mesopotamian Ubaid period, which I have dated at the turn from the 21st to the 20th century B.C., saw the invention of the fast potter's wheel[108] and a new mass-produced pottery called the "Uruk ware", named after the city of Uruk which began to flourish and grow very large during the following period — the Uruk period.[109] The new ceramics replaced the old ware slowly, and the transition to the new period was smooth in other ways too: "in all respects the Uruk culture appears as the development of conditions that existed during the Ubaid period"[110], "an intensification of the earlier way of life, a realization of its potentials"[111]. Certainly "there is no clear-cut break between the Ubaid culture and the Uruk culture and no sign of armed invasion and destruction".[112] The Uruk culture arose in the southern Iraqi alluvial lowlands while late Ubaidian cultural influences still lingered in the north (Amuq E).

In the early Uruk period the much increased and fast-growing population living in southern Iraqi rural villages started to regroup itself heavily within and around rapidly enlarging towns. This led to a reinforcement of the authority of the towns' traditional chiefs who ran the public building projects, controlled the labor force mobilization, and managed the redistribution and trade of excess agricultural and livestock production and the tribute exacted from provincial populations. As a result of this power and wealth concentrated over time in the hands of small elite groups, and societies became pronouncedly hierarchical. The surplus foodstuffs could also maintain the economies of various professional groups like craftsmen, mass production employees, construction workers, supervisors, merchants, soldiers, artists, architects, priests and record keepers. Technical aids like plows, carts and boats boosted the prolific grain agriculture and transportation.[113] The watering of the fields was being taken care of through artificial

---

[108] See Nissen 1988, 47, 48; Selz 2020, 169, 170.

[109] "The city of Uruk so dominated the new cultural phase that followed the Ubaid that it was named for it. During the Uruk Period, Uruk achieved the status of the first great city-state in Mesopotamia." Bourke 2018, 62.

[110] Roux 1992, 82, 83.

[111] Foster & Foster 2009, 16.

[112] Roux 1992, 67, 68.

[113] See Roaf 1990, 72. — "[…] waterborne transport in ancient Mesopotamia was at least 8 times more efficient than the most cost effective forms of overland carriage using donkeys." Algaze 2018, 86.

irrigation (dug canals), the maintenance of which required great amounts of communal effort. In addition to arable plains (as well as pasture lands) "the contribution of marshes and estuaries was particularly fundamental to the initial growth of early cities in the southernmost part of the alluvium".[114]

Over time a series of monumental temples[115] and other large buildings was built in the center of the city of Uruk which by the end of the period had reached an extraordinary size of 250 hectares (about one square mile or 2,5 square kilometers) — a small metropolis "many times larger than any other settlement observed in Iraq at the time", "a unique agglomeration".[116] The most famous of those archaic shrines is the so-called "White Temple" which was dedicated possibly to the sky-god An who was one of the major deities of the ancient Mesopotamians. This late Uruk period sanctuary was constructed atop a 40 feet (12 meters) high brick platform[117] and resembled the stepped temple-towers (ziggurats) of the later periods. The earliest temples of Uruk as well as the Ubaid period temples at Eridu were already built upon platforms, but those were low. With time the platforms were erected higher and higher until they exceeded in size the temples themselves.[118] This is the origin of the ziggurat-towers of the ancient Mesopotamian civilization, and they most probably did not have any real connection to the tower of Babel.[119]

---

[114] Pournelle & Algaze 2014, 8. See also Pournelle 2013, 22, 23, 27–29; Wilkinson 2013, 38. During the early and middle Uruk periods "polities in the southern alluvium of Mesopotamia, modern southern Iraq, and southwestern Iran developed enough societal complexity to warrant classifying them as states [...] Outside the alluvium, polities in the hills of modern western Iran, the steppeland and hills of modern southeastern Turkey, northern Iraq, and North Syria were also developing more complex societal systems, but, not of the same complexity as those of the southern alluvium" (Rothman 2002, 263, 264; see also Algaze 2018, 76–79, 81). On the development of the southern Mesopotamian urban society during the Uruk period see also Algaze 2008.

[115] For the ruling elite religion was also a means of supporting the existing social order (see Foster & Foster 2009, 28, 29).

[116] Foster & Foster 2009, 21. See also Nissen 2018, 61, 62, 64; Selz 2020, 167; Bartash 2020, 539. It has been estimated that Uruk could have had up to 40,000 or so inhabitants at that time (Nissen 2003; 2018, 64; see also Algaze 2013, 74, 89 note 4; 2018, 77). On the ancient city of Uruk see also Crüsemann et al. (eds.) 2019.

[117] This massive brick platform "must have been a striking sight, visible for miles around, rising from the flat terrain of southern Mesopotamia at a time when large-scale monuments were still rare and unusual structures" (Bahrani 2017, 44).

[118] See Roux 1992, 62, 70, 164; Postgate 1994, 25 (Figure 2:2); Foster & Foster 2009, 63; Bahrani 2017, 36, 37; Eichmann 2019, 97–99.

[119] "For those who take Genesis 11 to be an historical account, the tower [of Babel] can hardly have looked like a ziggurat. Ziggurats [...] evolved from simpler religious structures [...]" Hoerth 1998, 197.

Towards the end of the Uruk period the record keeping needs of the complex administrative systems of the southern Mesopotamian regimes led to the invention of writing which started to replace the earlier accounting methods based on counting tokens, seals and numerical clay tablets.[120] Writing was initially in a form of small, simplified drawings of everyday objects (pictograms) and abstract symbols for words and ideas, but in a short course of time they were gradually transformed to the cuneiform ("wedge-shaped") signs used in Mesopotamian texts until the beginning of the first millennium A.D.[121]

This new innovation was mastered at first only by a small class of scribes. Common people like Abraham, who lived during the period when the art of writing was introduced to the world, very unlikely possessed this noble skill or any long written texts. Nor is it certain that actual writing had existed in the pre-flood world. I consider it likely that even Noah did not use any writing. In my view the knowledge of the important events and persons of the past (e.g. the creation of the world, Adam and Eve, the genealogy from Adam to Noah, the flood, the confusion of languages and the dispersal at Babel — all these are recorded in Gen 1–11) was stored faithfully in the accurate memory of sagacious people like Abraham[122], in a similar way as the ancient Arabs used to preserve their oral "books" of poetry virtually unchanged over many generations.[123]

---

[120] See for example Roaf 1990, 70; Roux 1992, 73–76; Foster & Foster 2009, 30–33; Woods 2010b; Stiebing & Helft 2018, 43–46; Nissen 2019; Marzahn 2019; Selz 2020, 194–204, 220. — "[...] at the very end of the Uruk period, in level Uruk IVa, writing appeared, in all probability a local invention." Beaulieu 2018, 31. — "The invention of writing at Uruk — and it is plausible to think that it was invented in that city by a particular individual [...]" Potts 2019, 3. See also Nissen 2019, 150, 151.

[121] At the beginning writing, like its precursors (tokens, seals, numerical tablets), functioned independently of language and the texts contained only very brief bits of information. It was not until the so-called Early Dynastic period that the southern Mesopotamian scribes further developed "cuneiform to render spoken language. And only from this moment on was it possible to write coherent texts" (Nissen 2001, 178; see also Nissen & Heine 2009, 4, 5, 48, 57, 58; Woods 2010a, 18–22; 2010b, 33, 34, 43–45; Seri 2010, 87; Krebernik 2019; Bartash 2020, 531). The Early Dynastic period succeeded the Uruk period in southern Mesopotamia, only a short interlude called the Jemdet Nasr period coming between them. Both the Jemdet Nasr and the Early Dynastic periods will be discussed more later. The oldest-known language documented in cuneiform writing is Sumerian which according to Simo Parpola (2010; 2016; but see also Cunningham 2013, 96, 97) belongs to the so-called Uralic language family (as does also Finnish, for example).

[122] According to Josephus (JA, Book I:vii.1 (p. 77)) Abraham was "a man of ready intelligence on all matters, persuasive with his hearers, and not mistaken in his inferences".

[123] See Hoyland 2001, 212. See also Mackintosh-Smith 2019, 58–60, 84, 85, 102, 103.

The people who lived in Babel before the dispersal must have known a lot about the things recorded in the Book of Genesis' chapters 1–11. Surely it was the righteous men like Noah and Shem who saw to it that the sacred history and the fear of God were not forgotten. After the confusion of languages the scattered groups carried with them the learned traditions and the recent experiences to their new homelands — also to the southern part of Iraq where, unfortunately, that historical and religious heritage became soon blurred and corrupted, and the faith in the real creator God was suppressed under the emerging polytheistic paganism.[124] However, glimpses of the original traditions can still be seen in certain very old Mesopotamian myths and legends which contain some startling similarities with the stories and documentation of the first chapters of the Bible. The knowledge of the universal flood, for example, was preserved also among numerous tribes and nations all around the world.[125]

By divine providence, however, the real knowledge of the past was kept unaltered for a long time by pious individuals through many godly family lineages. Abraham must have been one of the guardians of the truth[126] who communicated the received old traditions to his own household and descendants who, in turn, continued to store them in memory over the years until they were finally edited and written down in the Book of Genesis by Moses — who, being under the influence of God's inspiration and counsel, was not dependent on his own intellect and the earthly sources only.[127]

---

[124] "For although they knew God, they neither glorified him as God nor gave thanks to him, but their thinking became futile and their foolish hearts were darkened." Rom 1:21 NIV. See also Jer 16:19, 20.

[125] See Bill Cooper (2011), *The Authenticity of the Book of Genesis*; Raúl López (1998), *The Antediluvian Patriarchs and the Sumerian King List*. See also Bill Cooper (1995), *After the Flood*; Wang & Nelson 1998; Martin 2009; Thong & Fu 2009; Forbes 2011; Campbell 2012, 33–39; Anderson & Edwards 2014, 2, 3; Hodge & Welch (eds.) 2014; Chaffey 2016; Kaiser & Wegner 2017, 44–46; Price & House 2017, 55–63; Liguori 2021. When the pagan Sumero-Akkadians composed their mythological stories and histories, they drew everything against the background of the natural environments, cities, societal systems and cultural features that were familiar to them and within which they were living themselves. See for example Kramer 1972; Roux 1992, 82, 85–121; Foster 2013.

[126] However, it seems to say in Josh 24:2 that Abraham used to be an idolater while he was still living in Mesopotamia, but, in my view, he had rejected the false gods already some time before God told him to leave his country (Gen 12:1). C. F. Keil (2011b, 167) conjectures that Abraham "was not deeply sunk in idolatry, though he had not remained entirely free from it in his father's house".

[127] On the authorship, date and structure of the Book of Genesis see for example Sarfati 2015, 7–32. Of course it is possible that at least some parts of the guarded tradition (e.g. Gen 5, "the book of the genealogy of Adam" NKJV; see also Kidner 1967, 80; Aalders 1981, 138; Wenham 1987, 122; Sarna 1989, 41; Hamilton 1990, 254; Mathews 1996, 306, 307; Waltke 2001, 113; Arnold 2009, 85; Leupold 2010, 144; Currid 2015, 161, 162; Hendel 2024, 244; but see also Cassuto 1961, 273; Westermann 1994, 355; Fischer 2018, 331, 332, 344, 364; NRSV; REB; CEV) existed already in some written form shortly before

Now, to continue on the main trajectory of our narration, Abraham[128] was born in 1996 B.C., a couple of years after the death of Noah.[129] His life commenced in southern Iraq at the same time with the onset of the Uruk period, during which "the cultural development already perceptible during the Ubaid period proceeded at a quicker pace and the Sumerian civilization finally blossomed",[130] as we saw above. However, the rise of this civilization could not have been possible without natural resources like timber, common as well as precious and semiprecious stones, and metals (copper, lead, gold, silver) which were imported into the raw-material-lacking southern alluvium from distant regions.[131] Around the mid-century, in order to secure access to these needed commodities and to regularize their flow, the powerful southern centers like Uruk, Ur, Eridu, Nippur and Larsa started to extend their politico-economic presence and cultural influence strongly to the north amongst the weaker native societies, characterized then by ceramics of the Amuq F type. A little earlier, in the second quarter of the century (in LC 3 or even late LC 2)[132], settlers from southern Iraq had begun to colonize the plains of southwestern Iran, thus inaugurating the period's massive population and culture diffusions collectively referred to as the "Uruk Expansion". In the words of Guillermo Algaze, "This expansion took a variety of forms in different areas, depending no doubt

---

Moses. Moses very likely used in his Hebrew texts the so-called proto-consonantal script, that is, the world's oldest consonantal letters that were invented in Egypt (by Israelites?) when the Israelites were living there. See also Courville 1971, 111, 112 (in volume 1); Douglas Petrovich (2016), *The World's Oldest Alphabet: Hebrew as the Language of the Proto-Consonantal Script*; Hughes 2020.

[128] His name was originally Abram but God changed it later to Abraham (Gen 17:5).

[129] Jones 2015, 278. Noah died when he was 950 years old (Gen 9:29). The Book of Genesis' chapter 11 demonstrates that after the flood human lifespan shortened exponentially over time (see Jones 2015, 74a; Holladay 2016) so that modern people live only about a tenth of the years that the antediluvians used to live. This life expectancy drop is best explained by genetics (see for example Sarfati 2015, 467–469, 685–688; but see also the chapter "Why Did People Live for about 900 Years before the Flood?" in Walt Brown's *In the Beginning*). See also John C. Sanford (2014), *Genetic Entropy*, 158–160, 168.

[130] Roux 1992, 66. — "The more we learn, the more we see this period as the real beginning of Mesopotamian civilization, which was to last until the early Christian era." Foster & Foster 2009, 33.

[131] "Natural resources were unevenly distributed [...] Southern Mesopotamia had the most dependable crops, and it had salt, along with bitumen [...], but it had stone only in a few places and no metal ores. It was not poor, however." Podany 2014, 9. The marshes and estuaries of South Mesopotamia provided "substantial and easily exploitable resources usable as food, fodder, fuel and raw materials (minimally including fish, reeds, dates, flax, salt, dyestuffs and shell) that were not available to peer societies away from the Mesopotamian delta region" (Pournelle & Algaze 2014, 8).

[132] See Algaze 2001, 46; 2013, 82, 83. LC = (Greater Mesopotamian) Late Chalcolithic, periods 1–5: LC 1 = terminal Ubaid/Ubaid-Uruk transitional period; LC 2 = early Uruk period; LC 3–4 = middle Uruk period; LC 5 = late Uruk period. See Rothman 2001, 5–9.

on distance away from the alluvium, ease of transport, and the varying nature of preexisting societies in the intruded areas."[133]

By the end of the third quarter of the century, in the late Uruk period (LC 5), the southern polities had succeeded in establishing many colonies, communities and stations in northern parts of Mesopotamia on strategically important locations along the main water and land routes. In this manner they were able to tap very effectively into the preexisting exchange networks leading from the resource rich north to the ever-hungry south. According to some scholars the southern Mesopotamian cities controlled the interregional trade and affected politically and culturally the peripheral local societies to such an extent that it can be said that there existed then a kind of Uruk "world system" or "economic empire" which reached into modern southeastern Turkey and western Iran.[134]

This hegemony, however, did not last a long time. The end of the Uruk period, which in my view correlates with the end of the 20th century B.C., saw a sudden collapse of the southern presence and influence in the regions where the Uruk population and culture had spread. Most of the Uruk settlements in the north were violently destroyed or just abandoned and never inhabited thereafter, but indigenous societies often continued to develop further in their own right, having greatly benefited socio-politically and economically from the contacts with the southern powers. Certain changes took place also within the southern Mesopotamian alluvium, but those will be discussed in more detail later.

During the time when the "Uruk empire" was still in its glory, Abraham, who was then 60–70 years old, received one day a word from God:

> Get thee out of thy country, and from thy kindred, and from thy father's house, unto a land that I will shew thee: And I will make of thee a great nation, and I will bless thee, and make thy name great; and thou shalt be a blessing: And I will bless them that bless thee, and curse him that curseth

---

[133] Algaze 2013, 82.

[134] See Guillermo Algaze (2005), *The Uruk World System*; see also Algaze 2001; 2013; Scarre et al. 2021, 85–89. Actually, besides having connections to the north and the east, the Sumerian cities of the Uruk period had exchange relationships also with areas in the far south via the Persian Gulf, so that "remarkably, for a brief period of time the trading network of the Uruk world stretched from Anatolia to eastern Oman" (Carter 2013, 579).

> thee: and in thee shall all families of the earth be blessed. (Gen 12:1–3 KJV;
> see also Acts 7:2–4)

It is told in Gen 11:31 that Abraham left "Ur of the Chaldeans" with his wife Sarah[135], his nephew Lot, and his father Terah to go to the land of Canaan.[136] Ur was a southern Mesopotamian city in an area where a people known as Chaldeans lived.[137] The name "Chaldeans" probably derived from Noah's grandson Arphaxad who was their great leader and forefather.[138] Abraham was also his descendant (Gen 11:10–26) and probably belonged to the Semitic Chaldean tribe.[139]

In my opinion Abraham and his relatives journeyed first toward the north until they came to Nineveh. From there they went on their way toward the west until they finally arrived in Haran (or Harran), a place located in modern southeastern Turkey some 600 miles (960 kilometers) northwest of Ur.[140]

After staying in Haran for a while Abraham, being then 75 years old (Gen 12:4), departed from there and took with him (Gen 12:5 NKJV) "Sarai his wife and Lot his brother's son, and all their possessions that they had gathered, and the people whom they had

---

[135] Actually, her name was at that time Sarai but God changed it later to Sarah (Gen 17:15).

[136] As a matter of fact, Gen 11:31 may imply that also other members of Terah's family left Ur at the same time and not only the persons who are specifically mentioned in the verse (see Cassuto 1964, 280, 281; but see also Mathews 2005, 103, 104). It is quite certain that Abraham, Sarah and Lot were living as members of Terah's household ("from thy father's house" Gen 12:1), and in fact "Mesopotamian society in the alluvial plain most probably comprised extended families, the basic social units for primary production (agriculture and livestock)" (Frangipane 2001, 310). — "[...] in the Uruk period, much if not most production [...] continued to take place within households [...] households were the principal locus of production and consumption in ancient Mesopotamia." Pollock 1999, 115, 117.

[137] A land situating in the lower part of the southern Mesopotamian alluvium is named *Kaldu* (Chaldea) first time in Assyrian annals from the early first millennium B.C. (Wiseman 1982), but this does not have to mean that there were no Chaldeans living in that region long before, even during the time of Abraham. Those ancient Chaldeans were a seminomadic people who herded their animals in the deserts between North Arabia and the Persian Gulf (cp. Job 1:17).

[138] This is confirmed by the first-century A.D. Jewish historian Josephus in his *Jewish Antiquities*, Book I:vi.4 (p. 71): "Arphaxades named those under his rule Arphaxadaeans, the Chaldaeans of to-day." The last three consonants of Arphaxad's Hebrew name אַרְפַּכְשַׁד (ʾarpakšaḏ) form almost perfectly the root for the Chaldeans' Hebrew name כַּשְׂדִּים (kaśdîm). See also Mathews 1996, 461; Day 2022, 185.

[139] In early times three ethno-linguistic groups lived close together within southern Iraq: the Sumerians, the Semites, and "a small, diffuse minority of uncertain origin" (Roux 1992, 80).

[140] Thus, they followed the better one of the two main routes which led from South Mesopotamia to Syria and the Mediterranean coast (see Roux 1992, 14; Gurney 1998, 164). Archaeological finds show that Haran was occupied already during the Uruk period (see Chavalas 2003, 379). Abraham's Ur was situated in southern Mesopotamia and not — as some have suggested — in the northern Levant close to Haran. See for example Waltke 2001, 200; Kitchen 2003, 316; Wiseman 2009, 969, 970; Currid 2015, 250; Day 2022, 208–210. But see also Hamilton 1990, 363–365; Beitzel 2009, 98–100; Walton 2009, 65–67; Steinmann 2019, 142. On the archaeology and history of Ur see Crawford 2015.

acquired in Haran, and they departed to go to the land of Canaan. So, they came to the land of Canaan" after journeying some 400 miles (640 kilometers) to the southwest of Haran across the modern-day Syria and Jordan.[141]

Abraham's arrival in the land of Canaan took place in the year 1921 B.C.[142] which was almost 300 years after the dispersal at Babel in 2215 B.C. (my estimation). That land — historically better known (broadly speaking) as the land of Israel or Palestine[143] — was inhabited at that time mostly by the descendants of Noah's grandson Canaan, "the Canaanites" (Gen 10:6, 15–19; 12:6). Their ancestors had left the plain of Shinar in southeastern Turkey and moved southwestward to the eastern Mediterranean region where they lived by hunting and gathering for many decades.[144] Eventually the increased family sizes, combined with the people's social desire to stick close together, drove many hunter-gatherer groups to look for a more sustainable though not necessarily easier way of subsistence: they started to establish more permanent settled communities on well-watered locations where it was possible to cultivate crops and raise domestic animals.[145] Wild animals and plants, however, still remained as an important if not the main source of food for some time to come.[146] The reasons for the transition to the Neolithic lifestyle must have, of course, varied among different groups of people living within different environmental, cultural and social circumstances.[147]

---

[141] See for example Rasmussen 2010, 90, 91.

[142] See Jones 2015, 24, 25, 278.

[143] In this book I prefer the name "Palestine" for that particular geographical area, but I do so without any political intention.

[144] For more on the post-Babel migrations of the descendants of Noah's three sons Shem, Ham and Japheth see Hodge 2013, 113–190.

[145] "Ethnographic studies show that the life of early farmers was more arduous than that of hunter-gatherers, especially in the resource-rich areas of the Near East, where food could be readily collected without much effort. The question of why people moved toward agriculture thus remains difficult to answer, and the desire to live in larger communities may have been the main driving force." Van De Mieroop 2016, 11.

[146] This is indicated also by the numerous aerodynamically shaped projectile points or "arrowheads" found in early Neolithic contexts. Other typical Neolithic stone tools were axes, adzes, chisels, picks, hoes, knives, sickles, and various stone vessels and pulverizing equipment. Most of the stone tool making methods used by the Epipalaeolithic peoples continued into the Neolithic period, and some new techniques also emerged (see Shea 2013, 222–232). As a possible side effect of the sedentary way of living Neolithic stone tools were more strongly form-function correlated, that is to say, more functionally specialized than their Palaeolithic counterparts (see Shea 2013, 44, 305, 306, 308).

[147] The hunter-gatherers living near the pottery making cultures of Mesopotamia were perhaps generally more ready to embrace a new sedentary way of life than those living in more distant areas. The time before the tragic turn at Babel had remained in the memory of many people, and some who were scraping a living as hunter-gatherers longed for a life like in the old good days. The knowledge and

Many early Neolithic settlements were established in the Jordan Valley in the land of Canaan or Palestine at the end of the 22nd century B.C., Jericho being one of them. The site of Jericho, today known as Tell es-Sultan, was inhabited already in the late Epipalaeolithic period but it was during the following Pre-Pottery Neolithic A period that it became a thriving village community. At the western margin of the present-day 10-acre mound the excavators discovered a large, approximately 27 feet (8 meters) high and almost equally wide, stone tower built against the inside of an enclosure wall which was reinforced on its outer side by a broad trench dug into the rock. These massive Pre-Pottery Neolithic structures were so well done that, according to Amihai Mazar, "Technical skill, planning, and construction ability at Jericho must have been at a level only slightly inferior to that in later, Bronze Age periods".[148] Georges Roux describes the Pre-Pottery Neolithic Jericho as a place "which, with its well-built houses and strong city-wall of undressed stones, must have looked like a small medieval town".[149]

In my view Pre-Pottery Neolithic life lasted in Jericho perhaps almost 100 years, until the last decades of the 21st century B.C. During that phase the mud brick houses of Jericho were renovated and rebuilt numerous times; consequently "The accumulation of the Pre-Pottery Neolithic debris [...] reached an unprecedented depth of 9–10 m[eters]"[150] (over 30 feet) at the site. Such a rapid pace of deposition was totally possible during the early post-flood centuries when there was a lot more rainfall and more storms in many areas compared to current much drier climatic conditions. Waters pouring from the sky

---

skills necessary to farming and herding had not been totally forgotten either. It could also happen in certain cases that, after some time and some serious problems, new agriculturists had to revert completely back to hunting and gathering.

[148] Amihai Mazar (1992), *Archaeology of the Land of the Bible*, 42. See also Kaiser & Wegner 2017, 55, 56. Jericho was by no means the only place with monumental architecture in those days: roughly contemporary constructions were, in my view, the megalithic temples of the Pre-Pottery Neolithic Göbekli Tepe and Nevalı Çori in southeastern Turkey (see Sagona & Zimansky 2009, 57–63; Schmidt 2011; 2012, 150–159; Landis (ed.) 2015, 28–30), "a curving wall with semi-circular projections suggesting towers" of the Pre-Pottery Neolithic Tell Maghzaliyeh in northwestern Iraq (Roux 1992, 45), and "a 3-metre-deep ditch doubled by a thick, buttressed mud wall" of the Samarran Tell es-Sawwan in central Iraq (Roux 1992, 54), for example.

[149] Roux 1992, 46. In the words of Alan H. Simmons (2007, 99) the PPNA Jericho "reflects an enormous degree of skill and planning that required considerable social organization". — "In addition, P. Dorrell has calculated that if Jericho was surrounded by a wall 600 meters long, 4 meters high, and 2 meters wide, only 1360 workdays of one builder (based on a rate of 3.3 cubic meters per day), or a week's work of 200 laborers, would have been required to construct it." Bar-Yosef 1992, 16. Ever wondered how long (or short) it took to build the tower of Babel?

[150] Mazar 1992, 40.

could erode the clayey walls and roofs fairly quickly so that houses had to be reconstructed frequently.[151] A whole village could become destroyed to the ground during a single violent storm, especially if the houses were made of poor-quality mud bricks. This notion gets support from a devastation that befell the village of Aqaba in southernmost Palestine, as reported by Nelson Glueck:[152]

> In April, 1940, a terrific rain- and hail-storm literally washed half of the mud-brick village away. Many of the mud-brick walls simply dissolved. A few days later, the natives began to make new mud-bricks, and dry them in the sun, preparatory to repairing the damage. Their bricks were made without any binding materials whatsoever, except lumps of dried mud from which the sand content had been more or less washed away by the rains. Small wonder that such bricks go to pieces during the first heavy rain! [...] the mud-brick walls of modern 'Aqabah crumble and collapse not long after they are built.

According to one of the excavators of Jericho, John Garstang, "mud bricks, such as were used throughout the life history of Jericho, were peculiarly liable to decay".[153]

Around the middle of the 21st century B.C., in my view, small pottery-making agrarian communities began to emerge in the fertile plains and valleys of Palestine.[154] As the key Palestinian Pottery Neolithic cultures can be named the so-called "Yarmukian", "Lodian", and "Wadi Rabah".[155] Both the Yarmukian and the Wadi Rabah cultures existed mainly in the northern parts of the land. The type site of the Lodian culture is Jericho (level IX, Pottery Neolithic A). Yarmukian and Wadi Rabah are generally

---

[151] See also Donovan A. Courville (1971), *The Exodus Problem and Its Ramifications*, 157–163 (in volume 2); A. J. M. Osgood (1986a), *A Better Model for the Stone Age*, 95–97; von Fange 1990, 206–232; 1994, 297–324; 2006, 32. Besides many village sites fast and thick stratification took place — mostly in purely natural ways — also in various caves and rockshelters, a good example being the northeastern Iraqi Shanidar Cave which was used as an occasional dwelling place by hunter-gatherers (also Neanderthals) since the Middle Palaeolithic period; for a cross section of the cave see for example Solecki 1971, 126; Redman 1978, 63; Nissen 1988, 17.

[152] Glueck 1940, 12.

[153] Garstang & Garstang 1948, 57.

[154] In my opinion the Pottery Neolithic period started in the northern parts of the Levant somewhat earlier than in the southern parts (see also Gopher 1995, 207; Bartl 2012, 388; Akkermans 2014, 142, 143; 2020, 68).

[155] On these cultures see Gopher 1995, for example.

considered as chronologically sequential traditions, in that order.[156] Nonetheless the two could have still been much overlapping temporally.

In my view the Wadi Rabah culture persisted until the late 20th century B.C. It was largely contemporary with the Palestinian Chalcolithic cultures, the most remarkable of them being the so-called "Ghassulian" which — again in my view — lasted about 100 years from the second quarter of the 20th century B.C. onward.[157] The Chalcolithic settlements of Palestine were situated emphatically — in contrast to the preceding and succeeding periods — in the land's peripheral areas such as the northern Negev, the Judean Desert, and the Golan Heights, areas which are today relatively arid.[158] Many Chalcolithic sites existed also in the Jordan Valley. For example, Teleilat Ghassul, a type site of the Ghassulian culture, was an economically and culturally important village/small town located at the southeastern end of the valley opposite to Jericho in the west.[159]

As the term "Chalcolithic" (from the Greek *chalkos*, "copper", and *lithos*, "stone")[160] implies tools and other objects made of copper began to appear in Palestine during that time.[161] In the early 1960s an ancient cache of various copper artifacts (over 400 in total)

---

[156] For differing views on the Pottery Neolithic cultures of Palestine see Simmons 2007, 200, 201; Sharon 2014, 49, 50.

[157] Suitably, Yosef Garfinkel (1999b, 5, 6) does not consider the Wadi Rabah culture as Pottery Neolithic but as early Chalcolithic. See also Goring-Morris & Belfer-Cohen 2014, 149, 151; Rowan 2014, 223, 224. Also, Syrian Halaf-influence has been noticed in the material remains of the Wadi Rabah culture (Mazar 1992, 53; Banning 2002, 48; Golden 2014, 13; Bourke 2018, 51; see also Akkermans 2014, 143). The Ghassulian culture, in turn, was influenced by the Ubaid culture (see Mazar 1992, 87, 88; Golden 2014, 10; see also Thuesen 1989, 435). Some pottery of the Yarmukian culture resembles the Hassuna ware of northern Iraq (see Amiran 1969, 20). All this confirms that effects of the Great Migration (see page 33 in this book) reached the southern Levant.

[158] See Mazar 1992, 60–63. See also Gonen 1992, 42–48; Greenberg 2019, 15, 17.

[159] "It is possible that the earliest levels at [Teleilat] Ghassul fall somewhere around the time of the Pottery Neolithic (PN) A-B transition at Jericho [...] The following phases [...] represent the early Chalcolithic [...] It is quite possible that this phase was contemporary with the 'Wadi Rabah' sites, yet lay outside the sphere of immediate 'Rabah' influence." Golden 2014, 23.

[160] Liddell & Scott 1994, 113, 776.

[161] "The Chalcolithic period was marked by the local inception of copper technology, although many aspects of material culture remained much the same as in the Neolithic (Wadi Rabah) period." Golden 2009, 45. See also Golden 2014, 10–12, 74, 95. On the copper production in the Chalcolithic period see Levy 2007, 39–45. Chalcolithic cultures used also stone tools, of course. As a matter of fact, stone tools continued to be produced a very long time after the end of the actual "Stone Age". See Rosen 1997; 2012, 249–253, 257, 258; OEBA, 2:369–372; Shea 2013, 285, 286. — "[...] the earliest gold in the southern Levant appears at a [Chalcolithic] cave tomb in the form of large, ring-shaped items, the function of which is not clear [...]" Golden 2009, 209. See also Levy 2007, 50; Golden 2014, 55–57. Cp. Job 42:11 (NKJV): "Then all his brothers, all his sisters, and all those who had been his acquaintances

from the Chalcolithic period was found in a remote cave in the Judean Desert.[162] It is very likely that those copper artifacts, being clearly ritualistic in character, had originally belonged to a small Ghassulian-Chalcolithic temple complex discovered at nearby En Gedi on the western shore of the Dead Sea. For some mysterious reason the temple complex was abandoned at the end of the period, and the rich cult equipment was hidden away by its priests.[163]

In my view the origin of the Palestinian Chalcolithic cultures was in the intermingling of the native Neolithic population with northern Mesopotamian and Anatolian immigrants who arrived in the land before the mid-20th century B.C.[164] Further, during the last decades of the century, more foreigners came into Palestine from the late Uruk (LC 5) Mesopotamia and Anatolia. Those people, in turn, contributed to the emergence of the Palestinian Early Bronze I (EB I) cultures.[165] Thus Abraham, who himself moved to the land around 1921 B.C., was just one of a large number of people who had left their

---

before, came to him and ate food with him in his house; and they consoled him and comforted him for all the adversity that the LORD had brought upon him. Each one gave him a piece of silver and each a ring of gold."

[162] See Bar-Adon (ed.) 1980; Tadmor 1986, 72–85; Gonen 1992, 66–71; NEAEHL, 3:822–827.

[163] See Ussishkin 1971; 2014; Mazar 1992, 66, 68, 72–75, 81. See also Kaiser & Wegner 2017, 62–64; Currid 2020, 121, 122. — "The enclosure at En-Gedi was not destroyed but was abandoned, and when the last worshipers left, they apparently took the cult furniture with them." NEAEHL, 2:405.

[164] See also Gonen 1992, 78, 79; Mazar 1992, 73, 75, 87, 88; Harney & May et al. 2018.

[165] "In the past, it was widely accepted that the EB I culture represented a massive immigration from outside Palestine […] There are also some indications of Mesopotamian influence in the local EB I culture, such as the bent cylindrical spouts of pottery 'teapots' and the appearance of cylinder seals. These elements could have arrived in Palestine via Sumerian colonies which are now known to have existed along the Upper Euphrates […] (such as at Habuba Kabira) […] Thus it appears that the material culture of EB I Palestine was an intermingling of new features — originating in Syria, Anatolia, and Mesopotamia — with elements rooted in the local culture of the preceding period. Probably, to some extent, ethnic and demographic changes occurred; it is possible that new peoples arrived in Palestine mainly from Syria and mixed with the remnants of the autochthonous population." Mazar 1992, 104, 105. See also Ben-Tor 1992, 93. One foreign ethnic group to arrive in the land of Canaan during the 20th century B.C. may have been the Horites (חֹרִי, ḥōrî) who are mentioned in Gen 14:6. It is possible to equate them with the extrabiblical Hurrians, a people who played a significant role in the ancient Near Eastern history (see for example TWOT, 323, 324; Walton et al. 2000, 172, 173; HALOT, 353; Harrison 2005, 63; Carpenter 2009, 434; HAHAT, 396, 397; Longman 2020, 95). The Hurrians' original homeland was, as has been proposed, in eastern Anatolia and Transcaucasia, but in later ancient times they had a strong presence also in northern Mesopotamia (see Bryce & Birkett-Rees 2016, 123, 124). One northern Palestinian EB I pottery group, namely the so-called "Gray Burnished ware" (see Amiran 1969, 47–49), may have had a Horite/Hurrian origin, at least in my opinion: "Though Gray Burnished Ware was locally made, both the shapes and the decoration were foreign to the Levant; their parallels have to be sought in northeastern Anatolia. This ware, therefore, can be taken as evidence of immigration of small population groups from eastern Anatolia to northern Palestine via Syria. The immigrants probably assimilated with the local population, but they continued to produce a limited number of shapes of their traditional pottery." Mazar 1992, 103. See also Golden 2002a, 95; Greenberg 2019, 36.

homelands, crossed the river Euphrates, and found a new domicile amongst the Canaanites.[166]

So, entering Palestine Abraham met a land of cultural mosaic containing local communities which represented different but contemporary traditions: late Pottery Neolithic, late Chalcolithic, and early Early Bronze I. Surely there survived also a few hunter-gatherer groups in some remote areas of the country. The view that different "cultural periods" did coexist for a while in Palestine gets support from the fact that "Some scholars [...] hold that the new culture [EB I] became entrenched in the northern and central parts of the country, while the Chalcolithic people still lived in the south".[167] Donovan A. Courville shows a great understanding when he suggests that "Chalcolithic is but a local phase at specific sites, falling entirely within the period of Neolithic and possibly extending into Early Bronze of Palestine".[168]

---

[166] In Gen 14:13 Abraham is called הָעִבְרִי (hā'iḇrî, hā being an article), "the Hebrew", an appellation which probably meant at that time "an immigrant from beyond the Euphrates" (Keil 2011a, 131; see also BDB, 720 (Strong's #5680); TWOT, 643; HAHAT, 917, 918; Mathews 1996, 460 note 107; 2005, 146). For sure Abraham was not the only "Hebrew" in the land of Canaan. In later ancient times a similar sounding term 'Apiru (often also spelled Ḫabiru), a social designation which could refer to foreigners, refugees, or even marauders, occurred in texts from all over the Near East. Gleason L. Archer (2007, 241) is probably right when he writes that "the Ḫabiru were 'people from the other side,' or 'migrants,' and this term may have been applied to those of diverse national origin. It is only in the Hebrew records that we find the name in the form 'ibrî (Hebrew) used to refer to a single racial stock, namely the descendants of Abraham, 'the Hebrew.' Thus Abraham may have been called 'the Ḫabiru' by the Canaanites because of his mode of life and because he was a foreigner; but then his descendants retained this designation in honor of their ancestor and transmuted it into an ethnic term." — "The designation of Abram as a 'Hebrew' may reflect a social status more than an ethnic identity." Walton 2009, 80. See also Wenham 1987, 313; Collins & Holden (eds.) 2020, 60, 61, 64, 66. But see also Arnold 2009, 147; Goldingay 2020, 235; Day 2022, 181, 182.

[167] Mazar 1992, 89. — "It is conceivable that at a certain time the northern Ghassulian culture had already been replaced by the culture of the beginning of the Early Bronze Age, while the southern Ghassulian culture continued to exist." Gonen 1992, 42.

[168] Courville 1971, 171 (in volume 2). The earliest occupation level (XX) of Megiddo belongs to the late Pottery Neolithic period. The succeeding stratum (XIX), in turn, belongs already to the Early Bronze I period, although some pieces of Chalcolithic pottery were found there too. Further, there was a temple in EB I Megiddo that resembled the Ghassulian-Chalcolithic temple at En Gedi. See Amiran 1969, 18, 19, 22; Ben-Tor 1992, 87, 88; Mazar 1992, 53, 54, 98, 145 (note 8); NEAEHL, 3:1005; AEHL, 329. In my view the cultural transition in Megiddo from the late PN to the EB I took place towards the end of the 20th century B.C, and the two above mentioned temples may have been in operation simultaneously — albeit only a very short period of time. At Jericho "Surprisingly, no Chalcolithic settlement is known to have existed" (Mazar 1992, 63); there, like at Megiddo, the late PN was succeeded by the EB I (or "Proto-Urban", in Kathleen M. Kenyon's terminology) (see NEAEHL, 2:678). The pottery of the late PN Jericho (level VIII, Pottery Neolithic B) has affinities with both the Wadi Rabah and Ghassulian ceramics (see Kenyon 1979, 51, 52, 57; Osgood 1986a, 95; Garfinkel 1999a; Golden 2014, 13). No doubt the late PN/early EB I Jericho and Megiddo were contemporary with the Ghassulian-Chalcolithic culture.

Abraham then passed through the land of Canaan towards the region of Negev in the southern part of the country (Gen 12:6–9). Next, about the year 1919 B.C., "there was a famine in the land, and Abram went down to Egypt to dwell there, for the famine *was* severe in the land" (Gen 12:10 NKJV).[169] In (northern) Egypt he became involved with a local ruler who is called "pharaoh" (Gen 12:14–20).[170] In my view the time of this pharaoh's reign belonged still to the late Pre-Dynastic Gerzean-Chalcolithic period of Egypt, for "The early part of EB I [of Palestine] can be associated with the late Pre-Dynastic Gerzean culture, while late EB I was contemporary with Dynasty 0 and the beginning of the First Dynasty".[171] The so-called First Dynasty of Egypt was not established until, in my estimation, the first quarter of the 19th century B.C. when its founder King Narmer put the whole country under his dominion.[172]

---

[169] In my view it was probably during this famine that Chalcolithic settlements in the northern Negev were abandoned and their people moved to other areas such as the central coastal plain where Chalcolithic settlements and burial sites have been found (see Mazar 1992, 84; Levy 1995, 235). In a later time, during another famine, Abraham's son Isaac also moved from Negev further north to the area of Gerar in the southern coastal plain (Gen 25:11; 26:1). — "The survey of [Chalcolithic] settlement sites noted that most of the sites were abandoned, with no evidence of violent struggle. Most were not resettled in the following period or in any succeeding period. This is especially true of the sites of the south and of the Golan. The impression is created of a sudden end to the period as a result of a catastrophe of some sort, either natural or inflicted by man, which forced the inhabitants to abandon their settlements and move on elsewhere." Gonen 1992, 79.

[170] This ruler's residence may have been at Tell el-Farkha in the eastern Nile Delta. See Gatto 2018, 179, 186, 187, 189. The meaning of the Egyptian royal title pharaoh is "great house", denoting the palace of the king (Shaw & Nicholson 2008, 248, 249; Kitchen 2009, 839). According to a Jewish tradition, "The Egyptian ruler, whose meeting with Abraham had proved so untoward an event, was the first to bear the name Pharaoh. The succeeding kings were named thus after him" (Ginzberg 1909, 225). — "It was probably towards the end of this [Pre-Dynastic] period that Abraham visited Egypt, a time before Egypt was unified when there was a local king in the East Delta and Canaan was in the Chalcolithic period." Porter 2022, 7.

[171] Mazar 1992, 108. See also Gophna 1995, 277. In my view the Chalcolithic period began in Egypt and Palestine about the same time. Further, utilizing and interpreting the information presented in Hendrickx & Vermeersch 2003 and Köhler 2020, the Epipalaeolithic and early Saharan Neolithic periods of Egypt correspond chronologically, by and large, to the Pre-Pottery Neolithic period of Palestine. The middle and late Saharan Neolithic periods, in turn, correlate roughly with the first half of the Palestinian Pottery Neolithic period. As the name implies the Saharan Neolithic peoples lived in the desert areas west of the Nile Valley. They produced pottery from the earliest phase on and herded livestock but, surprisingly, never practiced agriculture. Some Saharan Neolithic cultures continued into dynastic time. Agriculture was introduced to Egypt most probably from the Levant. The earliest crop cultivating cultures of Egypt, namely Faiyum A and Merimda in the northern Nile Valley and Badarian in the south, are unlikely to be older than the Yarmukian culture of Palestine. For more on the prehistoric Egypt from a good biblical-creationist perspective see Osgood 1986a, 100. Osgood's chronological chart "Figure 10" is commendable but in need of some improvement.

[172] By the designation "Dynasty 0" are meant very late Pre-Dynastic kings who reigned locally before the unification of Egypt. Many scholars put Narmer among the kings of the Dynasty 0, but others name him as the first king of the First Dynasty. Mizraim, Noah's grandson (Gen 10:6) whose name means "Egypt" in Hebrew, was the great ancestor of the Egyptians. Many biblical scholars identify Mizraim with Menes

By the time of Narmer's kingdom early hieroglyphic writing, used by scribes and artisans, had already appeared in Egypt. Concerning the origin of writing in Egypt Kathryn A. Bard writes:[173]

> Although some scholars believe that the Egyptian writing system was invented [...] with stimulus from Mesopotamia, where the earliest writing is found, the two writing systems are so different that it seems more likely that they are both the result of independent invention.

There were, however, some cultural innovations in the late Pre-Dynastic and First Dynasty periods of Egypt that were certainly influenced by the Mesopotamian civilization of the late Uruk period: cylinder seals, various artistic motifs, and niched architecture (buildings with niched facades), for example.[174] Amihai Mazar writes:[175]

> Sumerian influence on Egyptian culture was considerable during the Late Gerzean [late Pre-Dynastic] and Archaic [Early Dynastic] periods in Egypt. These international relations during one of the most creative periods in the history of the ancient Near East may indicate movements of people over long distances — both by land, from Mesopotamia westward through Syria to Palestine and Egypt, and by sea, connecting Elam and southern Mesopotamia with Egypt around Arabia.

Now, Sumerian Abraham also came "from Mesopotamia westward through Syria to Palestine and Egypt" during that particular time and, at least according to Josephus, "introduced them [Egyptians] to arithmetic and transmitted to them the laws of astronomy. For before the coming of Abraham the Egyptians were ignorant of these sciences, which thus travelled from the Chaldaeans into Egypt".[176]

---

who according to Manetho, the renowned 3rd century B.C. Egyptian priest and historian, was the first king of the First Dynasty of Egypt. In my opinion, however, Mizraim may have been a local chieftain/king during the Neolithic and Chalcolithic periods but never a king of Egypt in the true sense of the word. The semimythical Menes is often identified also with Narmer. See also Bestock 2020, 249, 257, 271, 272, 274; Tallet 2020, 435.

[173] Bard 2003, 74. See also Stauder 2010, 142. But see also Petrovich 2016, 2–4; Köhler 2020, 128.

[174] See for example Bard 2003, 62, 63; 2015, 112; Wilkinson 2002; Foster & Foster 2009, 29, 30; Van De Mieroop 2011, 47, 48; Hikade 2012, 834, 835; Stevenson 2013; Collins 2016, 48–51.

[175] Mazar 1992, 105.

[176] JA, Book I:viii.2 (p. 83). See also Kugel 1998, 249, 250, 259–261.

After staying in Egypt for a little while Abraham was sent out from there, and he returned to Negev (Gen 12:20; 13:1).[177] Very soon after that, in the final decade and a half of the 20th century B.C. (and even later), during the time when the originally southern Egyptian Gerzean/Naqada II culture consolidated its leading position in northern Egypt, a multitude of Egyptians also left the country and moved eastward to live in the northern Sinai and southern Palestine where numerous EB I sites containing a lot of pottery of the late Pre-Dynastic and First Dynasty periods have been found.[178] Kathryn A. Bard writes:[179]

> Not only did the Egyptians establish camps and way stations in the northern Sinai, but the ceramic evidence also suggests that they established a highly organized network of settlements in southern Palestine where an Egyptian population was in residence.

Among the Egyptian migrants who came to southern Palestine were also the Philistines[180] whom Abraham encountered at Gerar (Gen 20; 21; cp. Gen 26) in the southern coastal plain very soon after the promise of Isaac's birth (Gen 17; 18) and the destruction of Sodom and Gomorrah (Gen 19) in 1897 B.C.[181] Philistines originated from Casluhim/Casluhites who descended from Mizraim, the great progenitor of the Egyptians (Gen 10:13, 14). From Jer 47:4 and Amos 9:7 it can be inferred that the Philistines who lived in Palestine had come there from the country/coastland of Caphtor which probably referred to the northern Nile Delta region. Caphtorim/Caphtorites, who

---

[177] According to Sebastian Adams' *Adams' Synchronological Chart or Map of History* (Master Books edition 2008) Abraham went to Egypt in 1919 B.C. and returned from there in 1917 B.C. I think these year numbers are very likely correct.

[178] See Ben-Tor 1992, 93, 94; Mazar 1992, 106, 107. At Arad in the northeastern Negev, right above the Chalcolithic level V, inside the late EB I (or EB Ib) level IV, was revealed a fragment of an Egyptian jar inscribed with the name of Narmer (NEAEHL, 1:75, 76). The Chalcolithic Arad was abandoned probably towards the end of the 20th century B.C., and the EB Ib settlement was then established in the early 1800s. Incised inscriptions with the name of Narmer have been uncovered also at several other southern Palestinian late EB I sites (Mazar 1992, 106–108; AEHL, 361).

[179] Bard 2003, 62. — "Some scholars interpret the Egyptian finds in southern Palestine as merely representing trade relations; others argue for active Egyptian colonization in southern Canaan; still others claim that the Egyptians invaded the region." Mazar 1992, 107. See also de Miroschedji 2014, 312; Mumford 2014, 71; Greenberg 2019, 57–64; Bestock 2020, 253, 274.

[180] Andrew E. Steinmann (2019, 126) writes that "the name *Philistine* probably means 'migrant' or 'foreigner' (as it is often translated in the LXX)". LXX = Septuagint, pre-Christian Greek translation of the Old Testament. See also Keil 2011a, 106.

[181] Jones 2015, 47, 278. In my opinion the town of Gerar should be identified with Tell el-Hesi, a site located some 16 miles or 26 kilometers northeast of Gaza. Another possible site is Tel Erani, northeast of Tell el-Hesi.

were themselves a tribe sprung from Mizraim (Gen 10:13, 14), may have accounted for a proportion of the Egyptian migrants; at least they colonized the southern coastal plain of Palestine at some early period of time: "And the Avim, who dwelt in villages as far as Gaza — the Caphtorim, who came from Caphtor, destroyed them and dwelt in their place" (Deut 2:23 NKJV).[182] After settling down the Egyptian newcomers and their posterity became culturally "Canaanized" during the subsequent Early Bronze II and III periods.

Back in the land of the Canaanites Abraham ended up living close to Hebron in the country's central mountain range (Gen 13:18), but his nephew Lot chose to dwell in the plain of Jordan and its many cities (Gen 13:10–12), among which were also Sodom and Gomorrah. About that time Sodom and Gomorrah (as well as Admah, Zeboiim and Zoar) had been subject to Chedorlaomer king of Elam for twelve years but in the thirteenth year (1916 B.C.), after the years of the severe famine, they revolted (Gen 14:4). Next year, in my view in 1915 B.C.,[183] Chedorlaomer went with Amraphel king of Shinar, Arioch king of Ellasar, and Tidal king of Goyim to take a revenge on the rebels. These four kings came from far north with their powerful army and passed through the whole of Transjordan, defeating the Rephaim, the Zuzim, the Emim and the Horites who lived there (Gen 14:5, 6). Then, probably somewhere in the northern Negev, they smote in a battle a defending force of Amorites "who dwelt in Hazezon Tamar" (Gen 14:7 NKJV). But, Hazezon Tamar is just another name for En Gedi (2 Chr 20:2)![184] There is now an answer to the mystery why the Ghassulian-Chalcolithic temple complex at En Gedi was suddenly closed down and its cult furniture hidden in a secret place in the Judean Desert: because the priests did not want to give any opportunity for the attacking kings to loot

---

[182] On the origin of the Philistines in Palestine see also Osgood 1986b, 85, 86; Cooper 1995, 192, 193. Josephus [JA, Book I:vi.2 (p. 67)] writes that Mizraim "had eight sons, all of whom occupied the territory extending from Gaza to Egypt; but Phylistinus is the only one whose country has preserved the founder's name, for the Greeks call his portion Palestine". Some Caphtorites may have migrated also to the island of Crete, for later Egyptians called Cretans as *keftiu* (see for example Shaw & Nicholson 2008, 84). Some Egyptian predynastic stone vessels have been found in Crete and mainland Greece (see Burns 2010, 293, 294). — "They [Caphtorites] may be descendants of Mizraim who left Egypt and colonized Crete." Steinmann 2019, 126.

[183] According to James Ussher (2003, 25) this happened in 1912 B.C. (in 1913 B.C. according to Adams 2008).

[184] "[...] Hazezon Tamar. On the basis of 2 Chronicles 20:2, it is to be identified with the site of En Gedi on the western shore of the Dead Sea." Currid 2015, 281. See also Wenham 1987, 312; Mathews 2005, 143; Speiser 2007, 102; Steinmann 2019, 161; Goldingay 2020, 234.

their holy sanctuary, they decided to evacuate the temple precinct after the failure to repel the invaders (by the coalition army of Sodom, Gomorrah and the three other cities, if the smiting of Amorites [14:7] should be understood to have really occurred only after the battle in the Valley of Siddim [14:8–10]).[185]

After Chedorlaomer and the other kings with him had smashed the Amorite resistance, they won another fight against the five kings of Sodom, Gomorrah, Admah, Zeboiim and Zoar (Gen 14:8–10). "Then they took all the goods of Sodom and Gomorrah, and all their provisions, and went their way. They also took Lot, Abram's brother's son who dwelt in Sodom, and his goods, and departed" toward the north (Gen 14:11, 12 NKJV). The narrative then continues:

> Then one who had escaped came and told Abram the Hebrew, for he dwelt by the terebinth trees of Mamre the Amorite, brother of Eshcol and brother of Aner; and they *were* allies with Abram. Now when Abram heard that his brother was taken captive, he armed his three hundred and eighteen trained *servants* who were born in his own house, and went in pursuit as far as Dan. He divided his forces against them by night, and he and his servants attacked them and pursued them as far as Hobah, which *is* north of Damascus. So he brought back all the goods, and also brought back his brother Lot and his goods, as well as the women and the people. And the king of Sodom went out to meet him at the Valley of Shaveh (that *is,* the King's Valley), after his return from the defeat of Chedorlaomer and the kings who *were* with him. (Gen 14:13–17 NKJV)[186]

---

[185] The above told confirms the view that Abraham arrived in Palestine during the late Chalcolithic period. To my knowledge the first person to recognize the connection between the Chalcolithic En Gedi and Gen 14 was A. J. M. Osgood in his 1986 article *The Times of Abraham* (=Osgood 1986b). — "Another group of Ghassulian sites was in caves in the high cliffs of the Judaean mountains flanking the Dead Sea, and the finds from these sites included the most spectacular of all. It may be no coincidence that many of these caves contained pottery and other objects of two periods, the Ghassulian and those of refugees from the Romans in A.D. 135 after the Second Revolt of the Jews. The Ghassulians, like the Jews of the 2nd century A.D., may have taken refuge in these barren and almost inaccessible spots in the face of an approaching enemy." Kenyon 1979, 62. See also Ussishkin 1971, 39; Gonen 1992, 47, 48. Cp. Gen 14:10 (NKJV): "Now the Valley of Siddim *was full of* asphalt pits; and the kings of Sodom and Gomorrah fled; *some* fell there, and the remainder fled to the mountains."

[186] Abraham and his men probably did not use horses when they chased after the four kings, but there surely existed domestic horses in Palestine, at least in the northern Negev, already during the Chalcolithic period (Levy 1995, 232; 2002, 58). — "Further faunal remains of domesticated species include those of horse and donkey found at Ghassul and of camel found at Shiqmim." Gonen 1992, 62. See also Grigson 1995, 258, 259. Abraham also owned donkeys and camels (Gen 12:16; 24:10; for Jacob see Gen 30:43). — "Recently discovered evidence [in Egypt] [...] is in the form of a limestone receptacle shaped like a camel and complete with load, which confirms that the Arabian camel was domesticated by about the first dynasty [of Egypt] [...]" Rea 2009, 720. Terra-cotta figurine of a dromedary (one-

But who really were those four kings whom Abraham defeated, and what was the outcome of their failed military campaign? I believe that Amraphel, Arioch, Chedorlaomer and Tidal were great kings of different parts of Mesopotamia who had allied themselves with each other sometime after the beginning of the Uruk Expansion, maybe at the outset of the late Uruk period (LC 5). Amraphel was a king of Shinar in southeastern Turkey and perhaps northern Syria,[187] his capital being possibly Samsat.[188] Arioch king of Ellasar ruled probably in northern Iraq, and his capital was possibly Nineveh.[189] Chedorlaomer was a king of Elam in southwestern Iran (Khuzestan), his capital being either Susa or Chogha Mish.[190] Last but not least, Tidal reigned in Goyim (גּוֹיִם, gôyim), that is, Sumer.[191] He must have been the king of Uruk, "the most important city-state, colonial power and sophisticated centre of cultic and administrative capability in the whole of Mesopotamia" during the Uruk period.[192]

---

humped camel, the Arabian camel), from the late Ubaid period, has been found at Uruk (see Jantzen 2019, 263).

[187] See the discussion of the location of Shinar in Habermehl 2011, 26–30, 33–35. — "Some scholars have […] sought to identify Amraphel with Amorapil, who may have been the king of a territory known as Sanhar. This kingdom supposedly lay in northwestern Mesopotamia." Aalders 1981, 282.

[188] On Samsat in the Uruk period see Algaze 2005, 34–36, 46, 47, 49, 96, 97, 110, 132. Maybe Samsat can be identified with Erech/Uruk of Gen 10:10; it may have been named so after the southern Mesopotamian city. Nimrod, the first king of Shinar (Gen 10:10), was probably already dead in the late 1900s B.C. Ken Johnson's (2010, 124) identification of Nimrod with Hammurabi is a great historical and archaeological error. Hammurabi, the famous king of Babylon, will be discussed more in the next chapter. Greatly mistaken is also Douglas Petrovich (2013) who asserts that the proper candidate for historical Nimrod is Sargon of Akkad (of whom see later in this chapter).

[189] On Nineveh in the Uruk period see Algaze 2005, 37, 38, 41, 46–48, 52, 53, 57, 86, 96, 97, 110, 132. — "The name *Arioch* has parallels in names found in upper Mesopotamia […] we should probably locate *Ellasar* in that region." Steinmann 2019, 159.

[190] On southwestern Iran in the Uruk period see Algaze 2005, 11–18, 75, 76, 81.

[191] Goyim is the plural form of the word גּוֹי (gôy), "a nation/people", but in Gen 14:1, 9 Goyim is evidently a designation for a country. Now, "The Sumerians referred to themselves as the 'black-headed people' […] and called their homeland simply 'native land' (Sumerian: ki-en-gi […] In later sources, ki-en-gi is translated into Akkadian as *māt šumerim*, the 'Sumerian land' or short 'Sumer'" (Brisch 2013, 111). Also, the Sumerians wrote kalam "the country/land (of Sumer)" and ukú "the people (of Sumer)" in the same manner, using the same ideogram for both words (Roux 1992, 105). Thus, simple *Goyim*, "People", was a fitting Hebrew name for the land of the Sumerians who proudly called themselves only 'the (black headed) people' and "identified themselves with the earliest inhabitants of Mesopotamia and indeed with the initial population of the earth" (Roux 1992, 105). The Sumerians also "did believe that in some past age they had brought civilization to the rest of the world" (Foster & Foster 2009, 33).

[192] Matthews 2000c, 313. At that time Uruk may have functioned as the religious capital of Sumer (see Algaze 2001, 32, 33). Tidal may be identified with some of the kingly figures which are depicted in the iconographic art of the late Uruk period, for example the famous Uruk Vase (see for example Foster & Foster 2009, 22, 24, 25; see also Hamblin 2006, 37–40; Collins 2016, 38–40; Van De Mieroop 2016, 28–30; Stiebing & Helft 2018, 39; Vogel 2019; Selz 2020, 216–219).

These four kings, who are presented in Gen 14:1 in order from north to south, were the supreme potentates of their respective countries. Even though they may have had only a loose control of the countries' other elites who sometimes agreed to subservience only after harsh coercive measures, we can talk about four regional kingdoms which in concert dominated politics and economy over the whole of Mesopotamia and in many areas around it. The lead of this alliance, however, was in the hands of the southern authorities and especially the great city of Uruk which, in the words of Roger Matthews, was during the late Uruk period "the central power in an economic and political empire which reached up the Euphrates into northern Syria and Anatolia as well as into Iran to the east".[193]

As already told earlier in this chapter the southern Mesopotamian polities established colonies, communities and stations in northern parts of Mesopotamia on strategically important locations. Along the river Euphrates in northern Syria, in the vicinity of Tell Habuba Kabira, a new well-planned urban enclave comprised by Habuba Kabira-süd/South, Tell Qannas and Jebel Aruda was built in the earlier part of the late Uruk period (early LC 5).[194] The construction work began in the early 1930s B.C., in my view, and it was also then that lots of Mesopotamian and other people started to immigrate to Palestine, shortly launching its Early Bronze Age. Soon also the four allied kings became interested in the southern Levant, chiefly because of its resources like agricultural products, copper, bitumen, and labor force.[195] Around 1928 B.C. the kings

---

[193] Matthews 2000c, 313. See also Matthews 2003, 108–126, 132, 133, 148–150; Gibson 2010, 85; Van De Mieroop 2016, 40, 41; Beaulieu 2018, 31; Bourke 2018, 64; Stiebing & Helft 2018, 40; Potts 2019, 4. — "By the Late Uruk period [...] Uruk had reached more than 200 hectares in area, and was the greatest city of the age, with a population as high as 40,000 to 50,000 [...] Cities of this size could probably field armies of several thousand men, and perhaps up to 5000 with maximum effort, compared to the dozens or hundreds of men who composed earlier Neolithic tribal armies." Hamblin 2006, 36.

[194] See Strommenger 1980; Akkermans & Schwartz 2003, 190–197; Algaze 2005, 25–29; 2013, 84, 85; Butterlin 2019, 188–190. — "The level of planning and organisation that would have been needed to create Habuba [Kabira] is astonishing." Collins 2016, 45. — "[...] only one piece of evidence for Egyptian material in the Sumerian world has been proposed: a fragment of 'black incised' pottery (N-ware) [from Gerzean/Naqada II period; Roaf 1990, 68; Butterlin 2019, 189] found at Habuba Kabira-South [...], a type of ceramic created in Egypt's neighbouring Nubia. This fragment is, however, small (<5cm) and its identification is open to question." Stevenson 2013, 629. Syrian Amuq F pottery of the Uruk period has been identified at Buto in the northern Nile Delta (Bard 2003, 62; 2015, 112).

[195] If Abraham had not been able to rescue Lot and the other captured people from the hands of the four kings they probably would have ended up as slaves, for foreign captives "were among the resources flowing southwards in the Uruk period and [...] probably a primary source of the workers at the disposal of Uruk state administrators" (Algaze 2013, 87). See also Scott 2017, 157–160, 176; Bourke 2018, 63.

made a campaign of conquest to Palestine and put its villages and towns under tribute.[196] The region of Sodom and Gomorrah became evidently subject to Chedorlaomer while Tidal, Amraphel and Arioch got other areas. This Mesopotamian mastery over the southern Levant lasted for 12 years (Gen 14:4), after which happened a general revolt in 1916 B.C.[197]

To punish the rebels in the south the four kings went on to another military expedition in 1915 B.C. But after ravaging the eastern Palestine, on the way back to its base at Habuba Kabira in northern Syria,[198] the invading army was destroyed by the servants of Abraham (Gen 14:14, 15). This memorable defeat caused the dissolution of the Mesopotamian coalition which then led to the collapse of the Uruk empire. The Sumerian colonies, stations and outposts across Upper Mesopotamia were soon either abandoned or devastated by hostile forces.[199] In southern Mesopotamia the competing cities may have ended up having warlike conflicts; at least the monumental buildings in the center of Uruk were demolished, and settlement patterns within the alluvial plain faced substantial changes.[200] These events were a transition to a new short-lived period in southern Iraq called "Jemdet Nasr" which in my view lasted only a few decades. During the Jemdet Nasr period new cities were founded, but "between the cultural elements of that period and those of the Uruk period there is no fundamental difference, but simple variations in style and quality".[201]

---

[196] It can be inferred from the archaeology of the late Uruk Mesopotamia that long-distance, large-scale, organized warfare was practiced already at that time (see Hamblin 2006, 41, 42; Algaze 2013, 83–85; McMahon 2014, 177, 178; Selz 2020, 189, 190). — "Scholars tend to exaggerate the difficulties of moving goods and people in the ancient world. It should be remembered that on a clear day one can see the entire landscape from Nippur to the first three ranges of the Zagros, and that the distance can be walked in a few days. Also, before modern transportation, caravans (of camels, but also with horses and donkeys) moved at a walking pace from Zubair in southern Iraq to Aleppo in forty days or so [...] such relative ease of movement [...]" Gibson 2010, 88.
[197] "The names of other peoples whom the Elamites and their allies subdued — Rephaim, Zuzim, Emim, Horites, Amalekites, Amorites — would indicate that the uprising of the five southern kinglets was but one part of a massive effort to resist continued Mesopotamian control in Transjordan. The invading kings repress such attempted revolts in grandiose and unmitigated style." Hamilton 1990, 402.
[198] Ephraim A. Speiser (2007, 102) writes that "The Gen. Apocr. [Genesis Apocryphon] (column xxi, line 28) puts the starting point of the invasion somewhere on the Euphrates".
[199] "It has been suggested [...] that the origins of Early Bronze Age culture [in Palestine] should be sought in the north, perhaps as a result of population 'spillover' associated with the collapse of the Uruk colonies of northern Syria [...]" Golden 2009, 49.
[200] Algaze 2001, 77; 2005, 106; 2013, 88.
[201] Roux 1992, 76. — "In southern Mesopotamia, a clear regional culture developed during the Jemdet Nasr Tradition, which probably had some economic and political unity [...] Such cultural similarity had

From the Jemdet Nasr period there was a smooth shift to the so-called Early Dynastic period of southern Mesopotamia which lasted, in my opinion, roughly to the end of the 19th century B.C., that is to say, less than a hundred years.[202] During that period urbanization was more prominent than before, "with most of the population living in walled cities". There were "some twenty to thirty city-states, each with a principal center that linked smaller towns and villages dispersed across the countryside".[203] Armed conflicts between the city-states were not rare. Written documents began to be common in the later part of the period.[204]

Abraham's life can be summarized in the following manner: He was born at the beginning of the Uruk period, came to Palestine in the late Uruk period and lived there in the Jemdet Nasr and Early Dynastic periods until his death in 1821 B.C.[205] Abraham's

---

long been present in southern Mesopotamia by the time the Jemdet Nasr Tradition emerged, but it seems to have become more pronounced and focused during this period, which some scholars view as the aftermath of the collapse of the much more broadly distributed Uruk culture of the Late Chalcolithic Mesopotamia tradition." Peregrine 2002b, 237. In southwestern Iran the Uruk culture was replaced by the Proto-Elamite culture which encompassed also the central and eastern parts of Iran (see Nissen 2001, 175–177). At the same time northern Mesopotamia saw the emergence of the Ninevite 5 and western Early Bronze I cultures (see Nissen 2001, 175, 177; Frangipane 2001, 324). Ninevite 5 pottery has been found in the late EB I cemetery of ´Ein Assawir in Palestine (Greenberg 2019, 51).

[202] "[...] it is almost impossible to determine from surface material whether a site has been occupied only during the Jemdet Nasr period or continued into the Early Dynastic. This is because common Jemdet Nasr period pottery is the same as Early Dynastic I pottery without Early Dynastic idiosyncrasies. It is therefore impossible to differentiate between settlements founded in Jemdet Nasr or Early Dynastic I." Nissen 2001, 167.

[203] Peregrine 2002a, 112, 113. See also Bartash 2020, 538–541. Early Dynastic Ur, a leading city-state of the period, had a large cemetery which contained many "exceptionally rich tombs, known as the Royal Graves", several of which "reflect elaborate burial rituals, in which as many as seventy-four people went to their deaths in order to accompany the tomb's principal occupant into the netherworld" (Foster & Foster 2009, 36, 37; see also Zettler & Horne (eds.) 1998; Down 2010, 39–41; Bahrani 2017, 87–99). According to Georges Roux (1992, 137) "royal burials with human sacrifices fell into disuse at a very early date, probably during the Early Dynastic period". Royal tombs with human sacrifices are also known in Egypt, but only from the First Dynasty period (Bard 2003, 68; 2015, 121; Bestock 2020, 260, 292) which was, in my view, contemporary with the Early Dynastic period of southern Mesopotamia.

[204] Many Early Dynastic royal inscriptions have been found in southern Mesopotamia. Those inscriptions belong to kings of different city-states who reigned, in my view, approximately between the years 1875–1800 B.C. Some of those kings are mentioned by name in the ancient *Sumerian King List* which is a very much exaggerated and fictional portrayal of the early southern Mesopotamian history. It is also probable that many Early Dynastic kings did not use just one name during their regnal years, so royal inscriptions with different names may have actually belonged to the same king. The kings, events, and duration of the Early Dynastic period need a lot more investigation and reinterpretation from the biblical chronological perspective. — "Importantly, recent scholarship has confirmed that the value of the Sumerian King List, a later literary composition naming rulers and dynasties that existed in various recensions since at least the Ur III period, is minimal for the reconstruction of the history of the ED period [...] It is today universally accepted that royal and literary inscriptions must be used for historical reconstruction with the utmost care." Bartash 2020, 534, 535, 537.

[205] Jones 2015, 278.

wife, Sarah, had died 39 years earlier in 1860 B.C.,[206] in the late Early Bronze I period of Palestine. When she died, he bought a cave and buried her there (Gen 23); later also Abraham, Isaac and his wife Rebekah, and Jacob and his wife Leah were buried in that same cave (Gen 49:29–33). Now, against this background, it is fascinating — though not so surprising — to read that "The most common practice [in Palestine during the Early Bronze I period] was multiple burial — several generations of one family being buried in the same artificial or natural cave".[207] This kind of burial custom continued to be common in EB II and EB III.[208]

A huge cemetery containing thousands of graves dating to early EB I (or EB Ia) existed at Bab edh-Dhra', a site located just south of the Dead Sea.[209] In my view this necropolis belonged collectively to Sodom and Gomorrah (and other cities of that region) until they were destroyed (Gen 19) in 1897 B.C.[210] Shortly afterwards, in late EB I (or EB Ib), "new tombs were constructed by the people who founded the first permanent settlement at Bab edh-Dhra', which in the following EB II period was to develop into a fortified town". Those new tombs resembled certain Chalcolithic burial structures found in the northern Negev.[211]

Bab edh-Dhra' was not the only town that was fortified in the Early Bronze II period. In fact, EB II–III was the time when urban centers with massive city walls, temples, palaces and other public constructions emerged everywhere in Palestine.[212] In my view EB II must be dated from the mid-1800s to the very early 1600s B.C. This period of time

---

[206] Jones 2015, 278.
[207] Mazar 1992, 98, 99. See also Ben-Tor 1992, 88.
[208] Mazar 1992, 139.
[209] See Mazar 1992, 99, 100; Greenberg 2019, 40, 41.
[210] On the location and destruction of Sodom and Gomorrah see Möller 2010, 39–49. Perhaps these cities resembled Habuba Kabira-South in plan and architecture.
[211] See Mazar 1992, 82, 100. — "Bab edh-Dhra' is thus part of the pattern of emerging villages that developed throughout Palestine during the Early Bronze Age IB [...] the cultural material of these villages suggests vestiges of the area's earlier indigenous Chalcolithic populations [...]" NEAEHL, 1:133. See also A. J. M. Osgood (1988b), *From Abraham to Exodus*, 101, 103; Harrison 2012, 638; Greenberg 2019, 28.
[212] See Mazar 1992, 108, 111–114, 118–129. — "[...] most of the towns in Palestine [...] achieved urban status only at the beginning of the Early Bronze Age II; some places, however, such as Erani, Ai, and Tell el-Far'ah North, preceded the others and may be called towns already at the end of the Early Bronze Age I." Ben-Tor 1992, 86. Recent archaeological excavations at En Esur in the northern Sharon Plain, Israel, have revealed a very large (65 hectares) fortified EB Ib city. See for example Elad & Paz 2018; de Miroschedji 2018, 110, 112. — "[...] it may be surmised that the concept of fortification was tested in the late EB I but became universal only in the following EB II period." Greenberg 2019, 48.

corresponds to the Book of Genesis' chapters 24–50 which tell about the lives and doings of Isaac, Jacob and his twelve sons, of whom the most prominent is Joseph. Joseph, the second youngest son of Jacob, was treacherously sold into slavery to Egypt by his older brothers (Gen 37) in 1728 B.C.[213] There, after thirteen years, God made him "lord of all Egypt" (Gen 45:9 NKJV) at the age of 30 (Gen 41:46) in 1715 B.C:[214]

> And Pharaoh said to Joseph, "See, I have set you over all the land of Egypt." Then Pharaoh took his signet ring off his hand and put it on Joseph's hand; and he clothed him in garments of fine linen and put a gold chain around his neck. And he had him ride in the second chariot which he had; and they cried out before him, "Bow the knee!" So he set him over all the land of Egypt. Pharaoh also said to Joseph, "I *am* Pharaoh, and without your consent no man may lift his hand or foot in all the land of Egypt." (Gen 41:41–44 NKJV)

Joseph's duty as the pharaoh's right-hand man was to prepare Egypt for a seven-year famine which would come after seven years of plenty (Gen 41:33–36, 47–49).

> Then the seven years of plenty which were in the land of Egypt ended, and the seven years of famine began to come, as Joseph had said. The famine was in all lands, but in all the land of Egypt there was bread. So when all the land of Egypt was famished, the people cried to Pharaoh for bread. Then Pharaoh said to all the Egyptians, "Go to Joseph; whatever he says to you, do." The famine was over all the face of the earth, and Joseph opened all the storehouses and sold to the Egyptians. And the famine became severe in the land of Egypt. So all countries came to Joseph in Egypt to buy *grain,* because the famine was severe in all lands. (Gen 41:53–57 NKJV)

In the second year of the famine (Gen 45:6, 11), in 1706 B.C.,[215] Jacob with all his family moved from the land of Canaan to Egypt to live near to Joseph (Gen 45:10; 46). The pharaoh let them stay "in the best of the land [...] in the land of Goshen" (Gen 47:6 NKJV) in the eastern Nile Delta region. This pharaoh who ruled over the country at that time was certainly Djoser, the first king of the so-called Third Dynasty of Egypt.[216] He built the

---

[213] Jones 2015, 56a, 278.
[214] Jones 2015, 56a, 278.
[215] Jones 2015, 56a, 278.
[216] See Möller 2010, 67–98; Habermehl 2013; 2023, 565–567; Wyatt 2020, 33–46.

first pyramid in Egypt, the so-called Step Pyramid at Saqqara just south of the modern capital of Cairo.[217]

Selling grain to Egyptians and to foreigners made the pharaoh extremely rich:

> Now *there was* no bread in all the land; for the famine *was* very severe, so that the land of Egypt and the land of Canaan languished because of the famine. And Joseph gathered up all the money that was found in the land of Egypt and in the land of Canaan, for the grain which they bought; and Joseph brought the money into Pharaoh's house. (Gen 47:13, 14 NKJV)

Egyptians had to hand over also all their livestock and fields in exchange for grain; as a matter of fact, the peasants became virtual slaves of the pharaoh (Gen 47:15–25). All the wealth and power that Joseph had accumulated for the royalty during the great seven-year famine formed the basis of the prosperity of the subsequent dynasties and rulers who built more pyramids, many of them being a lot mightier than the Step Pyramid.[218] In my opinion all the great pyramids of Egypt were constructed approximately between the years 1700 and 1500 B.C. while the Israelites were living and increasing there.[219] Many dynasties must have been contemporary with each other during those couple centuries and also afterwards.[220] The history of Egypt from the beginning of the dynastic period to the rise of the so-called 18th Dynasty in the early 11th century B.C., in my view, needs very much more research and drastic reinterpretation.

The great seven-year famine in the final years of the 18th century B.C. hit hard also the very late EB II Palestine, causing major societal changes in the land. Some cities in

---

[217] See for example Bard 2015, 140–145; Bárta 2020, 329, 330, 337. In my view Djoser was roughly contemporary with Ur-Nammu, the founder of the so-called Third Dynasty of Ur, who built the famous Great Ziggurat of Ur, one of the first classic ziggurats (see Foster & Foster 2009, 62; Bahrani 2017, 158–160). The pyramids of Egypt and the ziggurats of Mesopotamia are an impressive testimony of the ingenuity of the ancient Near Eastern peoples. For more on the intelligence and technological achievements of the ancient man see Donald E. Chittick (2006), *The Puzzle of Ancient Man*; Don Landis (ed.) (2012), *The Genius of Ancient Man*; Don Landis (ed.) (2015), *The Secrets of Ancient Man*.

[218] "An examination of Egyptian history reveals it was during the time of Djoser that Egypt, for the first time, became an exceptionally powerful nation. The reason for that can be found in the story of Joseph." Wyatt 2020, 36.

[219] According to Josephus [JA, Book II:ix.1 (p. 253); see also page 65 in this book] the Egyptians put the Israelites to build pyramids and exhausted them with much labor.

[220] See also Courville 1971, 101, 104 Figure 2 (in volume 1); Habermehl 2013.

Palestine were destroyed or abandoned at the end of EB II, including Arad in the northeastern Negev. Numerous small settlements in the Negev as well as in southern Sinai became also empty of inhabitants about the same time.[221] Lots of people must have moved to other areas and countries. Surely Jacob and his family were not the only Canaanite people who found their safety in Egypt.

Without doubt the years 1707–1701 B.C. were unbearably hard also for many peoples who lived in Mesopotamia, especially in its northern parts. During the 1700s southern Mesopotamia was dominated by the so-called Dynasty of Akkad/Agade whose first king was the great conqueror Sargon.[222] He and his successors established a powerful Semitic-Sumerian empire which extended its rule over large areas in western Iran, northern Iraq and Syria. The very successful reign of Sargon's grandson Naram-Sin became "a byword for imperial grandeur in Mesopotamian tradition".[223] However, during the reign of Naram-Sin's son and successor Sharkalisharri ("king of all kings") the empire began to contract and crumble. The ultimate reason for this was most likely the same drought and famine which afflicted also Egypt and Palestine.[224] It was at that same time that Amorites and other peoples from Syria — surely to escape starvation — moved towards the heartlands of the Akkadian kingdom in the upper part of the southern Mesopotamian alluvium.[225] Soon a civil war broke out in the land, and in the end, after

---

[221] See Mazar 1992, 109, 114–117, 141. See also Osgood 1988b, 96, 97, 105–107; Ben-Tor 1992, 97. Note that Osgood's dates differ some 45 years from those of Jones' (2015), due to a somewhat different view of the biblical chronology. For certain good reasons the dates given by Jones are always to be preferred.

[222] The name for this dynasty is obtained from its capital Akkad or Agade which still remains unlocated archaeologically (see Schrakamp 2020, 612, 613; Michalowski 2020, 688, 702, 703).

[223] Foster & Foster 2009, 55. In my opinion Naram-Sin must have reigned in the late 18th century B.C. He implemented many administrative reforms and levied a 20-percent tax for the harvest of the cultivated lands (Foster & Foster 2009, 56). Interestingly, Joseph also ordered the Egyptians to give one-fifth of the harvest to the pharaoh (Gen 41:34; 47:24, 26).

[224] "But after Naram-Sin's death, the empire quickly disintegrated, and ended abruptly in the reign of his son Shar-kali-sharri [...] Incessant revolts by subject peoples, internal political instability, and a long period of severe drought may all have contributed to the empire's fall." Bryce & Birkett-Rees 2016, 73. See also Weiss 2002, 22; 2014, 371–376; McMahon 2012, 664–667; Bourke 2018, 90, 91.

[225] See also Akkermans & Schwartz 2003, 282, 283; Foster & Foster 2009, 60.

a brief[226] period of Gutian dominance,[227] the Dynasty of Akkad was succeeded in power by the so-called Third Dynasty of Ur which was founded, in my estimation, in the early 17th century B.C. by the city's former military governor Ur-Nammu (or Ur-Namma). The era of this new dynasty, which lasted until the end of the century, was a real golden age of Sumerian culture and literature.[228]

Jacob died in 1689 B.C., and Joseph died 54 years later in 1635 B.C.[229] Before his death Joseph spoke to his brethren the Israelites and said (Gen 50:24 NKJV): "I am dying; but God will surely visit you, and bring you out of this land to the land of which He swore to

---

[226] In my view the Gutian mastery over southern Mesopotamia lasted no more than a few decades, after which they were driven out of the country. The generally accepted opinion is that the Gutians dominated nearly a century, but this cannot be true in the light of the biblical chronology. The long period view is based on the Sumerian King List which is, in many respects, very exaggerated and unreliable historical document. — "About the Guti who overthrew the Akkadian empire and ruled over Mesopotamia for almost a hundred years we know next to nothing. The Sumerian King List gives 'the hordes of Gutium' twenty-one kings, but very few of them have left us inscriptions, and this, coupled with silence from other sources, points to a period of political unrest. The invaders were certainly not very numerous [...]" Roux 1992, 161. — "It is unclear how long this 'intermediate' period lasted, and because of the (almost complete) absence of written records it is difficult to reconstruct events between the Akkad dynasty and the Third Dynasty of Ur [...]" Brisch 2013, 122.

[227] The Gutians were a stockbreeding people from the Zagros Mountains in western Iran. They "took advantage of the disorder to enter the lowlands and set up kingdoms in some of the Sumerian and Akkadian cities" (Foster & Foster 2009, 60). — "The rise and fall of the Akkadian empire offers a perfect preview of the rise and fall of all subsequent Mesopotamian empires: rapid expansion followed by ceaseless rebellions, palace revolutions, constant wars on the frontiers, and in the end, the *coup de grâce* given by the highlanders: Guti now, Elamites, Kassites, Medes or Persians tomorrow." Roux 1992, 159.

[228] "[...] the Third Dynasty of Ur [...] represents one of the most brilliant periods in the history of ancient Iraq, for not only did Ur-Nammu and his successors restore the Akkadian empire throughout its length and breadth but they gave Mesopotamia a century of relative peace and prosperity and sponsored an extraordinary renaissance in all the branches of Sumerian art and literature." Roux 1992, 162. For more on the Dynasty of Akkad and the Third Dynasty of Ur see for example Roaf 1990, 96–107; Roux 1992, 146–178; Foster & Foster 2009, 51–70; Foster 2016; Schrakamp 2020; Michalowski 2020; Garfinkle 2022. In my view the Ur III dynasty was contemporary with the time of the so-called Palace G at Ebla (EB IVA2; see Welton 2020, 54, 55; Pinnock 2020, 74) in northwestern Syria. This palace had archive rooms containing thousands of clay cuneiform tablets written in Sumerian and the local Semitic language. On Ebla see also Pettinato 1981; 1991; Roaf 1990, 86, 87; Akkermans & Schwartz 2003, 235–246; Pinnock 2013; 2020; Matthiae 2020; Vacca & D'Andrea 2020, 124–127; Bartash 2020, 556–560, 579–583; Michalowski 2020, 700–702.

[229] Jones 2015, 278. Jacob's brother Esau may have also lived until the early 17th century B.C. The eight kings of Edom listed in Gen 36:31–39 reigned most likely during the 17th–15th centuries B.C., in EB III Palestine. See also Keil 2011a, 209–210; Leupold 2010, 572, 573. Job, the protagonist of the Book of Job in the Old Testament, was born probably in the late 1700s B.C., and his trial took place possibly around the mid-1600s. On the date of the life of Job see also Hodge 2013, 253–263; Jones 2015, 20, 278; Habermehl 2019a–c. — "Numerous indications scattered through the Book of Job indicate its great antiquity. Its whole outlook and atmosphere is essentially the same as in the early chapters of Genesis. Job probably lived sometime between Abraham and Moses [...]" Morris 2000, 33. In the Septuagint, in the epilogue of the Book of Job (42:17a–e), it is told that Job "had as father Zerah, from the sons of Esau [...] so that it made him fifth from Abraham" (verse 17c, LES).

Abraham, to Isaac, and to Jacob." These words came true 144 years later when the Israelites left the land of Egypt under the leadership of Moses. But this subject belongs already to the next chapter which concerns the latter half of the second millennium B.C. — the days of Moses, Joshua, and the judges of Israel.

CHAPTER 5: IN THE DAYS OF MOSES, JOSHUA AND THE JUDGES

While living in Egypt the Israelites prospered as a people: they "were fruitful and increased abundantly, multiplied and grew exceedingly mighty; and the land was filled with them" (Ex 1:7 NKJV). However, in order to curb their reproduction, the Egyptians "set taskmasters over them to afflict them with their burdens. And they built for Pharaoh supply cities, Pithom and Raamses" (Ex 1:11 NKJV). Josephus has this to say about the hard construction work done by the Israelites in the land of Egypt:[230]

> Those benefits which they [Egyptians] had received from Joseph being through lapse of time forgotten, and the kingdom having now passed to another dynasty, they grossly maltreated the Israelites and devised for them all manner of hardships. Thus they ordered them to divide the river into numerous canals, to build ramparts for the cities and dikes to hold the waters of the river and to prevent them from forming marshes when they overflowed its banks; and with the rearing of pyramid after pyramid they exhausted our race, which was thus apprenticed to all manner of crafts and became inured to toil.

Doing heavy work, however, did not discourage the Israelites (Ex 1:12). Even trying to kill all their newborn baby boys did not prevent them from growing very mighty, under God's providence (Ex 1:15–22). The descendants of Jacob had to endure hard servitude and violent oppression probably a little over a hundred years.[231] Finally, after staying in Egypt for a total of 215 years,[232] the pharaoh allowed the Israelites to leave the country, but only after ten tormenting and devastating plagues which God performed against the Egyptians through Moses and his brother Aaron (Ex 7–12).[233]

---

[230] JA, Book II:ix.1 (p. 251, 253).

[231] See Jones 2015, 55.

[232] See Jones 2015, 53–61; Carter & Sanders 2021. — "They left Egypt [...] 430 years after the coming of our forefather Abraham to Canaan, Jacob's migration to Egypt having taken place 215 years later." JA, Book II:xv.2 (p. 305). See also Ex 12:40 in LXX.D; Gal 3:16, 17.

[233] On the ten plagues and the historical time of the Exodus see also Courville 1971; Ashton & Down 2006, 98–102; Down 2006; Immanuel Velikovsky (2009), *Ages in Chaos I*, 23–70; Habermehl 2018. It is very difficult to determine which pharaoh of which dynasty was the pharaoh who let the Israelites go. In their book *Unwrapping the Pharaohs* (2006, 98, 206) John Ashton and David Down suggest that he may have been Neferhotep I of the so-called 13th Dynasty. Anne Habermehl (2013; 2023, 567–569) argues for Amenemhat IV of the so-called 12th Dynasty. I think Habermehl is probably right.

So over 600,000 army-fit men of Israel (twenty years old and above), besides all the others like women and children, went out of Egypt in 1491 B.C.[234] to go back to the land of Canaan to dwell there permanently (Ex 12:37; Num 1:44–47).[235] After they had crossed the Red Sea (Ex 14), that is, the Gulf of Aqaba between the Sinai Peninsula and northwest Saudi Arabia, God made them to wander in the wilderness for forty years (Num 32:13).[236] At the end of the forty years the Israelites came to a region bordering Canaan, east of the Jordan River, opposite Jericho (Num 33:38, 48; 36:13). From there, under the command of Joshua, they moved westward, crossed the river, and entered the land which God had promised to Abraham, Isaac, and Jacob, and their descendants (Deut 1:8; 34:4; Josh 3). A little earlier God had given instructions to the people, saying:

> When you have crossed the Jordan into the land of Canaan, then you shall drive out all the inhabitants of the land from before you, destroy all their engraved stones, destroy all their molded images, and demolish all their high places; you shall dispossess *the inhabitants of* the land and dwell in it, for I have given you the land to possess. (Num 33:51–53 NKJV; see also Deut 7:1, 2, 5; 20:16, 17)

The Israelites arrived in the land of Canaan in 1451 B.C.,[237] at the end of the Palestinian Early Bronze period. The first city to be vanquished was naturally Jericho which stood on the way to the inner country (Josh 6).[238] Kathleen M. Kenyon, the foremost excavator of

---

[234] Jones 2015, 24, 278.

[235] Thus, the number of the Israelites twenty years before the Exodus (or 1511 B.C., 195 years after Jacob's arrival in Egypt) was about 1,200,000 (600,000 males and 600,000 females). If there were originally some 100 persons in the family of Jacob when he came to Egypt in 1706 B.C., then the annual growth rate of the Israelites must have been almost five percent during the 195 years to reach the high population of 1,200,000 persons in 1511 B.C.: $100 \times 1.0494^{195} \approx 1{,}200{,}000$ (100 initial people, annual growth rate 4.94 % for 195 years). The Israelites in Egypt were getting married generally in their early teens and had fast lots of children. The verses Ex 1:7, 12, 20 are not exaggerating at all when they are telling about the Israelites multiplying exceedingly and growing very mighty despite their hardships.

[236] On the Exodus route see Möller 2010; Glen A. Fritz (2016), *The Lost Sea of the Exodus*; (2019), *The Exodus Mysteries*; Joel Richardson (2018), *Mount Sinai in Arabia*.

[237] Jones 2015, 278.

[238] "Jericho lay on the best route from the east to the central uplands. The Israelites under Joshua were following this route when Joshua sent his spies with the instructions 'go view the land, and Jericho'. The recent excavations have shown what importance the inhabitants of Jericho placed on their defences." Kenyon 1979, 90. The twelve men that Moses sent 38 years earlier to spy out the land of the Canaanites had reported large fortified cities and strong people of great size (Num 13; Deut 1:28). Indeed, there existed "mighty fortifications" (Mazar 1992, 140; see also de Miroschedji 2014, 309; 2020, 176; Kaiser & Wegner 2017, 75) in EB III Palestine ("[...] [EB III] period excels in the construction of massive fortifications [...]" Greenberg 2019, 99). A unique hoard of copper tools and weapons from the Early Bronze period has been found near Kfar Monash in the Sharon Plain, Israel. Interestingly, the hoard included gigantic spearheads, one measuring 26 inches or 66 centimeters in length and 4.4 pounds or 2 kilograms in weight. See Hestrin & Tadmor 1963; Ben-Tor 1992, 112–114; Mazar 1992, 134, 135;

the site in question, writes about the destruction of the last city of the Early Bronze period Jericho:[239]

> The final end of the Early Bronze Age civilization came with catastrophic completeness. The last of the Early Bronze Age walls of Jericho was built in a great hurry, using old and broken bricks, and was probably not completed when it was destroyed by fire. Little or none of the town inside the walls has survived subsequent denudation, but it was probably completely destroyed, for all the finds show that there was an absolute break, and that a new people took the place of the earlier inhabitants. Every town in Palestine that has so far been investigated shows the same break. The newcomers were nomads, not interested in town life, and they so completely drove out or absorbed the old population, perhaps already weakened and decadent, that all traces of the Early Bronze Age civilization disappeared.

Sounds like Kenyon has just — albeit inadvertently — essentially described the destruction of the city of Jericho and the conquest of the land of Canaan by the tent-

---

Greenberg 2019, 61, 62. Moses' spies described Canaan as a land that "truly flows with milk and honey" (Num 13:27 NKJV; see also Ex 3:8, 17; 13:5; 33:3; Deut 8:8). They had also brought with them "a branch with one cluster of grapes; they carried it between two of them on a pole. *They* also *brought* some of the pomegranates and figs" (Num 13:23 NKJV). Now in the *Story of Sinuhe* (an Egyptian narrative text written possibly — according to my estimation — in the early 1500s B.C.) a part of northern Canaan (or possibly the Beqa Valley in Lebanon; Charaf 2014, 446) is portrayed in the following way: "It was a good land, named Yaa. Figs were in it, and grapes. It had more wine than water. Plentiful was its honey, abundant its olives. Every (kind of) fruit was on its trees. Barley was there, and emmer. There was no limit to any (kind of) cattle." (See also Malamat 1998, 49, 50.) Read a translation of the entire story for example in Pritchard (ed.) 2011, 5–10 (the quoted text is on page 7); COS, 1:77–82. Other Egyptian literary works from around the same time include, for example, *Prophecy of Neferti* and *Teaching of Ptahhotep.*

[239] Kenyon 1979, 117, 118. See also Nigro 2019, 84, 99, 103; 2020. — "It is clear, therefore, that a new occupational wave had swept over the country at this time, putting an end to the E.B. [Early Bronze] population and laying the foundations for the eventual rise of new settlements in M.B. [Middle Bronze] and L.B. [Late Bronze] This was one of the greatest and most decisive migratory movements in the history of Palestine. After it one finds occupational continuity in most parts of the country down to the end of the Bronze Age." Aharoni 1979, 138. — "Although it has been demonstrated that internal factors played a role in the collapse of the Early Bronze Age culture, and that indigenous peoples continued to thrive in parts of the region [...] there is also evidence [...] that an infiltration of new peoples into Canaan may have been a factor." Golden 2009, 53.

dwelling Israelites, who emerged from the great wilderness after having wandered there

for forty years.[240] Amihai Mazar, in turn, writes:[241]

> The final annihilation or abandonment of these [Early Bronze] cities was
> one of the most fateful cultural crises in the history of Palestine: the
> entire Early Bronze Age urban culture in western Palestine collapsed
> within a short time, to be replaced by a totally different, nonurban
> pattern [...] It appears that the downfall of the cities was abrupt.
> Excavations at Megiddo, Beth-Yerah, 'Ai, Yarmuth, and other EB III sites
> have shown that they were abandoned or destroyed when they were at
> the peak of their urban development.

Before entering the Promised Land, the Israelites had defeated two Amorite kings who

reigned in upper Transjordan: Sihon of Heshbon and Og of Bashan (Num 21:21–35; Deut

2:26–3:11). In those days there lived Amorites not only in the hill country on either side

---

[240] See also Courville 1971, 87–94 (in volume 1); David Down (2010), *The Archaeology Book*, 16, 17;
David Down (2011), *Unveiling the Kings of Israel*, 60–62, 72–77. — "And your sons shall be shepherds in
the wilderness forty years, and bear the brunt of your infidelity, until your carcasses are consumed in
the wilderness." Num 14:33 NKJV — "How lovely are your tents, O Jacob, your encampments, O Israel!"
Num 24:5 ESV — "At the beginning of their history the Israelites, like their ancestors before them, lived
as nomads or semi-nomads, and when they came to settle down as a nation, they still retained some
characteristics of that earlier way of life." de Vaux 1973, 3.

[241] Mazar 1992, 141. See also pages 142, 158, 171, 227. See also Ben-Tor 1992, 123, 124; de Miroschedji
2018, 133, 134. For the best text dealing with the archaeology of the conquest of Palestine by the
Israelites at the end of the Early Bronze period see A. J. M. Osgood (1986c), *The Times of the Judges —
The Archaeology: (a) Exodus to Conquest*. The next city after Jericho to be destroyed was Ai (Josh 7; 8).
There is no doubt that the remains of biblical Ai (the name meaning "the mound of ruins") can be found
at et-Tell ("the mound") which is located some 10 miles or 16 kilometers northeast of Jerusalem "in the
southern part of the central hill country with a view of the arid hills stretching eastward toward the
Jordan valley" (Golden 2002a, 106). There is a *long narrow valley* or *gorge* (גַּיְא gay' Josh 8:11, "a ravine"
RSV, NRSV, ESV, ISV, NABRE, AMP, "a hollow" NJPS; see also TDOT, 11:206; Harrison 1979, 82; TWOT,
158, 159; Hubbard 2005, 22) called Wadi el-Jaya just north of et-Tell, and a *wide valley* or *plain* (עֵמֶק
'ēmeq Josh 8:13; see also TDOT, 11:205; TWOT, 158, 678; Woudstra 1981, 139, 140; NJB; NIDOTTE,
3:440; Howard 1998, 205; MED, 762; CDCH, 333; Wright 2020, 125, 127) just southeast of the site
"overlooking the Arabah" (Josh 8:14 NIV) or the Jordan Valley in the east (see also Howard 1998, 206;
Harstad 2004, 342, 343). The modern town of Deir Dibwan has been built on that plain. On the
archaeology of Ai/et-Tell, which was destroyed at the end of the Early Bronze period, see NEAEHL, 1:39–
45; AEHL, 21–23; Kennedy 2024, 172–179 (see especially pages 173, 175 and 177, on "a massive pile of
stones about six meters high [...] at the western edge of the site" (cp. Josh 8:28, 29; see also Marquet-
Krause 1949, 16; Callaway & Schoonover 1972, 41; Callaway 1980, 2, 18, 186, 187)). After its destruction
et-Tell remained abandoned a very long time, until the Iron Age (cp. Josh 8:28). — "In addition, other
geographical data in Joshua 7–8 concerning Ai — a place for the ambush party to the west of the city
(8:13), a valley to the north (8:13) [8:11], and a 'place overlooking the Arabah' to the east (8:14) — all fit
well with the et-Tell identification." Rasmussen 2010, 110. — "Many archeologists have identified Ai
with the site et-Tell [...] The geography of the area fits perfectly with the details found in Joshua 8."
Campbell 1983, 343. See also Mazar 1992, 331; Nelson 1997, 112; Finkelstein & Mazar 2007, 62; Hess
2008, 159, 173; Beitzel 2009, 117; Callaway & Shanks 2010, 64–66; Rösel 2011, 109, 110, 126–128;
Butler 2014, 405, 406; Petit 2014, 50–52; Rainey & Notley 2015, 125; Schlegel 2016, 38; Dessel 2017,
293.

of the Jordan River (Num 13:29; Josh 5:1; 10:6) but also in Syria and Iraq where they had many flourishing kingdoms. Amorites, a Semitic-speaking people originating probably from Syria, had been infiltrating southern Mesopotamia since the downfall of the Akkadian kingdom, but it was not until the finale of the Third Dynasty of Ur at the end of the 17th century B.C., in my view, that they managed to take over several important southern cities.[242]

About that time an Amorite dynasty was established also at the city of Babylon which "had never played a part in Sumerian politics".[243] However, under the rule of the most powerful king of that dynasty, Hammurabi, "Babylon became for the first time the political, religious, and economic heart of the land".[244] He ascended the throne, in my view, in the early 15th century B.C. (possibly in 1478 B.C.) and was therefore contemporary with Moses and the Israelites who left Egypt.[245] Today Hammurabi is best known for his law code (*Laws of Hammurabi*) which is not very much later than the Ten Commandments and the other ordinances that God gave to the Israelites at Mount Sinai (Ex 19–23) in 1491 B.C.[246]

One of Hammurabi's closest allies was Zimri-Lim, an Amorite king whose capital was Mari in eastern Syria, on the banks of the Euphrates. At Mari Zimri-Lim lived in a palace of "unprecedented size and splendor".[247] In the end the palace was burned down and destroyed by the troops of Hammurabi himself (possibly in 1445 B.C.), and the ruins concealed a vast archive of clay cuneiform tablets from which can be learnt much about

---

[242] "After the fall of the Third Dynasty of Ur, Amorites were to be found everywhere in Iraq, from the uplands east of the Tigris to the major urban centers of the alluvial plains." Foster & Foster 2009, 71. On the Amorites see also, for example, Bryce & Birkett-Rees 2016, 81–83; Fleming 2016; Burke 2021.

[243] Roux 1992, 184.

[244] Foster & Foster 2009, 77. See also Beaulieu 2018, 2, 34, 40, 41, 50, 57, 58, 76; Boivin 2022, 566, 567.

[245] On the historical time of Hammurabi see also Immanuel Velikovsky, *Hammurabi and the Revised Chronology*; Courville 1971, 233, 300, Figure 5 after p. 308 (in volume 2); Osgood 1986c, 74; 1988c, 116 (Figure 6); 2024, 411, 412.

[246] Jones 2015, 278. Read a translation of the laws of Hammurabi for example in Pritchard (ed.) 2011, 155–179; COS, 2:336–353. The earliest known law code comes from Ur-Nammu, the first king of the Third Dynasty of Ur, or his son and successor Shulgi (see Brisch 2013, 123; Van De Mieroop 2013, 282; read the laws of Ur-Nammu for example in Pritchard (ed.) 2011, 179–182; COS, 2:409, 410). For more on the life and achievements of Hammurabi see for example Roux 1992, 195, 197–207; Van De Mieroop 2005; Beaulieu 2018, 76–95.

[247] Bryce & Birkett-Rees 2016, 105. See also Roux 1992, 214–218; Bahrani 2017, 186–192.

the city's "daily affairs, its cultural and commercial activities, its alliances, and its fluctuating political and military fortunes".[248]

There is among the Mari tablets an accounting document (from the tenth year of Zimri-Lim's reign, possibly 1451 B.C., the year of the conquest of Canaan by the Israelites) which records allocations of tin to many high-ranking individuals, including the king of Hazor in northern Palestine.[249] The name of that king is also told, Ibni-Addu. Now this Ibni-Addu was probably the same person as the king of Hazor mentioned in Josh 11:1, Jabin, who led a large northern Canaanite military coalition against the invading Israelites — without success.[250]

The Israelites managed to capture a good portion of the Promised Land during the first seven years of the conquest.[251] The land thus entered a new archaeological and cultural

---

[248] Bryce & Birkett-Rees 2016, 105. — "More than twenty thousand cuneiform tablets were found in various rooms, including royal letters, administrative and omen texts. Accounts record the arrival of luxury products and foodstuffs sent by neighbouring kings, testifying to the city's importance; its contacts were far-flung, including Hazor in Palestine." Bienkowski 2000, 190. On Mari see also, for example, Roaf 1990, 116–119; Akkermans & Schwartz 2003, 262–267; 313–317; Margueron 2013; 2014; Butterlin 2016.

[249] See Malamat 1971; 1998, 46, 47; Sasson 2015, 50, 51. See also Podany 2010, 107, 108. — "The main function of tin was for alloying with copper to produce bronze [...] Some tin passed through Mari, from where texts mention onward shipment to Hazor in northern Palestine and Ugarit on the Syrian coast." Philip 2000, 292. — "The Mari texts refer directly to Hazor and Laish (Tel Dan) as the recipients of tin via a complex trading system [...]" Golden 2002b, 299. See also Malamat 1998, 41, 46, 47. Laish (later renamed Dan, Judg 18:29) was "a large, prosperous city at the end of the Early Bronze Age II and in the Early Bronze Age III" (NEAEHL, 1:324). See also Greenberg 2019, 215, 216. — "Bronze, an alloy of copper and tin, did not appear in the southern Levant before the end of the Early Bronze Age, and possibly only later. The new alloy did not see widespread use in the region until the ensuing Middle Bronze Age." Golden 2009, 217. See also Richard 2014, 341, 342, 344; 2020, 437; Greenberg 2019, 116, 123, 125. The total amount of tin and bronze brought to late EB III Palestine was probably relatively small, and most of it became recycled. Axes, nails and a knife made of iron have been found at Mari; Zimri-Lim "presented an iron ring as a gift to a neighboring king" (Bourke 2018, 112, 113).

[250] See also Osgood 1986c, 74; 1988c, 114, 115. — "Jabin of Hazor, mentioned in Joshua and Judges, may well have held a throne name: the West Semitic equivalent of Ibni-Addu would be Yabni-Baʻal/Hadad [...]" Sasson 2015, 51. See also, for example, Hess 2009, 49, 50; Sasson 2014, 252; Dozeman 2015, 462; ESVSB, 412 (the study note on Josh 11:1); NIVZSB, 439 (the study note on Judg 4:2); NLTSB, 425 (the study note on Judg 4:1–5:31). — "In several documents from this [Mari] archive Hazor appears to be one of the most important cities in the ancient Near East." Mazar 1992, 193, 194. Cp. Josh 11:10 (NKJV): "Joshua turned back at that time and took Hazor, and struck its king [Jabin] with the sword; for Hazor was formerly the head of all those [Canaanite] kingdoms." — "Hazor [...] was first settled in the EB2 and began to emerge as an important center in the EB3." Golden 2002a, 96. See also Golden 2009, 110; OEBA, 1:478. Hopefully one day in the future archaeologists working at Hazor will unearth there an EB III royal archive of texts and letters from the days of Ibni-Addu/Jabin, Zimri-Lim and Hammurabi. See also Zuckerman 2006; Bechar 2017.

[251] See Jones 2015, 87, 278.

period known as Middle Bronze I (MB I) which differed a lot from the previous EB III period, as we have already read.[252] But Amihai Mazar writes again:[253]

> The uniqueness of the [MB I] period, and its outstanding divergence from those preceding and succeeding it [...] In most of western Palestine, the change in the way of life between the two periods [EB III and MB I] was extreme: a thriving, hierarchical urban culture with a city-state political system, surplus economy, and foreign trade relations was replaced by an egalitarian society based on pastoralism and agriculture, without any distinct political system [...] the discontinuity from the previous period is expressed in the essential modes of life. The complete desertion of many Early Bronze sites, the poor villages constructed on some of the ruined cities, the establishment of new encampments on previously unsettled hills, the occupation of the arid Negev highland and northern and central Sinai, and the appearance of new burial customs are all demonstrative of a radical cultural break.

The archaeological information concerning the Palestinian Middle Bronze I period is obtained primarily from cemeteries.[254] In one MB I tomb near ʿAin Samiya, north of Jerusalem, was found a fine silver goblet which is decorated with mythological scenes derived possibly from *Enuma elish*.[255] *Enuma elish* ("When on high") is "the most complete and detailed story of creation that we possess [...] a long [Babylonian] poem in seven tablets originally composed during the Old Babylonian period [the era of Amorite rule] [...] though all the copies found so far were written during the first

---

[252] This new period has also been called "Intermediate Early Bronze–Middle Bronze Period" and "EB IV/MB I", for example. See Mazar 1992, 152; de Miroschedji 2018, 134 note 7. In the most recent literature, the MB I period is regularly referred to as the EB IV period. — "If one wishes to get a glimpse of what Israelite culture was like [...] he should look at the debris which belongs to early Middle Bronze when the Israelites had opportunity to settle down in their new home and utilize their inherent abilities as the situation provided opportunity." Courville 1971, 112 (in volume 1).

[253] Mazar 1992, 152, 170, 171. — "The contrast with the highly developed urban economy and society of Palestine in Early Bronze II–III [...] could hardly be more striking [...] EB IV [MB I] represents a brief but dramatic shift at the end of EB III, from an urban to a rural and pastoral nomadic pattern of social organization." Dever 1995, 289, 295. But see also Richard 2020.

[254] Mazar 1992, 151, 159. See also Greenberg 2019, 164, 165.

[255] See Gophna 1992, 154, 155, Plate 24; Mazar 1992, 167, 168; Greenberg 2019, 175, 176. See also Kaiser & Wegner 2017, 82, 83.

millennium B.C.".[256] Perhaps the silver goblet was a spoil of the (EB III) city of Hazor which was looted and destroyed by the Israelites (Josh 11:10–14).[257]

The "rural and pastoral nomadic" Middle Bronze I period was then followed by the Middle Bronze II period (MB II) which "began with the revival of urban life in the country — at first on a limited scale, and later more extensively".[258] The re-urbanization started in the northern coastal plain and spread later to the south and east; all this took place during the early part of MB II, or MB IIA. The impulse for this new phase, "distinguished by an almost total revolution in all aspects of material culture",[259] came probably from the Byblian (Byblos) Middle Bronze civilization in Lebanon which is situated just north of Palestine.[260]

I have dated the beginning of the MB IIA phase to the last two decades of the 15th century B.C., soon after the death of Joshua in 1424 B.C., approximately.[261] After he and the other elders had died, the Israelites "forsook the LORD God of their fathers, who had brought them out of the land of Egypt; and they followed other gods from *among* the gods of the people who *were* all around them, and they bowed down to them; and they provoked the LORD to anger" (Judg 2:12 NKJV). The Israelites also intermarried with the idolatrous Canaanite peoples who still dwelt in the land (Judg 3:1–6). Presumably any

---

[256] Roux 1992, 95. Read a translation of *Enuma elish* for example in Pritchard (ed.) 2011, 28–39; COS, 1:391–402. — "The standard version of the narrative dates from the 1st millennium B.C., but the true provenience of the epic is controversial." White 2009, 340.
[257] "[…] Damascus and Hazor. The Mari documents, in fact, speak of Babylonian emissaries living in the latter city." Morandi Bonacossi 2014, 429. See also Malamat 1960, 13, 14; Rainey & Notley 2015, 56. — "The 'Ain Samiya cup may […] have originated in EB III 'Ai […]" Greenberg 2019, 176. The Israelites had also plundered the city of Ai (Josh 8:2, 27).
[258] Mazar 1992, 174. — "The migrating Israelites were nomads, and when they entered their Promised Land they had no disposition to occupy the houses of the cities they conquered. Of course, as time went by they were threatened by invaders and found it necessary to move into cities where they were protected by city walls, so in the MB II period we find evidence of city dwelling." Down 2011, 75. There were already walled sites in Palestine in the MB I period (see Richard 2020, 427, 428).
[259] Mazar 1992, 175.
[260] See Mazar 1992, 188, 189. See also Greenberg 2019, 188, 189, 206–208, 221, 236. — "[…] there is strong evidence that the MBA [Middle Bronze Age] re-urbanization process in the southern Levant was influenced, if not directly caused, by Amorite elements from the north." Harrison 2012, 644. In many regions of Palestine, the early MB IIA material culture must have been contemporary with the late MB I material culture — at the end of the 15th century and in the early 14th century B.C., in my view. See also Ilan 1995, 299, 300, 304. Note that Ilan is using different terminology for the MB I and MB IIA periods. On the transition from the MB I to the MB II period see also D'Andrea 2020, 409, 410.
[261] Jones 2015, 90, 278.

kind of foreign influence on the early Israelite society and culture in Palestine was most pronounced in the northern parts of the country.[262]

God did not leave Israel's apostasy unpunished:

> And the anger of the LORD was hot against Israel. So He delivered them into the hands of plunderers who despoiled them; and He sold them into the hands of their enemies all around, so that they could no longer stand before their enemies [...] And they were greatly distressed. Nevertheless, the LORD raised up judges who delivered them out of the hand of those who plundered them. (Judg 2:14–16 NKJV)

Around the year 1418 B.C.[263], only about six years after the death of Joshua, "The anger of the LORD burned against Israel so that he sold them into the hands of Cushan-Rishathaim king of Aram Naharaim, to whom the Israelites were subject for eight years" (Judg 3:8 NIV). At the end of those eight years a judge of Israel named Othniel went out to war against the oppressors and defeated them (Judg 3:9, 10).

So Cushan-Rishathaim ruled in Aram Naharaim ("Aram of the two rivers"), that is, in the region of northern and northeastern Syria where the two rivers Balikh and Khabur (or Habur) flow from north to south until they join the river Euphrates.[264] Interestingly, some Palestinian MB IIA painted pottery resembles the so-called "Khabur ware".[265] This ware "is rarely found in the Khabur river valley itself but is predominantly located to the north and east on the upper Khabur plains and in northern Iraq [...] Although the pottery is unequivocally associated with cuneiform texts dated to the reign of Shamshi-Adad, it is not clear how much earlier it was manufactured".[266] Shamshi-Adad (or Samsi-Addu) was contemporary with Hammurabi of Babylon and Zimri-Lim of Mari, in the early 1400s

---

[262] See also Osgood 1988c, 109, 110.

[263] Jones 2015, 88, 91, 278.

[264] On Aram Naharaim see also, for example, Kitchen 1982, 67; Block 1999, 152; NUBD, 92; Andersen 2009, 289; Sasson 2014, 215; Arbino 2017, 21; Kaiser & Wegner 2017, 303, 304; NIVZSB, 437 (the study note on Judg 3:8).

[265] See Mazar 1992, 182–184, 228 (note 17). See also Amiran 1969, 113–115, 118; Golden 2002b, 299; Cohen 2014, 455. On the so-called "Levantine Painted ware", which most likely originated in the coastal regions of Lebanon and Syria and which clearly had a connection to the Khabur ware and the Palestinian MB IIA pottery, see for example Charaf 2014, 442; Greenberg 2019, 203–206; Marcus 2022, 803–806. See also Cooper 2020, 114–116, on the painted goblets from EB IVB Ebla and western Syria (mid-1500s B.C., in my view). Levantine Painted ware -like pottery probably began to appear in Palestinian coastal sites long before the Israelites entered the land.

[266] Akkermans & Schwartz 2003, 308, 309.

B.C. He was a mighty Amorite ruler whose kingdom at its greatest extent "embraced the northern half of Iraq and the whole of Transeuphrataean Syria. This vast territory has been, and is still frequently referred to as 'Assyria' or 'The First Assyrian Empire', but it should be called the 'Kingdom of Upper Mesopotamia'".[267] The Babylonian kingdom of Hammurabi began to expand and flourish in real earnest only after the death of Shamshi-Adad.[268] By the late 1400s B.C. at least a part of northern Syria had fallen under the rule of Cushan-Rishathaim; the origin of the Khabur ware -like pottery in MB IIA Palestine may well be, in part at least, in the short period of dominance of the land by him.[269]

There was a smooth cultural transition from the MB IIA phase to the next phase, MB IIB.[270] This transition took place, in my view, during the 13th century B.C. The transition from the MB IIB phase to the final phase of the Palestinian Middle Bronze period, namely MB IIC, took place between 1150 and 1050 B.C., approximately.[271]

During MB IIB–C there was "a thriving, prosperous urban culture" in Palestine.[272] Many cities were surrounded by thick walls and ramparts, and they had also great palaces and

---

[267] Roux 1992, 191. For a map of the extent of Shamshi-Adad's kingdom see Roaf 1990, 116; Bryce & Birkett-Rees 2016, 90, 91.

[268] Zimri-Lim ascended the throne of Mari only after Shamshi-Adad's death, possibly in 1460 B.C., 18 years after Hammurabi had ascended the throne of Babylon. See also Chart 4 at the end of this book.

[269] See also Osgood 1988c, 110–116. In his 27th year of reign, possibly in 1409 B.C., Hammurabi's son and successor Samsu-iluna was victorious over Yadih-abum whose capital was possibly Mari, or Terqa between Mari and the confluence of the Khabur and the Euphrates. In the same year (and maybe at the same time) Samsu-iluna also got a victory over a king named Muti-Hurshana (*mu-ti-ḫu-ur-ša-na*) about whom nothing is known. See Horsnell 1999, 220, 221; Charpin 2011, 44; Arkhipov 2022, 381, 382; Boivin 2022, 622–624. Now, could this Muti-Hurshana have been the same person as Cushan-Rishathaim whom Othniel defeated possibly in 1410 or 1409 B.C., after the eight years of oppression (Judg 3:7–11)? Cushan-Rishathaim, "Hebrew 'Cushan Double-Wickedness,' looks like a distorted name" (SBLSB, 380), being "likely a pejorative name created from the real name as a literary device meant to heighten Othniel's deliverance of Israel" (NIVZSB, 437; "'the twice wicked Moor' (?) disfigurement of a proper name" HALOT, 467). The consonants in the name Muti-Hurshana could just have been rearranged in a suitable way. KJV spells the name of the oppressor as Chushan-rishathaim, LXX.D Chusarsathom/-sathaim. — "The year: Samsuiluna, the king, at the command of Enlil and by the cleverness and strength which Marduk gave to him, (conquered) Iadiabum and Mutihurshana, kings who had become hostile against him, and crushed them with his fierce weapon." Horsnell 1999, 221.

[270] Mazar 1992, 191, 193.

[271] Some scholars, however, divide the MB II period into phases A and B only and incorporate the MB IIC phase within the MB IIB phase. See Kempinski 1992, 159; Cohen 2014, 453; Sharon 2014, 53, 54; Greenberg 2019, 181; Höflmayer 2022, 12, 13. In the most recent literature the MB IIA–C phases are regularly referred to as the MB I–III.

[272] Mazar 1992, 213. — "[…] a period of independence, prosperity and high cultural attainment […] MB IIB […]" McCarter 2010, 9. — "MBA2 [Middle Bronze Age 2] […] marked the high point of civilization in Canaan. Large urban centers thrived." Collins & Holden (eds.) 2020, 48. — "The later phases of the

temples.[273] A large building compound, "a massive 123-foot-wide fortification with wall and earthen embankment",[274] existed at MB IIB Shechem in central Palestine; "it is likely that a sanctuary room of some sort was part of the complex, along with other buildings".[275] Now this MB IIB fortification, situating at the western edge of the city, was most probably "the castle or citadel of the town of Shechem, which is called the tower of Shechem in vv. [Judg 9:]46–49",[276] and it probably contained also "the temple of El-Berith" (NIV) mentioned in Judg 9:4, 46.[277] The events told in the ninth chapter of the Book of Judges took place at the time when Abimelech, a son of Gideon the judge (see Judg 6–8), was made king by the Shechemites (Judg 9:6) and ruled over Israelites for three years (Judg 9:22) from 1218 B.C. onwards.[278]

Middle Bronze Age in Canaan are marked by a continuation of the developments begun in MB I [MB IIA], with increasing trends toward centralization of social, economic, and political systems, and further standardization of material culture." Cohen 2014, 459. See also Baker 2017, 193; Greenberg 2019, 180, 221, 222, 224.

[273] See Mazar 1992, 198–212. — "Virtually all of the major [Middle Bronze] cities, and even some smaller centers, were surrounded by massive earthworks, also known as earthen ramparts [...] In fact, these ramparts are what give most tell sites their characteristic sloping form today. In the case of cities, the earthen ramparts enclosed areas of urban development that included public buildings such as temples and palaces as well as residential structures." Golden 2009, 5, 54.

[274] AEHL, 460.

[275] NEAEHL, 4:1349. — "The complex was surrounded by massive thick walls and comprised inner courtyards and large rooms. It was defined by the excavator as a 'Courtyard Temple,' but in fact it was probably a large civil center, perhaps the residence of the local governor." Mazar 1992, 182. See also OEBA, 2:351, 352.

[276] Keil 2011b, 262. See also, for example, DBI, 880; Block 1999, 331, 332; Walton et al. 2000, 256; Butler 2009, 248; HAHAT, 626; Sasson 2014, 363, 398; Fischer 2018, 610; "the fort at Shechem" GNB, "Fortress of Shechem" CEV margin, "the fortress at Sh'khem" CJB, "the citadel of Shechem" EHV.

[277] "The *tower of Shechem* is clearly a fairly large area, possibly distinct from the city but adjacent to it, that in itself contained a *stronghold* dedicated to *El-Berith*, meaning 'god of the covenant' [...] those who sought refuge in this stronghold did not escape; the tower was burnt and the people inside were incinerated." Evans 2017, 113. See also Webb 2012, 290, 291.

[278] Jones 2015, 279. — "The area of Abimelech's reign was never very large, being confined to the environs of Shechem in the territory of the western half tribe of Manasseh." Kaiser & Wegner 2017, 310. — "The major settlement of the central hills was Shechem. This site dominated the entire hill country throughout the whole of the Middle Bronze Age [...]" Kempinski 1992, 172. The Israelites had destroyed the northern Palestinian city of Hazor (Josh 11:10, 11) at the end of the EB III period. However, Hazor was reconstructed to a new glory at the beginning of the MB IIB phase (see Mazar 1992, 194; NEAEHL, 2:595, 599; AEHL, 220, 221; Greenberg 2019, 189, 228, 229). The rebuilder of the city was probably "Jabin king of Canaan, who reigned in Hazor" (Judg 4:2 NKJV). This Jabin oppressed the people of Israel for 20 years (Judg 4:3), 1298–1278 B.C. (Jones 2015, 278, 279). The MB IIB phase may have started earlier in northern Palestine compared to the more southern parts of the land. A fragment of a cuneiform tablet (a letter) which can be dated to the Old Babylonian period has been unearthed at Hazor. The tablet begins with the words "To Ibni", that is for sure, Jabin. See Horowitz & Shaffer 1992; NEAEHL5, 1772. See also Ferguson 2006, 275; ESVASB, 304 (the study note on Josh 11:1).

During the 12th century B.C. God raised up still many judges to deliver the Israelites out of the hand of their enemies (Judg 10–16).[279] Under the leadership of the last judge, Samuel, the Israelites got a great victory over the Philistines (1 Sam 7) in 1101 B.C.[280] Not a long time after that the elders of the people asked Samuel to give them a king. They said to him: "We want a king over us. Then we will be like all the other nations, with a king to lead us and to go out before us and fight our battles" (1 Sam 8:19, 20 NIV). A short time later a man named Saul from the tribe of Benjamin was chosen the first king of all Israel (1 Sam 10). This started a new period in the history of the nation of Israel, a period which will be briefly reviewed in the next chapter.

---

[279] On the chronology of the judges see Jones 2015, 71–88, 278, 279, and Chart 4 in the CD-ROM.
[280] Jones 2015, 83, 279.

CHAPTER 6: IN THE DAYS OF THE KINGS

Saul began to reign in 1095 B.C.[281] He "fought against all his enemies on every side, against Moab, against the people of Ammon, against Edom, against the kings of Zobah, and against the Philistines [...] And he gathered an army and attacked the Amalekites, and delivered Israel from the hands of those who plundered them" (1 Sam 14:47, 48 NKJV).

Saul's bloodiest military act was the extermination of the southern Palestinian Amalekites (1 Sam 15) which took place in the final years of the 1070s B.C.[282] Israelites had confronted Amalekites for the first time soon after their departure from Egypt in 1491 B.C. (Ex 17:8–16). Put in a very simplified way, the Amalekites of those days invaded the land of Egypt and ruled parts of it oppressively for about 400 years. They were known by the Egyptians as *heka khasut*, "rulers of foreign lands",[283] the Greek form of the phrase being "Hyksos". In the end the Egyptians rose to a final revolt, and the Amalekites/Hyksos were expelled from the country and destroyed — largely by the Israelite army under the command of King Saul.[284]

---

[281] Jones 2015, 279.

[282] David was secretly anointed king by Samuel (1 Sam 16) in 1070 B.C., approximately (Jones 2015, 103, 279), probably soon after the destruction of the Amalekites.

[283] Shaw & Nicholson 2008, 154.

[284] On the Amalekites/Hyksos and their expulsion and destruction see also Courville 1971, 227–241 (in volume 1); Ashton & Down 2006, 102–107, 207; Velikovsky 2009, 71–113; Down 2011, 90; Lacey 2025. Probably around the same time ended also the period of Kassite domination in southern Iraq. The Kassites, a people who may have originated from the Zagros Mountains in western Iran, had gained power in northern Babylonia in the early 13th century B.C., in my view, around the time of the demise of the Amorite dynasty of Hammurabi. — "In both material culture and language, the end of the Old Babylonian period is often difficult to differentiate from the beginning of the Middle Babylonian (or Kassite) period, making it sometimes hardly possible to date artifacts, archaeological levels, and texts with precision." Boivin 2022, 567.

Saul was succeeded as king of Israel by David in 1055 B.C.[285] He reigned first at Hebron[286] and then at Jerusalem[287] (2 Sam 5:5). Because "the LORD gave victory to David wherever he went" (2 Sam 8:14 ESV) he got under his authority the Philistines, the Edomites, the Moabites, the Ammonites, and the Arameans. David was also on good terms with the king of Tyre, Hiram, who sent to Jerusalem "cedar logs and carpenters and stonemasons, and they built a palace for David" (2 Sam 5:11 NIV).

In the days of David's reign began the golden era of the kingdom of Israel which reached its peak during the reign of his son and successor, Solomon, who ascended the throne

---

[285] Jones 2015, 103, 279.

[286] One year after the Israelites had left Egypt (in 1491 B.C.) Moses sent twelve men to spy out the land of Canaan (Num 13). Those men witnessed many fortified cities (Num 13:28), including Hebron. It is stated in Num 13:22 that "Hebron was built seven years before Zoan" (NKJV). Zoan (or Tanis) was an Egyptian city located in the northeastern Nile Delta region. The quoted verse of The Book of Numbers implies that Zoan and the date of its foundation were well known to the Israelites — the city was most likely established during the time when the Israelites were living in Egypt. According to the same verse Hebron was built almost the same time as Zoan. Now, archaeological excavations at Hebron (Tell er-Rumeida) have demonstrated that the first massively fortified city dates to the EB III period (AEHL, 224; Ortiz 2005, 390; OEBA, 1:486, 487). I believe that Num 13:22 refers to this EB III Hebron and that it was built during the time when the Israelites were living in Egypt. In certain Egyptian inscriptions (the so-called Execration Texts) from the 16th and 15th centuries B.C. (the Palestinian late EB III period), in my view, the city of Hebron is possibly mentioned by the name of "Yanak". In the Old Testament the name "Anak" is strongly connected to the pre-Israelite Hebron: see Num 13:22; Josh 11:21; 14:12, 13, 15; 15:13, 14; 21:11; Judg 1:20. See also Kempinski 1992, 159, 160, 182, 183; Marcus 2022, 817–821; see then Courville 1971, 239–241 (in volume 1), 90, 91, 110–118 (in volume 2); Mazar 1992, 228 note 21; Marcus 2022, 827. During the MB II period Hebron was "the major settlement in the Judean Hills" (NEAEHL, 2:608); no wonder that Hebron was selected as David's first capital.

[287] David and his men captured Jerusalem from the Jebusites who lived there at the time (2 Sam 5:6–9; 1 Chr 11:4–8). The city was so well fortified that the Jebusites could taunt David by saying to him: "You will not get in here; even the blind and the lame can ward you off" (2 Sam 5:6 NIV). See also, for example, NBC, 324; ESVSB, 549 (the study note on 2 Sam 5:6–8); NIVZSB, 553 (the study note on 2 Sam 5:6); NLTSB, 527 (the study note on 2 Sam 5:7); Hoffner 2015, comments on 2 Sam 5:6–8; Steinmann 2017, 84, 88; Tsumura 2019, 96. In ancient times the most important source of water for Jerusalem was the Gihon Spring which is located in the Kidron Valley just east of the city. Archaeological excavations have revealed that "the Gihon Spring was heavily protected by a fortified enclosure with towers during Middle Bronze IIB" (AEHL, 261; see also Hoffmeier 2008, 90; NEAEHL5, 1801–1805; Bahat 2011, 18, 20; Galor & Bloedhorn 2013, 21, 23–26; OEBA, 1:414, 2:11, 12; Halpern 2017, 347, 348; Greenberg 2019, 226, 236–238; Collins & Holden (eds.) 2020, 52; Finkelstein 2024, 21, 22, 29–32, 262, 264, 362). Sections of Jerusalem's massive MB IIB city wall have also been uncovered (see AEHL, 261, 262; Galor & Bloedhorn 2013, 20–22). — "In the Middle Bronze Age [Jerusalem] [...] massive walls and towers of an impressive city fortification were built on the eastern slope of the City [...]" Finkelstein & Silberman 2006, 274. See also Down 2011, 97. — "Throughout its history, Jerusalem had several water systems, most of which centered on the Gihon Spring [...] the reference to the ṣinnôr [צִנּוֹר, in 2 Sam 5:8, "the water tunnel" GNB, NASB, CJB, NLT, NET, LSB, "the water supply" LEB; see also HALOT, 1038; HAHAT, 1125, 1126; Hoffner 2015, note 2479; Steinmann 2017, 83, 85, 88, 89; Tsumura 2019, 95, 97–99] must have been to another water system constructed in Middle Bronze Age II [...] that included a spring-fed pool and a guard tower made of cyclopean masonry [...]" Borowski 2005, 981. See also Long 2009, 433–435; ESVASB, 431–433; Kaiser & Wegner 2017, 370, 371; Currid 2020, 173.

in 1015 B.C.[288] Solomon built in Jerusalem a magnificent temple for God,[289] and palaces

for himself and his Egyptian queen (1 Kings 5–7). He also built

> Tadmor in the wilderness, and all the storage cities which he built in
> Hamath. He built Upper Beth Horon and Lower Beth Horon, fortified
> cities *with* walls, gates, and bars, also Baalath and all the storage cities
> that Solomon had, and all the chariot cities and the cities of the cavalry,
> and all that Solomon desired to build in Jerusalem, in Lebanon, and in all
> the land of his dominion. (2 Chr 8:4–6 NKJV)

Solomon "ruled over all the kingdoms from the Euphrates River to the land of the

Philistines, as far as the border of Egypt. These countries brought tribute and were

Solomon's subjects all his life" (1 Kings 4:21 NIV). He "excelled all the kings of the earth

in riches" (1 Kings 10:23 ESV),[290] and they "sought the presence of Solomon to hear his

wisdom, which God had put in his heart" (2 Chr 9:23 NKJV).

The most memorable royal visitor to Solomon was the queen of Sheba (1 Kings 10:1–13;

2 Chr 9:1–12). This queen was none other than the female pharaoh Hatshepsut of the

---

[288] Jones 2015, 104, 279. — "[…] [Solomon] saw Israel rise to heights it had never known before and would never know again […]" Merrill 2008, 330.

[289] The great temple of Solomon in Jerusalem pretty much resembled certain other temples in MB II Palestine. See Mazar 1992, 211, 212; Greenberg 2019, 226, 251, 252. In the time of the judges (MB IIA– late B/early C) the Israelites' main sanctuary (the tabernacle) was at Shiloh, located about 20 miles or 32 kilometers north of Jerusalem (Josh 18:1; 19:51; Judg 18:31; 21:19; 1 Sam 1–4). The late MB II Shiloh "was heavily fortified […] with a massive wall (10–18 feet) […] Among the remains of the city from this period were storage rooms and cultic vessels, indicating the presence of a shrine. This level was destroyed" (AEHL, 463; see also Mazar 1992, 205; NEAEHL, 4:1366, 1367; Gilmour 2005, 893; Down 2011, 81–83; OEBA, 2:365–367; Greenberg 2019, 243, 244) most probably by the Philistines after they had won the battle against the Israelites at Aphek/Ebenezer and captured from them the Ark of the Covenant (1 Sam 4; see also Ps 78:60; Jer 7:12–14; Provan et al. 2003, 184; Merrill 2008, 195, 196; Kaiser & Wegner 2017, 374), in 1122 B.C. (Jones 2015, 279).

[290] Solomon had a fleet of long voyage vessels called "ships of Tarshish" at the Red Sea (at Ezion-Geber; see Down 2011, 107; Kaiser & Wegner 2017, 408–410). Those ships brought for Solomon gold, silver, ivory, apes and peacocks far from the east (1 Kings 9:26–28; 10:22). Tarshish itself was "one of the islands (or coastal territories) to the west of Palestine" (HALOT, 1797; see also Gordon 1962, 517, 518; Day 2013, 154–165; Hendel 2024, 363); it may have been a Hebrew name for the island of Crete (see Jan Sammer, *New Light on the Dark Age of Greece*, the chapter *Where was Tarshish?*). Still in the days of Solomon Crete was the center of the prosperous Minoan civilization, now famous for its impressive palaces (especially Knossos), sophisticated art, and wide-ranging maritime trade (see for example Landis (ed.) 2015, 32–35, 40). Interestingly, in his fascinating study of the history of ancient kingdoms Sir Isaac Newton made Solomon contemporary with Minos (see Newton 2009, 47), the semimythical powerful king of Crete whose name lies behind the term "Minoan". On the chronology of the ancient Aegean/Greek world see also Courville 1971, 267–287 (in volume 2); Velikovsky, *The Dark Age of Greece*; Sammer, *New Light on the Dark Age of Greece*; Schorr, *Applying the Revised Chronology: Mycenae*; Sweeney 2009; Velikovsky 2009, 192–194. Some Minoan pottery, a few inscriptions, and floor and wall paintings have been found in MB II archaeological contexts in Palestine (see Mazar 1992, 210, 218; Yasur-Landau 2010, 833–835; Greenberg 2019, 234, 236).

so-called 18th Dynasty of Egypt which had come to power after the fall of the Hyksos.[291] Experiencing all the glory of Solomon's court in Jerusalem "took her breath away" (1 Kings 10:5 CSB). She then said to Solomon:

> It was a true report which I heard in my own land about your words and your wisdom. However I did not believe the words until I came and saw with my own eyes; and indeed the half was not told me. Your wisdom and prosperity exceed the fame of which I heard. (1 Kings 10:6, 7 NKJV)

"The Bible with justice depicts Solomon's reign as one of unexampled prosperity."[292] Archaeology has confirmed that there really was "extraordinary prosperity"[293] in late Middle Bronze II Palestine, "the golden age"[294] of Palestine's entire Bronze Age.[295] However, the numerous wars which took place in the days of Samuel, Saul, David, Solomon and his son and successor Rehoboam also left their traces in the land's archaeological record. Jonathan M. Golden writes:[296]

> By the end of the MBA [Middle Bronze Age] [...] there was a major breakdown in [...] settlement system [in Palestine] as virtually every urban center, especially in the central highlands, experienced destruction, abandonment, or significant depopulation. Many scholars now agree that this process of deurbanization may have taken over a century, and that while Egyptian interference may have hastened their demise, internal problems already threatened the stability of [...] cities.

A great tragedy befell Rehoboam's kingdom in his fifth year of reign, in 971 B.C.,[297] when Shishak king of Egypt "took the fortified cities of Judah and came to Jerusalem [...] and

---

[291] See Ashton & Down 2006, 116–123; Velikovsky 2009, 115–152; Down 2010, 29; 2011, 105, 106; Scott 2012. According to Josephus [JA, Book VIII:vi.5 (p. 305)] the queen of Sheba was "queen of Egypt and Ethiopia [...] thoroughly trained in wisdom and remarkable in other ways". On the meaning of "Sheba" (=Theba/Thebes, the ancient southern Egyptian capital city) see Scott 2012, 35–41, 98.

[292] Bright 1981, 217.

[293] Finkelstein 1988, 339. — "This was a time of great local prosperity [...] the luxurious funerary appointments of Middle Bronze II B–C exceed anything else known in the history of the country." Albright 1960, 87. See also Cohen 2014, 460; Greenberg 2019, 255–262.

[294] Tubb 1998, 64; Golden 2009, 5, 54.

[295] See also Mazar 1992, 174; Ashton & Down 2006, 109, 111, 112; Down 2010, 17; 2011, 101, 103, 104, 130.

[296] Golden 2002b, 296. See also Mazar 1992, 239, 240; Greenberg 2019, 263, 264. — "The Middle Bronze Age is considered alternately warlike (because of its tremendous fortifications [...] and its plethora of weapons in tomb and cultic offerings) and peaceful (because so few destruction levels have been discerned until the end of the period) [...] it is now widely accepted that [...] the process of site destruction and abandonment occurred over a fairly extended period of time — perhaps as long as 150 years [...]" Ilan 1995, 311, 314.

[297] Jones 2015, 279.

took away the treasures of the house of the LORD and the treasures of the king's house;
he took everything" (2 Chr 12:4, 9 NKJV). Shishak must be identified with Queen
Hatshepsut's successor Thutmosis III "who left the record of his conquests in the north.
On the temple wall at Karnak [in southern Egypt] is a list of the treasures he brought
back from his conquests, and they correspond very well with the articles known to have
been in Solomon's temple".[298]

As a result of Thutmosis' military campaigns in the north "Palestine and parts of
southern Syria, as well as major trade routes in the eastern Mediterranean" came under
Egyptian control.[299] At the same time the cultural transition from the Middle Bronze
period to the following period, Late Bronze (LB), was underway in Palestine.[300] This
transition, which may have already begun in the previous century, was so smooth that
"our ability to date and differentiate late MB and early LB material culture is severely
limited".[301]

In my consideration the Late Bronze period lasted in Palestine until the Assyrian and
Babylonian conquests and captivities in the late 8th century (2 Kings 17) and the early
6th century B.C. (2 Kings 25), respectively. The period after Late Bronze is called Iron Age.
However, numerous Iron Age -labeled settlements in Palestine, for example the city of
Samaria in the central hill country (founded by King Omri in the late 900s B.C.),[302] were
in reality contemporaneous with Late Bronze -labeled settlements. In other words, two
"cultural periods" coexisted in Palestine during the 10th–6th centuries B.C.,

---

[298] Down 2011, 110. See also Courville 1971, 265, 266, 268, 270–272 (in volume 1); Ashton & Down
2006, 124–131; Velikovsky 2009, 153–189; Down 2010, 29; Scott 2012, 131–162.
[299] Bard 2015, 229.
[300] "Indeed, a case can be made for ending the Middle Bronze Age with the campaign of Thutmose III,
when Canaan [Palestine] came finally and decidedly into the Egyptian orbit […] though apparently
retaining many of its social and political structures." Ilan 1995, 315. See also Mazar 1992, 232; Bourke
2014, 479; Panitz-Cohen 2014, 542. Even though it was a very bitter thing that Rehoboam's kingdom
became a vassal state of its Egyptian plunderer (2 Chr 12:5–8, 13), "There were still some good things in
the land of Judah" (2 Chr 12:12 NLT; "conditions were good in Judah" NASB, ESV, CSB). After Solomon's
death in 975 B.C. (Jones 2015, 77, 279) his kingdom was divided into two realms: the southern kingdom
of Judah ruled by Rehoboam, and the northern kingdom of Israel ruled by Jeroboam. See 1 Kings 11; 12.
On the chronology of the kings of Judah and Israel see Jones 2015, the chart at the end of his book, and
Chart 5C in the CD-ROM.
[301] Ilan 1995, 314. — "[…] the Late Bronze Age […] is but a direct continuation of the Middle Bronze Age
II, with Egyptian influence gaining dominance." Kempinski 1992, 210. See also Harrison 2012, 644. But
see also Greenberg 2019, 264, 284.
[302] 1 Kings 16:23, 24. Omri reigned 929–918 B.C. (see Jones 2015, the chart at the end of his book, and
Chart 5C in the CD-ROM). On the archaeology of Samaria see also Sweeney 2006, 92–95.

approximately. This is comparable with the situation in the Aegean/Greek world during almost the same period of time where the Late Bronze (Mycenaean) and Iron Age (Geometric) cultures were also concurrent, not consecutive as is usually wrongly taught.[303]

In 586 B.C.[304] Nebuchadnezzar, the king of Babylon, attacked against the city of Jerusalem and took it: "Then his army burned the Temple of God, tore down the walls of Jerusalem, burned all the palaces, and completely destroyed everything of value. The few who survived were taken as exiles to Babylon, and they became servants to the king and his sons until the kingdom of Persia came to power" (2 Chr 36:19, 20 NLT). Palestine was under Persian rule from the late 6th century B.C. until the conquest of the Near East by Alexander the Great and the Greeks in the late 4th century B.C.[305] It is Alexander the Great who finally links up the (biblical-creationist) history presented in this book with the classical and universally accepted history of the even later periods of the ancient Near East.

---

[303] See the literature mentioned in footnote 290, on page 79. The archaeology of Palestine's Late Bronze and Iron Age periods needs a lot more investigation and reinterpretation. On these periods in Palestine see also Courville 1971, 112 (in volume 1), 338, 345 (in volume 2); Velikovsky, *Beth-Shan*; 2010, 53–57; Sweeney 2008, 81–84; Down 2010, 13, 17; 2011, 129, 130. Note the differences between my views and David Down's views.

[304] Jones 2015, 280.

[305] It was during this period of Persian domination in Palestine that the Old Testament canon was completed. See Steinmann 1999. As good introductions to the books of the Old Testament I recommend Uuras Saarnivaara (1983), *Can the Bible Be Trusted?*, and Gleason L. Archer (2007), *A Survey of Old Testament Introduction*. When studying the Old Testament history, it is always good to have Floyd Nolen Jones's *The Chronology of the Old Testament* close at hand.

EPILOGUE

Much more could be told about the history of Palestine and the surrounding countries from the time of Solomon until the time of Alexander the Great, but I have decided to keep that part of the narration very short and simple. The main reason for this is that those centuries have already been dealt with so well and in great detail by others, especially Immanuel Velikovsky. I just ask an interested reader to get acquainted with the "important literature" mentioned in Chart 3 of this book. I also encourage studying other useful literature, Christian as well as secular, concerning the ancient Near Eastern history and archaeology, but great care must be taken to distinguish between facts and interpretations. Interpretations and datings which are not in agreement with the history and chronology of the Bible cannot be accepted. The unfortunate truth is that almost all existing Christian literature on the ancient Near Eastern history is teaching similar false chronologies and other incorrect views as the secular literature.

A person who is well versed in the study of the ancient Near Eastern history and archaeology will quickly notice the uniqueness of the chronological charts of this book. I am increasingly confident that if the Bible is really true (and it is) those charts have to be essentially correct. In the words of Immanuel Velikovsky, in whom I have great respect for,[306]

> I claim the right to fallibility in details and I eagerly welcome constructive criticism. However, before proclaiming that the entire structure must collapse because an argument can be made against this or that point, the critic should carefully weigh his argument against the whole scheme, complete with all its evidence. The historian who permits his attention to be monopolized by an argument directed against some detail, to the extent of overlooking the work as a whole and the manifold proofs on which it stands, will only demonstrate the narrowness of his approach to history. He will be like that "conscientious scientist," Professor Twist, in Ogden Nash's verse, who went on an expedition to the jungles, taking his bride with him. When, one day, the guide brought the tidings to him that an alligator had eaten her, the professor could not but smile. "You mean," he said, "a crocodile?"

---

[306] Velikovsky 2009, 12.

I address the above words especially to those Bible-believing (young-earth) creationists who might doubt the truthfulness of the historical reconstruction that is presented in this work. To them I also want to say: study the things yourselves, and make more coherent and convincing one, if you can.

I really hope that this little book could be inspiring many faithful Bible students to become keenly interested in investigating deeply the ancient history. There is still so much to explore, so much history and archaeology to be understood better than in current textbooks.[307] It is high time to clearly and convincingly show the people of the world that the whole Bible can be trusted historically. Dear almighty God, Yehovah, King of the universe, our merciful Lord and Savior, please help people to believe in You. Let great praises rise up to You from all the nations of the earth, through the firm testimonies of Your Holy Scriptures, in the name of Your only Son and our Lord and Savior, Jesus the Messiah. All glory and power to God forever and ever!

The wise will be put to shame;
they will be dismayed and snared.
They have rejected the word of the LORD,
so what wisdom do they really have?

Jer 8:9 CSB

For it is written:
*"I will destroy the wisdom of the wise,
And bring to nothing the understanding of the prudent."*

1 Cor 1:19 NKJV (Isa 29:14)

---

[307] A student who would like to study further, for example, the chronological relationships between the earliest cultures of Mesopotamia and the earliest cultures of Afghanistan, Pakistan and India can find much help in A. J. M. Osgood's article *A Better Model for the Stone Age – Part 2* (1988a), pages 87–94.

ABBREVIATIONS

Acts	The Acts of the Apostles (in the New Testament)
A.D.	*Anno Domini*, "in the year of the Lord"; after the birth of Christ
AEHL	Avraham Negev & Shimon Gibson (eds.), *Archaeological Encyclopedia of the Holy Land*, 2001
Amos	The Book of Amos (in the Old Testament)
AMP	Amplified Bible, 2015
B.C.	before the birth of Christ
BDB	Francis Brown et al., *The Brown-Driver-Briggs Hebrew and English Lexicon*, 1906 (2007)
BHQ-Gen	Abraham Tal (ed.), *Biblia Hebraica Quinta: Genesis*, 2016
BHS	Karl Elliger & Wilhelm Rudolph (eds.), *Biblia Hebraica Stuttgartensia*, 1997
B2000	Bibel 2000 (a Swedish translation of the Bible)
c.	*circa*, "approximately/about"
CDCH	David J. A. Clines (ed.), *The Concise Dictionary of Classical Hebrew*, 2009
CEB	Common English Bible, 2011
CEV	Contemporary English Version, 1995
1 Chr	The First Book of the Chronicles (in the Old Testament)
2 Chr	The Second Book of the Chronicles (in the Old Testament)
CJB	Complete Jewish Bible, 1998
1 Cor	The First Letter of Paul the Apostle to the Corinthians (in the New Testament)
COS	William W. Hallo & K. Lawson Younger Jr. (eds.), *The Context of Scripture*, 2003
cp.	compare with
CSB	Christian Standard Bible, 2017
DBI	Leland Ryken et al. (eds.), *Dictionary of Biblical Imagery*, 1998
Deut	The Book of Deuteronomy/The Fifth Book of Moses (in the Old Testament)

ed(s).	editor(s)
e.g.	*exempli gratia*, "for example"
EHV	Evangelical Heritage Version, 2019
ESV	English Standard Version, 2016
ESVASB	John D. Currid & David W. Chapman (eds.), *ESV Archaeology Study Bible*, 2017
ESVSB	Wayne Grudem et al. (eds.), *ESV Study Bible*, 2008
et al.	*et alii*, "and others"
etc.	*et cetera*, "and so forth"
Ex	The Book of Exodus/The Second Book of Moses (in the Old Testament)
Gal	The Letter of Paul the Apostle to the Galatians (in the New Testament)
Gen	The Book of Genesis/The First Book of Moses (in the Old Testament)
GNB	Good News Bible, 1976
HAHAT	D. Rudolf Meyer & Herbert Donner (eds.), *Wilhelm Gesenius: Hebräisches und Aramäisches Handwörterbuch über das Alte Testament*, 2013
HALOT	Ludwig Koehler & Walter Baumgartner, *The Hebrew and Aramaic Lexicon of the Old Testament*, 2001
Heb	The Letter to the Hebrews (in the New Testament)
i.e.	*id est*, "that is"
Isa	The Book of Isaiah (in the Old Testament)
ISV	International Standard Version, 2011
JA	Josephus, *Jewish Antiquities*
Jer	The Book of Jeremiah (in the Old Testament)
Job	The Book of Job (in the Old Testament)
Jon	The Book of Jonah (in the Old Testament)
Josh	The Book of Joshua (in the Old Testament)
Judg	The Book of Judges (in the Old Testament)
1 Kings	The First Book of the Kings (in the Old Testament)
2 Kings	The Second Book of the Kings (in the Old Testament)
KJV	King James Version, 1611 (1769)

LEB	Lexham English Bible, 2012
LES	Ken M. Penner et al. (eds.), *The Lexham English Septuagint*, 2019
LSB	Legacy Standard Bible, 2021
LXX	Septuagint [Rahlfs (ed.) 2006]
LXX.B	Lancelot Charles Lee Brenton, *The Septuagint Version of the Old Testament: English Translation*, 1870
LXX.D	Wolfgang Kraus & Martin Karrer (eds.), *Septuaginta Deutsch*, 2009
2 Macc	The Second Book of the Maccabees (apocryphal/deuterocanonical)
MED	William D. Mounce et al. (eds.), *Mounce's Complete Expository Dictionary of Old and New Testament Words*, 2006
MEV	Modern English Version, 2014
NABRE	New American Bible, Revised Edition, 2010
NASB	New American Standard Bible, 1995
NBC	D. A. Carson et al. (eds.), *New Bible Commentary*, 1994
NEAEHL	Ephraim Stern (ed.), *The New Encyclopedia of Archaeological Excavations in the Holy Land*, 1993
NEAEHL5	Ephraim Stern (ed.), *The New Encyclopedia of Archaeological Excavations in the Holy Land, Supplementary Volume 5*, 2008
NET	The NET Bible (New English Translation), netbible.org
NETS	Albert Pietersma & Benjamin G. Wright (eds.), *A New English Translation of the Septuagint*, 2009
NIDOTTE	Willem A. VanGemeren et al. (eds.), *New International Dictionary of Old Testament Theology and Exegesis*, 1997
NIV	New International Version, 2011
NIVZSB	D. A. Carson et al. (eds.), *NIV Zondervan Study Bible*, 2015
NJB	New Jerusalem Bible, 1985
NJPS	Tanakh: The Holy Scriptures: The New JPS Translation According to the Traditional Hebrew Text, 1985
NKJV	New King James Version, 1982
NLT	New Living Translation, 2015
NLTSB	Sean A. Harrison et al. (eds.), *NLT Study Bible*, 2017

NRSV	New Revised Standard Version, 1989
NRSVue	New Revised Standard Version, Updated Edition, 2021
NUBD	Merrill F. Unger et al., *The New Unger's Bible Dictionary*, 2006
Num	The Book of Numbers/The Fourth Book of Moses (in the Old Testament)
OEBA	Daniel M. Master et al. (eds.), *The Oxford Encyclopedia of the Bible and Archaeology*, 2013
OSB	St. Athanasius Academy of Orthodox Theology, *The Orthodox Study Bible*, 2008 [St. Athanasius Academy Septuagint]
p.	page(s)
Ps	The Book of Psalms (in the Old Testament)
REB	Revised English Bible, 1989
Rom	The Letter of Paul the Apostle to the Romans (in the New Testament)
RSV	Revised Standard Version, 1971
1 Sam	The First Book of Samuel (in the Old Testament)
2 Sam	The Second Book of Samuel (in the Old Testament)
SBLSB	Steven L. McKenzie et al. (eds.), *The SBL Study Bible*, 2023
sic	*sic erat scriptum*, "thus was it written (in the original text)"
TDOT	G. Johannes Botterweck et al. (eds.), *Theological Dictionary of the Old Testament*, 2006
TWOT	R. Laird Harris et al. (eds.), *Theological Wordbook of the Old Testament*, 1980

BIBLIOGRAPHY

Aalders, G. Ch.
1981   Genesis. Volume 1. Bible Student's Commentary. Translated by William
            Heynen. Grand Rapids, MI: Regency Reference Library/Zondervan.

Adams, Sebastian
2008   Adams' Synchronological Chart or Map of History. Master Books edition.
            Green Forest, AR: Master Books.

Aharoni, Yohanan
1979   The Land of the Bible: A Historical Geography. Revised and enlarged
            edition. Translated and edited by A. F. Rainey. Philadelphia, PA: The
            Westminster Press.

Akkermans, Peter M. M. G.
2014   The Northern Levant during the Neolithic Period: Damascus and Beyond.
            — The Oxford Handbook of the Archaeology of the Levant, c. 8000–332
            BCE. Edited by Margreet L. Steiner & Ann E. Killebrew. Oxford, England:
            Oxford University Press. 134–146.
2020   Prehistoric Western Asia. — The Oxford History of the Ancient Near East.
            Volume 1. Edited by Karen Radner et al. New York, NY: Oxford University
            Press. 27–94.

Akkermans, Peter M. M. G. & Schwartz, Glenn M.
2003   The Archaeology of Syria: From Complex Hunter-Gatherers to Early Urban
            Societies (c. 16,000–300 BC). New York, NY: Cambridge University Press.

Albright, William F.
1960   The Archaeology of Palestine. Revised edition. Harmondsworth, England:
            Penguin Books.

Algaze, Guillermo
2001   The Prehistory of Imperialism: The Case of Uruk Period Mesopotamia. —
            Uruk Mesopotamia and Its Neighbors: Cross-Cultural Interactions in the
            Era of State Formation. Edited by Mitchell S. Rothman. Santa Fe, NM:
            School of American Research Press. 27–83.
2005   The Uruk World System: The Dynamics of Expansion of Early
            Mesopotamian Civilization. Second edition. Chicago, IL: University of
            Chicago Press.
2008   Ancient Mesopotamia at the Dawn of Civilization: The Evolution of an
            Urban Landscape. Chicago, IL: University of Chicago Press.
2013   The End of Prehistory and the Uruk Period. — The Sumerian World. Edited
            by Harriet Crawford. New York, NY: Routledge. 68–94.
2018   The Tyranny of Friction. — Prehistory and Protohistory of Ancient
            Civilizations. Origini XLII, 2018–2. Edited by Marcella Frangipane & Linda R.
            Manzanilla. Rome, Italy: Gangemi Editore. 73–92.

Alter, Robert
2018   The Hebrew Bible: A Translation with Commentary. 3 volumes. New York, NY: W. W. Norton & Company.

Amiran, Ruth
1969   Ancient Pottery of the Holy Land: From Its Beginnings in the Neolithic Period to the End of the Iron Age. Jerusalem, Israel: Massada Press.

Andersen, H. G.
2009   Aram Naharaim. — The Zondervan Encyclopedia of the Bible. Revised, full-color edition. 5 volumes. Edited by Merrill C. Tenney & Moisés Silva. Grand Rapids, MI: Zondervan. 1:289.

Anderson, Clive & Edwards, Brian
2014   Evidence for the Bible. Leominster, England: Day One Publications.

Arbino, Gary P.
2017   Introduction to the Geography and Archaeology of the Ancient Near East. — The Old Testament in Archaeology and History. Edited by Jennie Ebeling et al. Waco, TX: Baylor University Press. 15–44.

Archer, Gleason L.
2007   A Survey of Old Testament Introduction. Revised and expanded edition. Chicago, IL: Moody Publishers.

Arkhipov, Ilya
2022   The Middle East after the Fall of Ur: from Assur to the Levant. — The Oxford History of the Ancient Near East. Volume 2. Edited by Karen Radner et al. New York, NY: Oxford University Press. 310–407.

Arnold, Bill T.
2009   Genesis. The New Cambridge Bible Commentary. New York, NY: Cambridge University Press.

Ashton, John F.
2012   Evolution Impossible: 12 Reasons Why Evolution Cannot Explain the Origin of Life on Earth. Green Forest, AR: Master Books.

Ashton, John & Down, David
2006   Unwrapping the Pharaohs: How Egyptian Archaeology Confirms the Biblical Timeline. Green Forest, AR: Master Books.

Bahat, Dan
2011   The Carta Jerusalem Atlas. Third updated and expanded edition. Jerusalem, Israel: Carta Jerusalem.

Bahrani, Zainab
2017   Mesopotamia: Ancient Art and Architecture. London, England: Thames & Hudson.

Baker, Jill
2017   Archaeology and the Canaanites. — The Old Testament in Archaeology and
              History. Edited by Jennie Ebeling et al. Waco, TX: Baylor University Press.
              185–211.

Bandstra, Barry
2008   Genesis 1–11: A Handbook on the Hebrew Text. Waco, TX: Baylor
              University Press.

Banning, Edward
2002   Ceramic Neolithic: Late or Pottery Neolithic. — Encyclopedia of Prehistory.
              Volume 8: South and Southwest Asia. Edited by Peter N. Peregrine &
              Melvin Ember. New York, NY: Kluwer Academic/Plenum Publishers. 40–55.

Bar-Adon, Pessaḥ (ed.)
1980   The Cave of the Treasure: The Finds from the Caves in Naḥal Mishmar.
              Translated by I. Pommerantz. Jerusalem, Israel: Israel Exploration Society.

Bard, Kathryn A.
2003   The Emergence of the Egyptian State (c. 3200–2686 BC). — The Oxford
              History of Ancient Egypt. Edited by Ian Shaw. Oxford, England: Oxford
              University Press. 57–82.
2015   An Introduction to the Archaeology of Ancient Egypt. Second edition.
              Chichester, England: Wiley-Blackwell.

Bárta, Miroslav
2020   Egypt's Old Kingdom: A View from Within. — The Oxford History of the
              Ancient Near East. Volume 1. Edited by Karen Radner et al. New York, NY:
              Oxford University Press. 316–396.

Bartash, Vitali
2020   The Early Dynastic Near East. — The Oxford History of the Ancient Near
              East. Volume 1. Edited by Karen Radner et al. New York, NY: Oxford
              University Press. 531–611.

Bartl, Karin
2012   Varieties of Early Village and Town Life: The Northern Levant. — A
              Companion to the Archaeology of the Ancient Near East. 2 volumes. Edited
              by D. T. Potts. Chichester, England: Wiley-Blackwell. 1:375–395.

Bar-Yosef, Ofer
1992   The Neolithic Period. — The Archaeology of Ancient Israel. Edited by
              Amnon Ben-Tor. Translated by R. Greenberg. New Haven, CT: Yale
              University Press. 10–39.

Batten, Don & Catchpoole, David & Sarfati, Jonathan & Wieland, Carl
2012   The Creation Answers Book. Fourth edition. Powder Springs, GA: Creation
              Book Publishers.

Baumgardner, John R.
2005   14C Evidence for a Recent Global Flood and a Young Earth. —
            Radioisotopes and the Age of the Earth: Results of a Young-Earth
            Creationist Research Initiative. Edited by L. Vardiman & A. A. Snelling & E.
            F. Chaffin. El Cajon, CA: Institute for Creation Research; Chino Valley, AZ:
            Creation Research Society. 587–630.

Beaulieu, Paul-Alain
2018   A History of Babylon, 2200 BC–AD 75. Chichester, England: Wiley-
            Blackwell.

Bechar, Shlomit
2017   How to Find the Hazor Archives (I Think). — Biblical Archaeology Review
            43/2: 55–60, 70.

Beitzel, Barry J.
2009   The New Moody Atlas of the Bible. Chicago, IL: Moody Publishers.

Ben-Tor, Amnon
1992   The Early Bronze Age. — The Archaeology of Ancient Israel. Edited by
            Amnon Ben-Tor. Translated by R. Greenberg. New Haven, CT: Yale
            University Press. 81–125.

Bestock, Laurel
2020   Early Dynastic Egypt. — The Oxford History of the Ancient Near East.
            Volume 1. Edited by Karen Radner et al. New York, NY: Oxford University
            Press. 245–315.

Bienkowski, Piotr
2000   Mari. — Dictionary of the Ancient Near East. Edited by Piotr Bienkowski &
            Alan Millard. Philadelphia, PA: University of Pennsylvania Press. 189, 190.

Block, Daniel I.
1999   Judges, Ruth. The New American Commentary. Volume 6. Nashville, TN:
            B&H Publishing Group.

Boivin, Odette
2022   The Kingdom of Babylon and the Kingdom of the Sealand. — The Oxford
            History of the Ancient Near East. Volume 2. Edited by Karen Radner et al.
            New York, NY: Oxford University Press. 566–655.

Borowski, Oded
2005   Water and Water Systems. — Dictionary of the Old Testament: Historical
            Books. Edited by Bill T. Arnold & H. G. M. Williamson. Downers Grove, IL:
            InterVarsity Press. 980–984.

Botterweck, G. Johannes et al. (eds.)
2006   Theological Dictionary of the Old Testament. 15 volumes (1974–2006).
            Translated by J. T. Willis et al. Grand Rapids, MI: Eerdmans. [Volume 16,
            Aramaic Dictionary, published in 2018.]

Bourke, Stephen J.
2014   The Southern Levant (Transjordan) during the Middle Bronze Age. — The
            Oxford Handbook of the Archaeology of the Levant, c. 8000–332 BCE.
            Edited by Margreet L. Steiner & Ann E. Killebrew. Oxford, England: Oxford
            University Press. 465–481.
2018   The Middle East: The Cradle of Civilization. Revised and updated edition.
            Stephen Bourke as chief consultant. London, England: Thames & Hudson.

Bowman, Sheridan
1990   Radiocarbon Dating. Berkeley, CA: University of California Press/British
            Museum.

Boyd, Steven W. & Snelling, Andrew A. (eds.)
2014   Grappling with the Chronology of the Genesis Flood: Navigating the Flow
            of Time in Biblical Narrative. Green Forest, AR: Master Books.

Braidwood, Robert J.
1960   Concluding Address. — City Invincible: A Symposium on Urbanization and
            Cultural Development in the Ancient Near East. Edited by Carl H. Kraeling
            & Robert M. Adams. Chicago, IL: University of Chicago Press. 224–246.

Braidwood, Robert J. & Braidwood, Linda
1960   Excavations in the Plain of Antioch I: The Earlier Assemblages, Phases A–J.
            Chicago, IL: The Oriental Institute of the University of Chicago.

Brandt, Michael
2013   Stone Tools from the Early Tertiary in Europe: A Contradiction to Any
            Evolutionary Theory about the Origin of Man and to Long Geological
            Periods of Time. — Answers Research Journal 6: 231–264.

Brayford, Susan
2007   Genesis. Septuagint Commentary Series. Leiden, Netherlands: Brill.

Brenton, Lancelot Charles Lee
1870   The Septuagint Version of the Old Testament: English Translation. London,
            England: Samuel Bagster & Sons.

Bright, John
1981   A History of Israel. Third edition. London, England: SCM Press.

Brisch, Nicole
2013   History and Chronology. — The Sumerian World. Edited by Harriet
            Crawford. New York, NY: Routledge. 111–127.

Brown, Francis & Driver, Samuel R. & Briggs, Charles A.
2007   The Brown-Driver-Briggs Hebrew and English Lexicon: With an Appendix
            Containing the Biblical Aramaic. Reprinted from the 1906 edition originally
            published by Houghton, Mifflin and Company, Boston. Peabody, MA:
            Hendrickson.

Brown, Walt
—   In the Beginning: Compelling Evidence for Creation and the Flood.
               Continually updated online edition.
               creationscience.com/onlinebook/IntheBeginningTOC.html

Bryce, Trevor & Birkett-Rees, Jessie
2016   Atlas of the Ancient Near East: From Prehistoric Times to the Roman
               Imperial Period. New York, NY: Routledge.

Burdukiewicz, Jan Micha & Ronen, Avraham (eds.)
2003   Lower Palaeolithic Small Tools in Europe and the Levant. Oxford, England:
               British Archaeological Reports.

Burke, Aaron A.
2021   The Amorites and the Bronze Age Near East: The Making of a Regional
               Identity. New York, NY: Cambridge University Press.

Burns, Bryan E.
2010   Society and Culture: Trade. — The Oxford Handbook of the Bronze Age
               Aegean. Edited by Eric H. Cline. Oxford, England: Oxford University Press.
               291–304.

Butler, Trent C.
2009   Judges. Word Biblical Commentary. Volume 8. Nashville, TN: Thomas
               Nelson.
2014   Joshua 1–12. Word Biblical Commentary. Volume 7A. Grand Rapids, MI:
               Zondervan.

Butterlin, Pascal
2016   Mari (Deir ez-Zor). — A History of Syria in One Hundred Sites. Edited by
               Youssef Kanjou & Akira Tsuneki. Oxford, England: Archaeopress
               Archaeology. 228–231.
2019   The Expansion of Uruk Culture. — Uruk: First City of the Ancient World.
               Edited by Nicola Crüsemann et al. Los Angeles, CA: J. Paul Getty Museum.
               185–191.

Callaway, Joseph A.
1980   The Early Bronze Age Citadel and Lower City at Ai (et-Tell). Cambridge, MA:
               American Schools of Oriental Research.

Callaway, Joseph A. & Schoonover, Kermit
1972   The Early Bronze Age Citadel at Ai (Et-Tell). — Bulletin of the American
               Schools of Oriental Research 207: 41–53. jstor.org/stable/3218846

Callaway, Joseph A. & Shanks, Hershel
2010   The Settlement in Canaan: The Period of the Judges. — Ancient Israel:
               From Abraham to the Roman Destruction of the Temple. Third edition.
               Edited by Hershel Shanks. Washington, DC: Biblical Archaeology Society.
               59–83.

Calvet, Yves
1987   La Phase 'Oueili de l'Époque d'Obeid. — Préhistoire de la Mésopotamie: La
            Mésopotamie préhistorique et l'exploration récente du djebel Hamrin.
            Edited by Jean-Louis Huot. Paris, France: Centre National de la Recherche
            Scientifique. 129–151.

Campbell, Charlie H.
2012   Archaeological Evidence for the Bible: Exciting Discoveries Verifying
            Persons, Places and Events in the Bible. Carlsbad, CA: The Always Be Ready
            Apologetics Ministry.

Campbell, Donald K.
1983   Joshua. — The Bible Knowledge Commentary: Old Testament. An
            Exposition of the Scriptures by Dallas Seminary Faculty. Edited by John F.
            Walvoord & Roy B. Zuck. Colorado Springs, CO: David C. Cook. 325–371.

Carpenter, Eugene E.
2009   Deuteronomy. — Zondervan Illustrated Bible Backgrounds Commentary:
            Old Testament. 5 volumes. Edited by John H. Walton. Grand Rapids, MI:
            Zondervan. 1:418–547.

Carr, David M.
2021   Genesis 1–11. International Exegetical Commentary on the Old Testament.
            Stuttgart, Germany: Kohlhammer.

Carson, D. A. et al. (eds.)
1994   New Bible Commentary. Fourth edition. Nottingham, England: Inter-
            Varsity Press.
2015   NIV Zondervan Study Bible. Grand Rapids, MI: Zondervan.

Carter, Robert
2013   The Sumerians and the Gulf. — The Sumerian World. Edited by Harriet
            Crawford. New York, NY: Routledge. 579–599.

Carter, Robert & Hardy, Chris
2015   Modelling Biblical Human Population Growth. — Journal of Creation 29/1:
            72–79. creation.com/biblical-human-population-growth-model

Carter, Robert & Sanders, Lita
2021   How Long Were the Israelites in Egypt? Using Their Own Family Tree to
            Resolve a Debate. creation.com/how-long-were-the-israelites-in-egypt

Carter, Robert A. & Philip, Graham
2010   Deconstructing the Ubaid. — Beyond the Ubaid: Transformation and
            Integration in the Late Prehistoric Societies of the Middle East. Edited by
            Robert A. Carter & Graham Philip. Chicago, IL: The Oriental Institute of the
            University of Chicago. 1–22.

Cassuto, Umberto
1961   A Commentary on the Book of Genesis. Part One. From Adam to Noah.
            Translated by Israel Abrahams. Jerusalem, Israel: The Magnes Press.
1964   A Commentary on the Book of Genesis. Part Two. From Noah to Abraham.
            Translated by Israel Abrahams. Jerusalem, Israel: The Magnes Press.

Chaffey, Tim
2016   Humanity's Shared History Reflecting the Truth of Genesis 1–11. —
            Searching for Adam: Genesis and the Truth about Man's Origin. Edited by
            Terry Mortenson. Green Forest, AR: Master Books. 445–458.

Chambers, Nathan J.
2020   Reconsidering Creation Ex Nihilo in Genesis 1. University Park, PA:
            Eisenbrauns.

Charaf, Hanan
2014   The Northern Levant (Lebanon) during the Middle Bronze Age. — The
            Oxford Handbook of the Archaeology of the Levant, c. 8000–332 BCE.
            Edited by Margreet L. Steiner & Ann E. Killebrew. Oxford, England: Oxford
            University Press. 434–450.

Charpin, Dominique
2011   Le "pays de Mari et des bédouins" à l'époque de Samsu-iluna de Babylone.
            — Revue d'Assyriologie et d'archéologie Orientale 105: 41–59.
            jstor.org/stable/42580239

Chavalas, Mark W.
2003   Haran. — Dictionary of the Old Testament: Pentateuch. Edited by T.
            Desmond Alexander & David W. Baker. Downers Grove, IL: InterVarsity
            Press. 379–381.

Chittick, Donald E.
2006   The Puzzle of Ancient Man: Evidence for Advanced Technology in Past
            Civilizations. Third edition. Newberg, OR: Creation Compass.

Clarey, Tim
2015   Dinosaurs: Marvels of God's Design. The Science of the Biblical Account.
            Green Forest, AR: Master Books.

Clarke, Joanne
2014   Cyprus during the Neolithic Period. — The Oxford Handbook of the
            Archaeology of the Levant, c. 8000–332 BCE. Edited by Margreet L. Steiner
            & Ann E. Killebrew. Oxford, England: Oxford University Press. 183–199.

Clines, David J. A. (ed.)
2009   The Concise Dictionary of Classical Hebrew. Sheffield, England: Sheffield
            Phoenix Press.

Cohen, Susan L.
2014   The Southern Levant (Cisjordan) during the Middle Bronze Age. — The
               Oxford Handbook of the Archaeology of the Levant, c. 8000–332 BCE.
               Edited by Margreet L. Steiner & Ann E. Killebrew. Oxford, England: Oxford
               University Press. 451–464.

Collins, C. John
2006   Genesis 1–4: A Linguistic, Literary, and Theological Commentary.
               Phillipsburg, NJ: P&R Publishing.

Collins, Paul
2016   Mountains and Lowlands: Ancient Iran and Mesopotamia. Oxford,
               England: Ashmolean Museum.

Collins, Steven & Holden, Joseph M. (eds.)
2020   The Harvest Handbook of Bible Lands. Eugene, OR: Harvest House
               Publishers.

Cooper, Bill
1995   After the Flood: The Early Post-Flood History of Europe Traced Back to
               Noah. Chichester, England: New Wine Press.
2011   The Authenticity of the Book of Genesis: A Study in Three Parts.
               Portsmouth, England: Creation Science Movement.

Cooper, Lisa
2014   The Northern Levant (Syria) during the Early Bronze Age. — The Oxford
               Handbook of the Archaeology of the Levant, c. 8000–332 BCE. Edited by
               Margreet L. Steiner & Ann E. Killebrew. Oxford, England: Oxford University
               Press. 278–291.
2020   The Northern Levantine "Caliciform" Tradition. — New Horizons in the
               Study of the Early Bronze III and Early Bronze IV of the Levant. Edited by
               Suzanne Richard. University Park, PA: Eisenbrauns. 111–119.

Cosner, Lita
2013   How Does the Bible Teach 6,000 Years? — Creation 35/1: 54, 55.
               creation.com/6000-years

Courville, Donovan A.
1971   The Exodus Problem and Its Ramifications: A Critical Examination of the
               Chronological Relationships between Israel and the Contemporary Peoples
               of Antiquity. 2 volumes. Loma Linda, CA: Challenge Books.

Crawford, Harriet
2015   Ur: The City of the Moon God. London, England: Bloomsbury Academic.

Cremo, Michael A. & Thompson, Richard L.
1998   Forbidden Archeology: The Hidden History of the Human Race. Los
               Angeles, CA: Bhaktivedanta Book Publishing.

Crüsemann, Nicola et al. (eds.)
2019   Uruk: First City of the Ancient World. Los Angeles, CA: J. Paul Getty
            Museum.

Cummings, Vicki
2014   Hunting and Gathering in a Farmers' World. — The Oxford Handbook of
            the Archaeology and Anthropology of Hunter-Gatherers. Edited by Vicki
            Cummings & Peter Jordan & Marek Zvelebil. Oxford, England: Oxford
            University Press. 767–786.

Cunningham, Graham
2013   The Sumerian Language. — The Sumerian World. Edited by Harriet
            Crawford. New York, NY: Routledge. 95–110.

Cuozzo, Jack
1998   Buried Alive: The Startling, Untold Story about Neanderthal Man. Green
            Forest, AR: Master Books.

Currid, John D.
2015   A Study Commentary on Genesis. Volume 1: Genesis 1:1–25:18. EP Study
            Commentary. Darlington, England: EP Books.
2020   The Case for Biblical Archaeology: Uncovering the Historical Record of
            God's Old Testament People. Phillipsburg, NJ: P&R Publishing Company.

Currid, John D. & Chapman, David W. (eds.)
2017   ESV Archaeology Study Bible. Wheaton, IL: Crossway.

Curtis, John
1982   Arpachiyah. — Fifty Years of Mesopotamian Discovery: The Work of the
            British School of Archaeology in Iraq 1932–1982. Edited by John Curtis.
            London, England: British School of Archaeology in Iraq. 30–36.

D'Andrea, Marta
2020   About Stratigraphy, Pottery, and Relative Chronology: Some
            Considerations for a Refinement of the Archaeological Periodization of the
            Southern Levantine Early Bronze Age IV. — New Horizons in the Study of
            the Early Bronze III and Early Bronze IV of the Levant. Edited by Suzanne
            Richard. University Park, PA: Eisenbrauns. 395–416.

Day, John
2013   From Creation to Babel: Studies in Genesis 1–11. London, England:
            Bloomsbury T&T Clark.
2022   From Creation to Abraham: Further Studies in Genesis 1–11. London,
            England: T&T Clark.

Delitzsch, Franz
1888   A New Commentary on Genesis. Volume 1. Translated by Sophia Taylor.
            Edinburgh, Scotland: T. & T. Clark.

de Miroschedji, Pierre

2014   The Southern Levant (Cisjordan) during the Early Bronze Age. — The Oxford Handbook of the Archaeology of the Levant, c. 8000–332 BCE. Edited by Margreet L. Steiner & Ann E. Killebrew. Oxford, England: Oxford University Press. 307–329.

2018   The Urbanization of the Southern Levant in Its Near Eastern Setting. — Prehistory and Protohistory of Ancient Civilizations. Origini XLII, 2018–2. Edited by Marcella Frangipane & Linda R. Manzanilla. Rome, Italy: Gangemi Editore. 109–148.

2020   Monumental Architecture and Sociopolitical Developments in the Southern Levant of the Early Bronze Age. — New Horizons in the Study of the Early Bronze III and Early Bronze IV of the Levant. Edited by Suzanne Richard. University Park, PA: Eisenbrauns. 169–194.

Dessel, J. P.

2017   Looking for the Israelites: The Archaeology of Iron Age I. — The Old Testament in Archaeology and History. Edited by Jennie Ebeling et al. Waco, TX: Baylor University Press. 275–298.

de Vaux, Roland

1973   Ancient Israel: Its Life and Institutions. Translated by John McHugh. London, England: Darton, Longman and Todd.

Dever, William G.

1995   Social Structure in the Early Bronze IV Period in Palestine. — The Archaeology of Society in the Holy Land. Edited by Thomas E. Levy. London, England: Leicester University Press. 282–296.

DeYoung, Don

2005   Thousands…Not Billions: Challenging an Icon of Evolution, Questioning the Age of the Earth. Green Forest, AR: Master Books.

Dillmann, August

1897   Genesis: Critically and Exegetically Expounded. Volume 1. Translated by Wm. B. Stevenson. Edinburgh, Scotland: T. & T. Clark.

Down, David

2006   Archaeological Evidence for the Exodus. — The Big Argument: Does God Exist? Edited by John Ashton & Michael Westacott. Green Forest, AR: Master Books. 257–272.

2010   The Archaeology Book. Green Forest, AR: Master Books.

2011   Unveiling the Kings of Israel. Green Forest, AR: Master Books.

Dozeman, Thomas B.

2015   Joshua 1–12: A New Translation with Introduction and Commentary. The Anchor Yale Bible. Volume 6B. New Haven, CT: Yale University Press.

Eichmann, Ricardo
2019   Uruk's Early Monumental Architecture. — Uruk: First City of the Ancient
                World. Edited by Nicola Crüsemann et al. Los Angeles, CA: J. Paul Getty
                Museum. 97–107.

Elad, Itai & Paz, Yitzhak
2018   'En Esur (Asawir): Preliminary Report. — Hadashot Arkheologiyot:
                Excavations and Surveys in Israel 130. jstor.org/stable/26691671

Elliger, Karl & Rudolph, Wilhelm (eds.)
1997   Biblia Hebraica Stuttgartensia. Fifth revised edition, edited by Adrian
                Schenker. Stuttgart, Germany: Deutsche Bibelgesellschaft.

Evans, Mary J.
2017   Judges and Ruth: An Introduction and Commentary. Tyndale Old
                Testament Commentaries. Volume 7. Downers Grove, IL: IVP Academic.

Faura, Josep-Miquel & Molist, Miquel
2017   The Appearance and Development of Painted Ceramics at Seventh
                Millennium Tell Halula (Syria). — Painting Pots – Painting People: Late
                Neolithic Ceramics in Ancient Mesopotamia. Edited by Walter Cruells &
                Inna Mateiciucová & Olivier Nieuwenhuyse. Oxford, England: Oxbow
                Books. 70–82.

Ferguson, Paul
2006   The Historical Reliability of the Old Testament. — The Big Argument: Does
                God Exist? Edited by John Ashton & Michael Westacott. Green Forest, AR:
                Master Books. 273–296.

Finkelstein, Israel
1988   The Archaeology of the Israelite Settlement. Jerusalem, Israel: Israel
                Exploration Society.
2024   Jerusalem the Center of the Universe: Its Archaeology and History (1800–
                100 BCE). Atlanta, GA: SBL Press.

Finkelstein, Israel & Mazar, Amihai
2007   The Quest for the Historical Israel: Debating Archaeology and the History
                of Early Israel. Edited by Brian B. Schmidt. Atlanta, GA: Society of Biblical
                Literature.

Finkelstein, Israel & Silberman, Neil Asher
2006   David and Solomon: In Search of the Bible's Sacred Kings and the Roots of
                the Western Tradition. New York, NY: Free Press.

Fischer, Georg
2018   Genesis 1–11. Herders Theologischer Kommentar zum Alten Testament.
                Freiburg im Breisgau, Germany: Herder.

Fleming, Daniel E.
2016   The Amorites. — The World around the Old Testament: The People and
               Places of the Ancient Near East. Edited by Bill T. Arnold & Brent A. Strawn.
               Grand Rapids, MI: Baker Academic. 1–30.

Forbes, Brian
2011   From Noah to Hercules: What History Says about Early Man. Mustang, OK:
               Tate Publishing.

Foster, Benjamin R.
2013   Sumerian Mythology. — The Sumerian World. Edited by Harriet Crawford.
               New York, NY: Routledge. 435–443.
2016   The Age of Agade: Inventing Empire in Ancient Mesopotamia. New York,
               NY: Routledge.

Foster, Benjamin R. & Foster, Karen Polinger
2009   Civilizations of Ancient Iraq. Princeton, NJ: Princeton University Press.

Fox, Everett
1983   In the Beginning: A New English Rendition of the Book of Genesis. New
               York, NY: Schocken Books.

Frangipane, Marcella
2001   Centralization Processes in Greater Mesopotamia: Uruk "Expansion" as the
               Climax of Systemic Interactions among Areas of the Greater
               Mesopotamian Region. — Uruk Mesopotamia and Its Neighbors: Cross-
               Cultural Interactions in the Era of State Formation. Edited by Mitchell S.
               Rothman. Santa Fe, NM: School of American Research Press. 307–347.

Freeman, Travis R.
2008   Do the Genesis 5 and 11 Genealogies Contain Gaps? — Coming to Grips
               with Genesis: Biblical Authority and the Age of the Earth. Edited by Terry
               Mortenson & Thane H. Ury. Green Forest, AR: Master Books. 283–313.

Fritz, Glen A.
2016   The Lost Sea of the Exodus: A Modern Geographical Analysis. Second
               edition. San Antonio, TX: GeoTech.
2019   The Exodus Mysteries: Of Midian, Sinai and Jabal al-Lawz. San Antonio, TX:
               GeoTech.

Froman, Craig (ed.)
2016   How Many Animals Were on the Ark? Understanding the Animal Kinds.
               Green Forest, AR: Master Books.

Fruchtenbaum, Arnold G.
2009   The Book of Genesis: Exposition from a Messianic Jewish Perspective.
               Ariel's Bible Commentary. San Antonio, TX: Ariel Ministries.

Galor, Katharina & Bloedhorn, Hanswulf
2013   The Archaeology of Jerusalem: From the Origins to the Ottomans. New
              Haven, CT: Yale University Press.

Garfinkel, Yosef
1999a   Ghassulian Chalcolithic Presence at Jericho. — Levant 31: 65–69.
1999b   Neolithic and Chalcolithic Pottery of the Southern Levant. Jerusalem,
              Israel: The Hebrew University of Jerusalem.

Garfinkle, Steven J.
2022   The Kingdom of Ur. — The Oxford History of the Ancient Near East. Volume
              2. Edited by Karen Radner et al. New York, NY: Oxford University Press.
              121–189.

Garner, Paul
2015   The New Creationism: Building Scientific Theories on a Biblical Foundation.
              Darlington, England: EP Books.

Garstang, John & Garstang, J. B. E.
1948   The Story of Jericho. New revised edition. London, England: Marshall,
              Morgan & Scott.

Gatto, Maria Carmela
2018   The Origin of Urban Societies in the Nile Valley. — Prehistory and
              Protohistory of Ancient Civilizations. Origini XLII, 2018–2. Edited by
              Marcella Frangipane & Linda R. Manzanilla. Rome, Italy: Gangemi Editore.
              177–192.

Gertz, Jan Christian
2018   Das erste Buch Mose (Genesis): Die Urgeschichte Gen 1–11. Das Alte
              Testament Deutsch. Volume 1. Göttingen, Germany: Vandenhoeck &
              Ruprecht.

Gibbons, William J. & Hovind, Kent
1999   Claws Jaws and Dinosaurs (Living Dinosaurs). Pensacola, FL: Creation
              Science Evangelism.

Gibson, McGuire
2010   The Dead Hand of Deimel. — Beyond the Ubaid: Transformation and
              Integration in the Late Prehistoric Societies of the Middle East. Edited by
              Robert A. Carter & Graham Philip. Chicago, IL: The Oriental Institute of the
              University of Chicago. 85–92.

Gill, John
1810   Exposition of the Old and New Testaments. 9 volumes. London, England:
              Mathews & Leigh. biblestudytools.com/commentaries/gills-exposition-of-the-
              bible

Gilmour, Garth H.
2005   Shiloh. — Dictionary of the Old Testament: Historical Books. Edited by Bill
            T. Arnold & H. G. M. Williamson. Downers Grove, IL: InterVarsity Press.
            893–895.

Ginzberg, Louis
1909   The Legends of the Jews. Volume 1: From the Creation to Jacob. Translated
            by Henrietta Szold & Paul Radin. Philadelphia, PA: The Jewish Publication
            Society.

Gish, Duane T.
2009   Dinosaurs by Design. Green Forest, AR: Master Books.

Glueck, Nelson
1940   The Third Season of Excavation at Tell el-Kheleifeh. — Bulletin of the
            American Schools of Oriental Research 79: 2–18. jstor.org/stable/1355316

Golden, Jonathan M.
2002a   Early Bronze Age: Early Canaanite Period, Proto-Canaanite, Proto-Urban.
            — Encyclopedia of Prehistory. Volume 8: South and Southwest Asia. Edited
            by Peter N. Peregrine & Melvin Ember. New York, NY: Kluwer
            Academic/Plenum Publishers. 86–111.
2002b   Middle Bronze Age: Middle Bronze II A–B, Middle Canaanite Period. —
            Encyclopedia of Prehistory. Volume 8: South and Southwest Asia. Edited
            by Peter N. Peregrine & Melvin Ember. New York, NY: Kluwer
            Academic/Plenum Publishers. 293–305.
2009   Ancient Canaan and Israel: An Introduction. New York, NY: Oxford
            University Press.
2014   Dawn of the Metal Age: Technology and Society during the Levantine
            Chalcolithic. New York, NY: Routledge.

Goldingay, John
2020   Genesis. Baker Commentary on the Old Testament: Pentateuch. Grand
            Rapids, MI: Baker Academic.

Gonen, Rivka
1992   The Chalcolithic Period. — The Archaeology of Ancient Israel. Edited by
            Amnon Ben-Tor. Translated by R. Greenberg. New Haven, CT: Yale
            University Press. 40–80.

Gopher, Avi
1995   Early Pottery-Bearing Groups in Israel – The Pottery Neolithic Period. —
            The Archaeology of Society in the Holy Land. Edited by Thomas E. Levy.
            London, England: Leicester University Press. 205–225.

Gophna, Ram
1992   The Intermediate Bronze Age. — The Archaeology of Ancient Israel. Edited
            by Amnon Ben-Tor. Translated by R. Greenberg. New Haven, CT: Yale
            University Press. 126–158.

1995   Early Bronze Age Canaan: Some Spatial and Demographic Observations. —
             The Archaeology of Society in the Holy Land. Edited by Thomas E. Levy.
             London, England: Leicester University Press. 269–280.

Gordon, Cyrus H.
1962   Tarshish. — The Interpreter's Dictionary of the Bible: An Illustrated
             Encyclopedia. 4 volumes. Edited by George Arthur Buttrick et al. Nashville,
             TN: Abingdon Press. 4:517, 518.

Goring-Morris, A. Nigel & Belfer-Cohen, Anna
2014   The Southern Levant (Cisjordan) during the Neolithic Period. — The Oxford
             Handbook of the Archaeology of the Levant, c. 8000–332 BCE. Edited by
             Margreet L. Steiner & Ann E. Killebrew. Oxford, England: Oxford University
             Press. 147–169.

Graves, David E.
2014   Biblical Archaeology: An Introduction with Recent Discoveries that Support
             the Reliability of the Bible. Moncton, Canada: David E. Graves.

Greenberg, Raphael
2019   The Archaeology of the Bronze Age Levant: From Urban Origins to the
             Demise of City-States, 3700–1000 BCE. Cambridge, England: Cambridge
             University Press.

Grigson, Caroline
1995   Plough and Pasture in the Early Economy of the Southern Levant. — The
             Archaeology of Society in the Holy Land. Edited by Thomas E. Levy. London,
             England: Leicester University Press. 245–268.

Grudem, Wayne et al. (eds.)
2008   ESV Study Bible. Wheaton, IL: Crossway.

Grumet, Zvi
2017   Genesis: From Creation to Covenant. Jerusalem, Israel: Maggid Books.

Gurney, Oliver
1998   Sultantepe and Harran. — Ancient Anatolia: Fifty Years' Work by the British
             Institute of Archaeology at Ankara. Edited by Roger Matthews. London,
             England: British Institute of Archaeology at Ankara. 163–176.

Gut, Renate Vera
1995   Das prähistorische Ninive: Zur relativen Chronologie der frühen Perioden
             Nordmesopotamiens. 2 volumes. Mainz, Germany: Philipp von Zabern.

Habermehl, Anne
2011   Where in the World Is the Tower of Babel? — Answers Research Journal 4:
             25–53.
2013   Revising the Egyptian Chronology: Joseph as Imhotep, and Amenemhat IV
             as Pharaoh of the Exodus. — The Proceedings of the International

Conference on Creationism. Volume 7. Edited by Mark Horstemeyer. Pittsburgh, PA: Creation Science Fellowship. Article 38.

2018   The Ipuwer Papyrus and the Exodus. — The Proceedings of the International Conference on Creationism. Volume 8. Edited by John H. Whitmore. Pittsburgh, PA: Creation Science Fellowship. 1–6.

2019a   Job—Part 1: Did He Really Live during the Ice Age?

2019b   Job—Part 2: The Septuagint Coda and Other Sources.

2019c   Job—Part 3: Job's Land of Edom. independent.academia.edu/AHabermehl

2023   Synchronization of the Biblical and Egyptian Timelines. — Answers Research Journal 16: 561–576.

Hallo, William W. & Younger, K. Lawson, Jr. (eds.)

2003   The Context of Scripture: Canonical Compositions, Monumental Inscriptions and Archival Documents from the Biblical World. 3 volumes (1997–2003). Leiden, Netherlands: Brill.

Halpern, Baruch

2017   The United Monarchy: David between Saul and Solomon. — The Old Testament in Archaeology and History. Edited by Jennie Ebeling et al. Waco, TX: Baylor University Press. 337–362.

Ham, Ken

2012   The Lie: Evolution/Millions of Years. Revised and expanded edition. Green Forest, AR: Master Books.

2021   Creation to Babel: A Commentary for Families. Green Forest, AR: Master Books.

Ham, Ken (ed.)

2006   The New Answers Book 1: Over 25 Questions on Creation/Evolution and the Bible. Green Forest, AR: Master Books.

2008   The New Answers Book 2: Over 30 Questions on Creation/Evolution and the Bible. Green Forest, AR: Master Books.

2010   The New Answers Book 3: Over 35 Questions on Creation/Evolution and the Bible. Green Forest, AR: Master Books.

2013   The New Answers Book 4: Over 30 Questions on Creation/Evolution and the Bible. Green Forest, AR: Master Books.

Ham, Ken & Hodge, Bodie

2016   A Flood of Evidence: 40 Reasons Noah and the Ark Still Matter. Green Forest, AR: Master Books.

Ham, Ken & Ware, A. Charles

2010   One Race One Blood: A Biblical Answer to Racism. Green Forest, AR: Master Books.

Hamblin, William J.

2006   Warfare in the Ancient Near East to 1600 BC: Holy Warriors at the Dawn of History. New York, NY: Routledge.

Hamilton, Victor P.
1990   The Book of Genesis: Chapters 1–17. The New International Commentary
            on the Old Testament. Grand Rapids, MI: Eerdmans.

Hardy, Chris & Carter, Robert
2014   The Biblical Minimum and Maximum Age of the Earth. — Journal of
            Creation 28/2: 89–96. creation.com/biblical-age-of-the-earth

Harney, Éadaoin & May, Hila et al.
2018   Ancient DNA from Chalcolithic Israel Reveals the Role of Population
            Mixture in Cultural Transformation. — Nature Communications 9, article
            number 3336. nature.com/articles/s41467-018-05649-9

Harris, R. Laird & Archer, Gleason L. & Waltke, Bruce K. (eds.)
1980   Theological Wordbook of the Old Testament. Chicago, IL: Moody
            Publishers.

Harrison, R. K.
1979   Ai. — The International Standard Bible Encyclopedia. Revised edition. 4
            volumes (1979–1988). Edited by Geoffrey W. Bromiley et al. Grand Rapids,
            MI: Eerdmans. 1:81–84.
2005   Old Testament Times: A Social, Political, and Cultural Context. Exclusive
            full-color edition. Grand Rapids, MI: Baker Books.

Harrison, Sean A. et al. (eds.)
2017   NLT Study Bible. Carol Stream, IL: Tyndale House Publishers.

Harrison, Timothy P.
2012   Bronze Age Cities of the Plains and the Highlands: The Southern Levant. —
            A Companion to the Archaeology of the Ancient Near East. 2 volumes.
            Edited by D. T. Potts. Chichester, England: Wiley-Blackwell. 1:629–646.

Harstad, Adolph L.
2004   Joshua. Concordia Commentary. St. Louis, MO: Concordia Publishing
            House.

Hendel, Ronald
2024   Genesis 1–11: A New Translation with Introduction and Commentary. The
            Anchor Yale Bible. Volume 1A. New Haven, CT: Yale University Press.

Hendrickx, Stan & Vermeersch, Pierre
2003   Prehistory: From the Palaeolithic to the Badarian Culture (c.700,000–4000
            BC). — The Oxford History of Ancient Egypt. Edited by Ian Shaw. Oxford,
            England: Oxford University Press. 16–40.

Hess, Richard S.
2008   Joshua: An Introduction and Commentary. Tyndale Old Testament
            Commentaries. Volume 6. Downers Grove, IL: IVP Academic.

2009   Joshua. — Zondervan Illustrated Bible Backgrounds Commentary: Old Testament. 5 volumes. Edited by John H. Walton. Grand Rapids, MI: Zondervan. 2:2–93.

Hestrin, Ruth & Tadmor, Miriam
1963   A Hoard of Tools and Weapons from Kfar Monash. — Israel Exploration Journal 13/4: 265–288. jstor.org/stable/27924950

Hikade, Thomas
2012   Egypt and the Near East. — A Companion to the Archaeology of the Ancient Near East. 2 volumes. Edited by D. T. Potts. Chichester, England: Wiley-Blackwell. 2:833–850.

Hillman, Gordon & Davies, M. Stuart
1990   Measured Domestication Rates in Wild Wheats and Barley under Primitive Cultivation, and Their Archaeological Implications. — Journal of World Prehistory 4: 157–222.

Hodder, Ian
2006   The Leopard's Tale: Revealing the Mysteries of Çatalhöyük. London, England: Thames & Hudson.

Hodge, Bodie
2013   Tower of Babel: The Cultural History of Our Ancestors. Green Forest, AR: Master Books.
2023   Dinosaurs, Dragons, and the Bible. Green Forest, AR: Master Books.

Hodge, Bodie & Welch, Laura (eds.)
2014   The Flood of Noah: Legends and Lore of Survival. Green Forest, AR: Master Books.

Hoerth, Alfred J.
1998   Archaeology and the Old Testament. Grand Rapids, MI: Baker Academic.

Hoffmeier, James K.
2008   The Archaeology of the Bible. Oxford, England: Lion Books.

Hoffner, Harry A., Jr.
2015   1 & 2 Samuel. Evangelical Exegetical Commentary. Bellingham, WA: Lexham Press.

Holladay, Philip M.
2016   An Exponential Decay Curve in Old Testament Genealogies. — Answers Research Journal 9: 257–262.

Horowitz, Wayne & Shaffer, Aaron
1992   A Fragment of a Letter from Hazor. — Israel Exploration Journal 42/3/4: 165–167. jstor.org/stable/27926269

Horsnell, Malcolm J. A.
1999   The Year-Names of the First Dynasty of Babylon. Volume 2: The Year-Names Reconstructed and Critically Annotated in Light of their Exemplars. Hamilton, ON: McMaster University Press.

Howard, David M., Jr.
1998   Joshua. The New American Commentary. Volume 5. Nashville, TN: B&H Publishing Group.

Hoyland, Robert G.
2001   Arabia and the Arabs: From the Bronze Age to the Coming of Islam. New York, NY: Routledge.

Höflmayer, Felix
2022   Establishing an Absolute Chronology of the Middle Bronze Age. — The Oxford History of the Ancient Near East. Volume 2. Edited by Karen Radner et al. New York, NY: Oxford University Press. 1–46.

Hubbard, Robert L., Jr.
2005   Ai. — Dictionary of the Old Testament: Historical Books. Edited by Bill T. Arnold & H. G. M. Williamson. Downers Grove, IL: InterVarsity Press. 20–22.

Hughes, James R.
2020   The World's Oldest Alphabet. creation.com/oldest-alphabet

Huot, Jean-Louis
1989   'Ubaidian Village of Lower Mesopotamia: Permanence and Evolution from 'Ubaid 0 to 'Ubaid 4 as seen from Tell el'Oueili. — Upon This Foundation: The 'Ubaid Reconsidered. Edited by Elizabeth F. Henrickson & Ingolf Thuesen. Copenhagen, Denmark: Museum Tusculanum Press. 19–40.
1996   Oueili, Travaux de 1987 et 1989. Paris, France: Recherche sur les Civilisations.

Ilan, David
1995   The Dawn of Internationalism – The Middle Bronze Age. — The Archaeology of Society in the Holy Land. Edited by Thomas E. Levy. London, England: Leicester University Press. 297–319.

Isaacs, Darek
2010   Dragons or Dinosaurs? Alachua, FL: Bridge-Logos.

Jacob, Benno
2000   Das Buch Genesis: Das erste Buch der Tora, übersetzt und erklärt. Stuttgart, Germany: Calwer.
2007   The First Book of the Bible: Genesis. Augmented edition. Abridged, edited and translated by Ernest I. Jacob & Walter Jacob. Brooklyn, NY: KTAV Publishing House.

James, Peter et al.
1991   Centuries of Darkness: A Challenge to the Conventional Chronology of Old
                World Archaeology. London, England: Jonathan Cape.

Jantzen, Heinz
2019   Animal Terra-Cotta Figurines and Model Objects: Environment and
                Everyday Life in Uruk. — Uruk: First City of the Ancient World. Edited by
                Nicola Crüsemann et al. Los Angeles, CA: J. Paul Getty Museum. 262, 263.

Jeanson, Nathaniel T.
2017   Replacing Darwin: The New Origin of Species. Green Forest, AR: Master
                Books.
2022   Traced: Human DNA's Big Surprise. Green Forest, AR: Master Books.

Jeanson, Nathaniel T. & Tomkins, Jeffrey P.
2016   Genetics Confirms the Recent, Supernatural Creation of Adam and Eve. —
                Searching for Adam: Genesis and the Truth about Man's Origin. Edited by
                Terry Mortenson. Green Forest, AR: Master Books. 287–330.

Johnson, Ken
2010   Ancient Post-Flood History: Historical Documents That Point to Biblical
                Creation. Revised edition. Gardner, KS: Biblefacts Ministries.

Jones, Floyd Nolen
2015   The Chronology of the Old Testament. Revised, color edition. Green Forest,
                AR: Master Books.

Jordan, Peter & Cummings, Vicki
2014   Introduction. — The Oxford Handbook of the Archaeology and
                Anthropology of Hunter-Gatherers. Edited by Vicki Cummings & Peter
                Jordan & Marek Zvelebil. Oxford, England: Oxford University Press. 1–29.

Josephus
—   Jewish Antiquities. Books I–III. Translated by H. St. J. Thackeray. Loeb
                Classical Library 242. Published in 1930. Cambridge, MA: Harvard
                University Press.
—   Jewish Antiquities. Books VII–VIII. Translated by Ralph Marcus. Loeb
                Classical Library 281. Published in 1934. Cambridge, MA: Harvard
                University Press.

Kaiser, Walter C., Jr. & Wegner, Paul D.
2017   A History of Israel: From the Bronze Age through the Jewish Wars. Revised
                edition. Nashville, TN: B&H Academic.

Kaminski, Carol M.
2004   From Noah to Israel: Realization of the Primaeval Blessing After the Flood.
                London, England: T&T Clark International.

Keil, C. F.
2011a   Pentateuch. Commentary on the Old Testament. Volume 1 of 10 volumes
             by C. F. Keil & F. Delitzsch. Updated and reprinted from the English edition
             originally published by T. & T. Clark, Edinburgh, Scotland, 1866–91.
             Peabody, MA: Hendrickson.
2011b   Joshua, Judges, Ruth, 1 and 2 Samuel. Commentary on the Old Testament.
             Volume 2 of 10 volumes by C. F. Keil & F. Delitzsch. Updated and reprinted
             from the English edition originally published by T. & T. Clark, Edinburgh,
             Scotland, 1866–91. Peabody, MA: Hendrickson.

Keith, M. L. & Anderson, G. M.
1963   Radiocarbon Dating: Fictitious Results with Mollusk Shells. — Science
             141/3581: 634–637.

Kempinski, Aharon
1992   The Middle Bronze Age. — The Archaeology of Ancient Israel. Edited by
             Amnon Ben-Tor. Translated by R. Greenberg. New Haven, CT: Yale
             University Press. 159–210.

Kennedy, Titus
2024   The Essential Archaeological Guide to Bible Lands: Uncovering Biblical Sites
             of the Ancient Near East and Mediterranean World. Eugene, OR: Harvest
             House Publishers.

Kenyon, Kathleen M.
1979   Archaeology in the Holy Land. Fourth edition. London, England: Ernest
             Benn.

Kidner, Derek
1967   Genesis: An Introduction and Commentary. Tyndale Old Testament
             Commentaries. London, England: Inter-Varsity Press.

Kitchen, K. A.
1982   Aram, Aramaeans. — New Bible Dictionary. Second edition. Edited by J. D.
             Douglas et al. Leicester, England: Inter-Varsity Press. 67–69.
2003   On the Reliability of the Old Testament. Grand Rapids, MI: Eerdmans.
2009   Pharaoh. — The Zondervan Encyclopedia of the Bible. Revised, full-color
             edition. 5 volumes. Edited by Merrill C. Tenney & Moisés Silva. Grand
             Rapids, MI: Zondervan. 4:839–842.

Koehler, Edward W. A.
2006   A Summary of Christian Doctrine: A Popular Presentation of the Teachings
             of the Bible. Third revised edition. Prepared for publication by Brent W.
             Kuhlman. St. Louis, MO: Concordia Publishing House.

Koehler, Ludwig & Baumgartner, Walter
2001   The Hebrew and Aramaic Lexicon of the Old Testament. Study edition. 2
             volumes. Edited by Walter Baumgartner & Johann Jakob Stamm & M. E. J.
             Richardson et al. Leiden, Netherlands: Brill.

Köhler, E. Christiana
2020   Prehistoric Egypt. — The Oxford History of the Ancient Near East. Volume
               1. Edited by Karen Radner et al. New York, NY: Oxford University Press. 95–
               162.

Kramer, Samuel Noah
1972   Sumerian Mythology: A Study of Spiritual and Literary Achievement in the
               Third Millennium B.C. Revised edition. Philadelphia, PA: University of
               Pennsylvania Press.

Kraus, Wolfgang & Karrer, Martin (eds.)
2009   Septuaginta Deutsch: Das griechische Alte Testament in deutscher
               Übersetzung. Stuttgart, Germany: Deutsche Bibelgesellschaft.
2011   Septuaginta Deutsch: Erläuterungen und Kommentare zum griechischen
               Alten Testament. Band I: Genesis bis Makkabäer. Stuttgart, Germany:
               Deutsche Bibelgesellschaft.

Krebernik, Manfred
2019   Early Cuneiform and Its Relation to Language. — Uruk: First City of the
               Ancient World. Edited by Nicola Crüsemann et al. Los Angeles, CA: J. Paul
               Getty Museum. 167–173.

Kugel, James L.
1998   Traditions of the Bible: A Guide to the Bible as It Was at the Start of the
               Common Era. Cambridge, MA: Harvard University Press.

Kuhn, Steven L. & Clark, Amy E.
2014   Stone Tool Technology. — The Oxford Handbook of the Archaeology and
               Anthropology of Hunter-Gatherers. Edited by Vicki Cummings & Peter
               Jordan & Marek Zvelebil. Oxford, England: Oxford University Press. 607–
               624.

Kulikovsky, Andrew S.
2009   Creation, Fall, Restoration: A Biblical Theology of Creation. Geanies House,
               Scotland: Mentor.

Lacey, Troy
2025   The Hyksos – Does the Bible Shed Light on Who They Were? — Answers
               Research Journal 18: 97–124.

Landis, Don (ed.)
2012   The Genius of Ancient Man: Evolution's Nightmare. Green Forest, AR:
               Master Books.
2015   The Secrets of Ancient Man: Revelations from the Ruins. Green Forest, AR:
               Master Books.

Lee, Robert E.
1981   Radiocarbon Ages in Error. — Anthropological Journal of Canada 19/3: 9–
               29.

Legge, Anthony J.
1986   Seeds of Discontent: Accelerator Dates on Some Charred Plant Remains
            from the Kebaran and Natufian Cultures. — Archaeological Results from
            Accelerator Dating. Edited by J. A. J. Gowlett & R. E. M. Hedges. Oxford,
            England: Oxford University Committee for Archaeology. 13–21.

Leick, Gwendolyn
2002   Mesopotamia: The Invention of the City. London, England: Penguin Books.

Leupold, H. C.
2010   Exposition of Genesis. Volumes 1 and 2. Chillicothe, OH: DeWard
            Publishing Company.

Levy, Thomas E.
1995   Cult, Metallurgy and Rank Societies – Chalcolithic Period (ca. 4500–3500
            BCE). — The Archaeology of Society in the Holy Land. Edited by Thomas E.
            Levy. London, England: Leicester University Press. 226–244.
2002   Chalcolithic. — Encyclopedia of Prehistory. Volume 8: South and
            Southwest Asia. Edited by Peter N. Peregrine & Melvin Ember. New York,
            NY: Kluwer Academic/Plenum Publishers. 56–74.
2007   Journey to the Copper Age: Archaeology in the Holy Land. San Diego, CA:
            San Diego Museum of Man.

Lev-Yadun, Simcha & Gopher, Avi & Abbo, Shahal
2000   The Cradle of Agriculture. — Science 288/5471: 1602–1603.

Liddell, H. G. & Scott, R.
1994   Greek-English Lexicon. Abridged edition. Oxford, England: Clarendon
            Press.

Liguori, Nick
2021   Echoes of Ararat: A Collection of over 300 Flood Legends from North and
            South America. Green Forest, AR: Master Books.

Line, Peter
2020   New *Homo erectus* Crania Associated with Stone Tools Raise Issues. —
            Journal of Creation 34/2: 55–61. creation.com/homo-erectus-with-stone-tools

Lisle, Jason
2015   Understanding Genesis: How to Analyze, Interpret, and Defend Scripture.
            Green Forest, AR: Master Books.

Lloyd, Seton
1984   The Archaeology of Mesopotamia: From the Old Stone Age to the Persian
            Conquest. Revised edition. London, England: Thames & Hudson.

Long, V. Philips
2009   2 Samuel. — Zondervan Illustrated Bible Backgrounds Commentary: Old
            Testament. 5 volumes. Edited by John H. Walton. Grand Rapids, MI:
            Zondervan. 2:412–491.

Longman, Tremper, III
2020   Genesis. — The Baker Illustrated Bible Background Commentary. Edited by
            J. Scott Duvall & J. Daniel Hays. Grand Rapids, MI: Baker Books. 81–119.

López, Raúl
1998   The Antediluvian Patriarchs and the Sumerian King List. — Journal of
            Creation 12/3: 347–357. answersingenesis.org/bible-history/the-antediluvian-
            patriarchs-and-the-sumerian-king-list/

Lubenow, Marvin L.
1994   Axing Evolutionary Ideas – Stone Dead! — Creation 16/3: 28–30.
            creation.com/axing-evolutionary-ideas-stone-dead
2004   Bones of Contention: A Creationist Assessment of Human Fossils. Revised
            and updated edition. Grand Rapids, MI: Baker Books.

Mackintosh-Smith, Tim
2019   Arabs: A 3,000-Year History of Peoples, Tribes and Empires. New Haven,
            CT: Yale University Press.

Malamat, Abraham
1960   Hazor "The Head of All Those Kingdoms". — Journal of Biblical Literature
            79/1: 12–19. jstor.org/stable/3264495
1971   Syro-Palestinian Destinations in a Mari Tin Inventory. — Israel Exploration
            Journal 21/1: 31–38. jstor.org/stable/27925249
1998   Mari and the Bible. Leiden, Netherlands: Brill.

Mallowan, Max
1977   Mallowan's Memoirs: The Autobiography of Max Mallowan. London,
            England: Collins.

Manning, Sturt W.
2010   Eruption of Thera/Santorini. — The Oxford Handbook of the Bronze Age
            Aegean. Edited by Eric H. Cline. Oxford, England: Oxford University Press.
            457–474.

Marcus, Ezra S.
2022   Middle Kingdom Egypt and the Eastern Mediterranean. — The Oxford
            History of the Ancient Near East. Volume 2. Edited by Karen Radner et al.
            New York, NY: Oxford University Press. 777–853.

Margueron, Jean-Claude
2013   The Kingdom of Mari. — The Sumerian World. Edited by Harriet Crawford.
            New York, NY: Routledge. 517–537.
2014   Mari: Capital of Northern Mesopotamia in the Third Millennium. The
            Archaeology of Tell Hariri on the Euphrates. Oxford, England: Oxbow
            Books.

Marquet-Krause, Judith
1949   Les Fouilles de 'Ay (Et-Tell) 1933–1935. Paris, France: Librairie Orientaliste
            Paul Geuthner.

Martin, Charles
2009   Flood Legends: Global Clues of a Common Event. Green Forest, AR: Master
               Books.

Marzahn, Joachim
2019   On the Beginnings of Writing. — Uruk: First City of the Ancient World.
               Edited by Nicola Crüsemann et al. Los Angeles, CA: J. Paul Getty Museum.
               164, 165.

Master, Daniel M. et al. (eds.)
2013   The Oxford Encyclopedia of the Bible and Archaeology. 2 volumes. Oxford,
               England: Oxford University Press.

Mathews, Kenneth A.
1996   Genesis 1–11:26. The New American Commentary. Volume 1A. Nashville,
               TN: B&H Publishing Group.
2005   Genesis 11:27–50:26. The New American Commentary. Volume 1B.
               Nashville, TN: B&H Publishing Group.

Matthews, Roger
2000a   Halaf, (Tell). — Dictionary of the Ancient Near East. Edited by Piotr
               Bienkowski & Alan Millard. Philadelphia, PA: University of Pennsylvania
               Press. 137, 138.
2000b   The Early Prehistory of Mesopotamia: 500,000 to 4,500 BC. Turnhout,
               Belgium: Brepols.
2000c   Uruk. — Dictionary of the Ancient Near East. Edited by Piotr Bienkowski &
               Alan Millard. Philadelphia, PA: University of Pennsylvania Press. 312–313.
2002   Halafian. — Encyclopedia of Prehistory. Volume 8: South and Southwest
               Asia. Edited by Peter N. Peregrine & Melvin Ember. New York, NY: Kluwer
               Academic/Plenum Publishers. 138–150.
2003   The Archaeology of Mesopotamia: Theories and Approaches. New York,
               NY: Routledge.

Matthiae, Paolo
2020   The Problem of the Ebla Destruction at the End of Early Bronze Age IVB:
               Stratigraphic Evidence, Radiocarbon Datings, Historical Events. — New
               Horizons in the Study of the Early Bronze III and Early Bronze IV of the
               Levant. Edited by Suzanne Richard. University Park, PA: Eisenbrauns. 91–
               110.

Mazar, Amihai
1992   Archaeology of the Land of the Bible: 10,000–586 B.C.E. New York, NY:
               Doubleday.

McCarter, P. Kyle, Jr.
2010   The Patriarchal Age: Abraham, Isaac and Jacob. — Ancient Israel: From
               Abraham to the Roman Destruction of the Temple. Third edition. Edited by
               Hershel Shanks. Washington, DC: Biblical Archaeology Society. 1–34.

McKenzie, Steven L. et al. (eds.)
2023   The SBL Study Bible. New York, NY: HarperOne.

McMahon, Augusta
2005   From Sedentism to States, 10,000–3000 BCE. — A Companion to the
            Ancient Near East. Edited by Daniel C. Snell. Malden, MA: Blackwell. 20–
            33.
2012   The Akkadian Period: Empire, Environment, and Imagination. — A
            Companion to the Archaeology of the Ancient Near East. 2 volumes. Edited
            by D. T. Potts. Chichester, England: Wiley-Blackwell. 2:649–667.
2014   State Warfare and Pre-state Violent Conflict: Battle's Aftermath at Late
            Chalcolithic Tell Brak. — Preludes to Urbanism: The Late Chalcolithic of
            Mesopotamia. Edited by Augusta McMahon & Harriet Crawford.
            Cambridge, England: McDonald Institute for Archaeological Research.
            175–188.

Mellaart, James
1967   Çatal Hüyük: A Neolithic Town in Anatolia. New York, NY: McGraw-Hill.
1975   The Neolithic of the Near East. London, England: Thames & Hudson.

Merrill, Eugene H.
2008   Kingdom of Priests: A History of Old Testament Israel. Second edition.
            Grand Rapids, MI: Baker Academic.

Meyer, D. Rudolf & Donner, Herbert (eds.)
2013   Wilhelm Gesenius: Hebräisches und Aramäisches Handwörterbuch über
            das Alte Testament. Eighteenth, complete edition. Heidelberg, Germany:
            Springer.

Michalowski, Piotr
2020   The Kingdom of Akkad in Contact with the World. — The Oxford History of
            the Ancient Near East. Volume 1. Edited by Karen Radner et al. New York,
            NY: Oxford University Press. 686–764.

Moore, Andrew M. T.
2014   Post-Glacial Transformations among Hunter-Gatherer Societies in the
            Mediterranean and Western Asia. — The Oxford Handbook of the
            Archaeology and Anthropology of Hunter-Gatherers. Edited by Vicki
            Cummings & Peter Jordan & Marek Zvelebil. Oxford, England: Oxford
            University Press. 456–478.

Moorey, P. R. S.
1999   Ancient Mesopotamian Materials and Industries: The Archaeological
            Evidence. Winona Lake, IN: Eisenbrauns.

Morandi Bonacossi, Daniele
2014   The Northern Levant (Syria) during the Middle Bronze Age. — The Oxford
            Handbook of the Archaeology of the Levant, c. 8000–332 BCE. Edited by
            Margreet L. Steiner & Ann E. Killebrew. Oxford, England: Oxford University
            Press. 414–433.

Morris, Henry M.
2000   The Remarkable Record of Job: The Ancient Wisdom, Scientific Accuracy, and Life-Changing Message of an Amazing Book. Green Forest, AR: Master Books.
2002   The Biblical Basis for Modern Science. Green Forest, AR: Master Books.
2009   The Genesis Record: A Scientific and Devotional Commentary on the Book of Beginnings. Grand Rapids, MI: Baker Books.

Morris, Henry M. & Morris, Henry M., III
1996   Many Infallible Proofs: Evidences for the Christian Faith. Green Forest, AR: Master Books.

Morris, Henry M., III
2016   The Book of Beginnings: A Practical Guide to Understanding Genesis. Dallas, TX: Institute for Creation Research.

Morris, Henry M., III et al.
2013   Creation Basics and Beyond: An In-Depth Look at Science, Origins, and Evolution. Dallas, TX: Institute for Creation Research.

Morris, John
2007   The Young Earth: The Real History of the Earth – Past, Present, and Future. Revised and expanded edition. Green Forest, AR: Master Books.
2009   The Ice Age: Causes and Consequences. — Acts & Facts 38/8: 15. icr.org/article/4788/385

Mortenson, Terry (ed.)
2016   Searching for Adam: Genesis and the Truth about Man's Origin. Green Forest, AR: Master Books.

Mortenson, Terry & Ury, Thane H. (eds.)
2008   Coming to Grips with Genesis: Biblical Authority and the Age of the Earth. Green Forest, AR: Master Books.

Mounce, William D. et al. (eds.)
2006   Mounce's Complete Expository Dictionary of Old and New Testament Words. Grand Rapids, MI: Zondervan.

Möller, Lennart
2010   The Exodus Case: New Discoveries of the Historical Exodus. Fourth extended edition. Copenhagen, Denmark: Scandinavia Publishing House.

Mumford, Gregory D.
2014   Egypt and the Levant. — The Oxford Handbook of the Archaeology of the Levant, c. 8000–332 BCE. Edited by Margreet L. Steiner & Ann E. Killebrew. Oxford, England: Oxford University Press. 69–89.

Negev, Avraham & Gibson, Shimon (eds.)
2001   Archaeological Encyclopedia of the Holy Land. Revised and updated edition. New York, NY: Continuum.

Nelson, Richard D.
1997   Joshua: A Commentary. The Old Testament Library. Louisville, KY: Westminster John Knox Press.

Newton, Isaac
2009   Newton's Revised History of Ancient Kingdoms: A Complete Chronology. Edited by Larry Pierce & Marion Pierce. Green Forest, AR: Master Books.

Nieuwenhuyse, Olivier
2007   Plain and Painted Pottery: The Rise of Neolithic Ceramic Styles on the Syrian and Northern Mesopotamian Plains. Turnhout, Belgium: Brepols.

Nieuwenhuyse, Olivier (ed.)
2018   Relentlessly Plain: Seventh Millennium Ceramics at Tell Sabi Abyad, Syria. Oxford, England: Oxbow Books.

Nigro, Lorenzo
2019   Tell es-Sultan/ancient Jericho in the Early Bronze Age II–III. — Conceptualizing Urban Experiences: Tell es-Sultan and Tall al-Ḥammām Early Bronze Cities across the Jordan. Edited by Elisabetta Gallo. Rome, Italy: Sapienza University of Rome. 79–108.
2020   Tell es-Sultan/Jericho in the Early Bronze Age III: Apogee of an Unusual "Palatial Society" in Palestine. — New Horizons in the Study of the Early Bronze III and Early Bronze IV of the Levant. Edited by Suzanne Richard. University Park, PA: Eisenbrauns. 195–212.

Nissen, Hans J.
1988   The Early History of the Ancient Near East: 9000–2000 B.C. Translated by Elizabeth Lutzeier, with Kenneth J. Northcott. Chicago, IL: University of Chicago Press.
2001   Cultural and Political Networks in the Ancient Near East during the Fourth and Third Millennia B.C. — Uruk Mesopotamia and Its Neighbors: Cross-Cultural Interactions in the Era of State Formation. Edited by Mitchell S. Rothman. Santa Fe, NM: School of American Research Press. 149–179.
2003   Uruk and the Formation of the City. — Art of the First Cities: The Third Millennium B.C. from the Mediterranean to the Indus. Edited by Joan Aruz. New York, NY: The Metropolitan Museum of Art. 11–20.
2018   The City of Uruk and Its Hinterland. — Prehistory and Protohistory of Ancient Civilizations. Origini XLII, 2018–2. Edited by Marcella Frangipane & Linda R. Manzanilla. Rome, Italy: Gangemi Editore. 61–71.
2019   The Invention and Early Uses of Writing in Mesopotamia. — Uruk: First City of the Ancient World. Edited by Nicola Crüsemann et al. Los Angeles, CA: J. Paul Getty Museum. 149–153.

Nissen, Hans J. & Heine, Peter
2009   From Mesopotamia to Iraq: A Concise History. Translated by Hans J. Nissen. Chicago, IL: University of Chicago Press.

Nissen, Henri
2017   Noah's Ark: Ancient Accounts and New Discoveries. Second edition. Copenhagen, Denmark: Scandinavia Publishing House.

Oard, Michael J.
1990   An Ice Age Caused by the Genesis Flood. El Cajon, CA: Institute for Creation Research.
2019   The Deep Time Deception: Examining the Case for Millions of Years. Powder Springs, GA: Creation Book Publishers.

Oard, Michael J. & Oard, Beverly
1993   Life in the Great Ice Age. Green Forest, AR: Master Books.

Oard, Michael J. & Reed, John K.
2017   How Noah's Flood Shaped Our Earth. Powder Springs, GA: Creation Book Publishers.

Oard, Michael J. & Reed, John K. (eds.)
2009   Rock Solid Answers: The Biblical Truth Behind 14 Geologic Questions. Green Forest, AR: Master Books.

Oates, David & Oates, Joan
1976   The Rise of Civilization. Oxford, England: Elsevier–Phaidon.

Oates, Joan
1983   Ubaid Mesopotamia Reconsidered. — The Hilly Flanks and Beyond: Essays on the Prehistory of Southwestern Asia. Edited by T. Cuyler Young & Philip E. L. Smith & Peder Mortensen. Chicago, IL: The Oriental Institute of the University of Chicago. 251–281.
2012   Varieties of Early Village and Town Life: Southern Mesopotamia. — A Companion to the Archaeology of the Ancient Near East. 2 volumes. Edited by D. T. Potts. Chichester, England: Wiley-Blackwell. 1:466–484.

Odaka, Takahiro
2003   Fine Painted Wares in the Neolithic Northern Levant: The Earliest Evidence from Tell Ain el-Kerkh, the Rouj Basin. — Orient Express 2003/3: 80–81.
2017   Decoration of Neolithic Pottery in the Northern Levant: A View from the Rouj Basin. — Painting Pots – Painting People: Late Neolithic Ceramics in Ancient Mesopotamia. Edited by Walter Cruells & Inna Mateiciucová & Olivier Nieuwenhuyse. Oxford, England: Oxbow Books. 177–185.

O'Donnell, Phillip
2006   Dinosaurs: Dead or Alive? Maitland, FL: Xulon Press.

Ogden, J. G.
1977   The Use and Abuse of Radiocarbon Dating. — Annals of the New York Academy of Sciences 288: 167–173.

Ortiz, Steven M.
2005   Hebron. — Dictionary of the Old Testament: Historical Books. Edited by Bill
              T. Arnold & H. G. M. Williamson. Downers Grove, IL: InterVarsity Press.
              390–392.

Osgood, A. J. M.
1986a   A Better Model for the Stone Age. — Journal of Creation 2/1: 88–102.
              creation.com/a-better-model-for-the-stone-age
1986b   The Times of Abraham. — Journal of Creation 2/1: 77–87. creation.com/the-
              times-of-abraham
1986c   The Times of the Judges – The Archaeology: (a) Exodus to Conquest. —
              Journal of Creation 2/1: 56–76. creation.com/the-times-of-the-judges-the-
              archaeology-exodus-to-conquest
1988a   A Better Model for the Stone Age – Part 2. — Journal of Creation 3/1: 73–
              95. creation.com/a-better-model-for-the-stone-age-part-2
1988b   From Abraham to Exodus. — Journal of Creation 3/1: 96–108.
              creation.com/from-abraham-to-exodus
1988c   The Times of the Judges – The Archaeology: (b) Settlement and Apostasy.
              — Journal of Creation 3/1: 109–121. creation.com/the-time-of-the-judges-
              the-archaeology-b-settlement-and-apostasy
2024   The Place of Dynasty VI and of the Exodus in Egyptian History: Further
              Comments. — Answers Research Journal 17: 409–419.

Panitz-Cohen, Nava
2014   The Southern Levant (Cisjordan) during the Late Bronze Age. — The Oxford
              Handbook of the Archaeology of the Levant, c. 8000–332 BCE. Edited by
              Margreet L. Steiner & Ann E. Killebrew. Oxford, England: Oxford University
              Press. 541–560.

Parpola, Simo
2010   Sumerian: A Uralic Language (I). — Language in the Ancient Near East:
              Proceedings of the 53e Rencontre Assyriologique Internationale. Edited by
              L. Kogan et al. Winona Lake, IN: Eisenbrauns. 181–210.
2016   Etymological Dictionary of the Sumerian Language I–II. Publications of the
              Foundation for Finnish Assyriological Research 16. Winona Lake, IN: The
              Neo-Assyrian Text Corpus Project. [Part III published in 2022.]

Peasnall, Brian
2002   Ubaid. — Encyclopedia of Prehistory. Volume 8: South and Southwest Asia.
              Edited by Peter N. Peregrine & Melvin Ember. New York, NY: Kluwer
              Academic/Plenum Publishers. 372–390.

Penner, Ken M. et al. (eds.)
2019   The Lexham English Septuagint. Second edition. Bellingham, WA: Lexham
              Press.

Peregrine, Peter N.
2002a   Early Dynastic Mesopotamia: Sumerian. — Encyclopedia of Prehistory.
              Volume 8: South and Southwest Asia. Edited by Peter N. Peregrine &

Melvin Ember. New York, NY: Kluwer Academic/Plenum Publishers. 112–115.

2002b   Jemdet Nasr. — Encyclopedia of Prehistory. Volume 8: South and Southwest Asia. Edited by Peter N. Peregrine & Melvin Ember. New York, NY: Kluwer Academic/Plenum Publishers. 236–238.

Perkins, Ann Louise
1949   The Comparative Archeology of Early Mesopotamia. Chicago, IL: University of Chicago Press.

Petit, Lucas P.
2014   An Archaeological Historiography of Khirbet Et-Tell and the Ongoing Search of the Biblical City of 'Ai'. — Archaeology in the 'Land of Tells and Ruins': A History of Excavations in the Holy Land Inspired by the Photographs and Accounts of Leo Boer. Edited by Bart Wagemakers. Oxford, England: Oxbow Books. 41–59.

Petrovich, Douglas
2013   Identifying Nimrod of Genesis 10 with Sargon of Akkad by Exegetical and Archaeological Means. — Journal of the Evangelical Theological Society 56/2: 273–305.
2016   The World's Oldest Alphabet: Hebrew as the Language of the Proto-Consonantal Script. Jerusalem, Israel: Carta Jerusalem.

Pettinato, Giovanni
1981   The Archives of Ebla: An Empire Inscribed in Clay. Garden City, NY: Doubleday.
1991   Ebla: A New Look at History. Baltimore, MD: Johns Hopkins University Press.

Pettitt, Paul
2014   The European Upper Palaeolithic. — The Oxford Handbook of the Archaeology and Anthropology of Hunter-Gatherers. Edited by Vicki Cummings & Peter Jordan & Marek Zvelebil. Oxford, England: Oxford University Press. 279–309.

Philip, Graham
2000   Tin. — Dictionary of the Ancient Near East. Edited by Piotr Bienkowski & Alan Millard. Philadelphia, PA: University of Pennsylvania Press. 292.

Pierce, Larry
1999   In the Days of Peleg: Ancient Documents Are Consistent with the Total Accuracy of the Bible's Chronology. — Creation 22/1: 46–49. creation.com/in-the-days-of-peleg

Pietersma, Albert & Wright, Benjamin G. (eds.)
2009   A New English Translation of the Septuagint. Oxford, England: Oxford University Press.

Pinnock, Frances
2013   Ebla. — The Sumerian World. Edited by Harriet Crawford. New York, NY: Routledge. 538–555.
2020   Ebla in the Mid-to-Late Third Millennium BCE: Architecture and Chronology. — New Horizons in the Study of the Early Bronze III and Early Bronze IV of the Levant. Edited by Suzanne Richard. University Park, PA: Eisenbrauns. 72–90.

Podany, Amanda H.
2010   Brotherhood of Kings: How International Relations Shaped the Ancient Near East. Oxford, England: Oxford University Press.
2014   The Ancient Near East: A Very Short Introduction. Oxford, England: Oxford University Press.

Pollock, Susan
1999   Ancient Mesopotamia: The Eden that Never Was. Cambridge, England: Cambridge University Press.

Porter, Robert M.
2022   The Place of the Exodus in Egyptian History. — Answers Research Journal 15: 1–9.

Postgate, J. N.
1994   Early Mesopotamia: Society and Economy at the Dawn of History. New York, NY: Routledge.

Potts, Timothy
2019   Introduction to the English-Language Edition – Uruk: The Last "First City". — Uruk: First City of the Ancient World. Edited by Nicola Crüsemann et al. Los Angeles, CA: J. Paul Getty Museum. 1–5.

Pournelle, Jennifer R.
2013   Physical Geography. — The Sumerian World. Edited by Harriet Crawford. New York, NY: Routledge. 13–32.

Pournelle, Jennifer R. & Algaze, Guillermo
2014   Travels in Edin: Deltaic Resilience and Early Urbanism in Greater Mesopotamia. — Preludes to Urbanism: The Late Chalcolithic of Mesopotamia. Edited by Augusta McMahon & Harriet Crawford. Cambridge, England: McDonald Institute for Archaeological Research. 7–34.

Powell, James
2022   Decoding a World Navel "Visual Language" through Ideational Cognitive Archaeology. — Answers Research Journal 15: 301–337.

Pratico, Gary D. & Van Pelt, Miles V.
2007   Basics of Biblical Hebrew Grammar. Second edition. Grand Rapids, MI: Zondervan.

Price, Randall & House, H. Wayne
2017   Zondervan Handbook of Biblical Archaeology. Grand Rapids, MI: Zondervan.

Price, T. Douglas & Gebauer, Anne Birgitte
1995   New Perspectives on the Transition to Agriculture. — Last Hunters – First Farmers: New Perspectives on the Prehistoric Transition to Agriculture. Edited by T. Douglas Price & Anne Birgitte Gebauer. Santa Fe, NM: School of American Research Press. 3–19.

Pritchard, James B. (ed.)
2011   The Ancient Near East: An Anthology of Texts and Pictures. Princeton, NJ: Princeton University Press.

Provan, Iain & Long, V. Philips & Longman, Tremper, III
2003   A Biblical History of Israel. Louisville, KY: Westminster John Knox Press.

Rahlfs, Alfred (ed.)
2006   Septuaginta. Revised edition, edited by Robert Hanhart. Stuttgart, Germany: Deutsche Bibelgesellschaft.

Rainey, Anson F. & Notley, R. Steven
2015   The Sacred Bridge: Carta's Atlas of the Biblical World. Second emended and enhanced edition. Jerusalem, Israel: Carta Jerusalem.

Rasmussen, Carl G.
2010   Zondervan Atlas of the Bible. Revised edition. Grand Rapids, MI: Zondervan.

Rea, John
2009   Camel. — The Zondervan Encyclopedia of the Bible. Revised, full-color edition. 5 volumes. Edited by Merrill C. Tenney & Moisés Silva. Grand Rapids, MI: Zondervan. 1:719–722.

Redman, Charles L.
1978   The Rise of Civilization: From Early Farmers to Urban Society in the Ancient Near East. San Francisco, CA: W. H. Freeman and Company.

Reed, John K.
2014   Rocks Aren't Clocks: A Critique of the Geologic Timescale. Powder Springs, GA: Creation Book Publishers.

Richard, Suzanne
2014   The Southern Levant (Transjordan) during the Early Bronze Age. — The Oxford Handbook of the Archaeology of the Levant, c. 8000–332 BCE. Edited by Margreet L. Steiner & Ann E. Killebrew. Oxford, England: Oxford University Press. 330–352.

2020   New Vistas on the Early Bronze Age IV of the Southern Levant: A Case for "Rural Complexity" in the Permanent Sedentary Sites. — New Horizons in the Study of the Early Bronze III and Early Bronze IV of the Levant. Edited by Suzanne Richard. University Park, PA: Eisenbrauns. 417–453.

Richardson, Joel
2018   Mount Sinai in Arabia: The True Location Revealed. WinePress Media.

Riede, Felix
2014   The Resettlement of Northern Europe. — The Oxford Handbook of the Archaeology and Anthropology of Hunter-Gatherers. Edited by Vicki Cummings & Peter Jordan & Marek Zvelebil. Oxford, England: Oxford University Press. 556–581.

Riggs, Alan C.
1984   Major Carbon-14 Deficiency in Modern Snail Shells from Southern Nevada Springs. — Science 224/4644: 58–61.

Roaf, Michael
1990   Cultural Atlas of Mesopotamia and the Ancient Near East. New York, NY: Facts On File.

Rosen, Steven A.
1997   Lithics after the Stone Age: A Handbook of Stone Tools from the Levant. Walnut Creek, CA: AltaMira Press.
2012   Lithic Industries during the Holocene Period. — A Companion to the Archaeology of the Ancient Near East. 2 volumes. Edited by D. T. Potts. Chichester, England: Wiley-Blackwell. 1:236–260.

Rosenberg, A. J.
1993   The Book of Genesis: A New English Translation of the Text, Rashi, and a Commentary Digest. Volume 1. Brooklyn, NY: The Judaica Press.

Rothman, Mitchell S.
2001   The Local and the Regional: An Introduction. — Uruk Mesopotamia and Its Neighbors: Cross-Cultural Interactions in the Era of State Formation. Edited by Mitchell S. Rothman. Santa Fe, NM: School of American Research Press. 3–26.
2002   Late Chalcolithic Mesopotamia: Uruk. — Encyclopedia of Prehistory. Volume 8: South and Southwest Asia. Edited by Peter N. Peregrine & Melvin Ember. New York, NY: Kluwer Academic/Plenum Publishers. 261–270.

Roux, Georges
1992   Ancient Iraq. Third edition. London, England: Penguin Books.

Rowan, Yorke M.
2014   The Southern Levant (Cisjordan) during the Chalcolithic Period. — The
              Oxford Handbook of the Archaeology of the Levant, c. 8000–332 BCE.
              Edited by Margreet L. Steiner & Ann E. Killebrew. Oxford, England: Oxford
              University Press. 223–236.

Rösel, Hartmut N.
2011   Joshua. Historical Commentary on the Old Testament. Leuven, Belgium:
              Peeters.

Rösel, Martin
1994   Übersetzung als Vollendung der Auslegung: Studien zur Genesis-
              Septuaginta. Berlin, Germany: Walter de Gruyter.

Rupe, Christopher & Sanford, John
2019   Contested Bones. First edition, second printing. Waterloo, NY: FMS
              Publications.

Ruppert, Lothar
2003   Genesis: Ein kritischer und theologischer Kommentar. 1. Teilband: Gen
              1,1–11,26. Forschung zur Bibel. Second edition. Würzburg, Germany:
              Echter Verlag.

Ryken, Leland & Wilhoit, James C. & Longman, Tremper, III (eds.)
1998   Dictionary of Biblical Imagery. Downers Grove, IL: IVP Academic.

Saarnivaara, Uuras
1983   Can the Bible Be Trusted? Old and New Testament Introduction and
              Interpretation. Minneapolis, MN: Osterhus Publishing House.

Safar, Fuad & Mustafa, Mohammad Ali & Lloyd, Seton
1981   Eridu. Baghdad, Iraq: State Organization of Antiquities and Heritage.

Sagona, Antonio & Zimansky, Paul
2009   Ancient Turkey. New York, NY: Routledge.

Sailhamer, John H.
2008   Genesis. — The Expositor's Bible Commentary. Revised edition. 13
              volumes. Edited by Tremper Longman III & David E. Garland. Grand Rapids,
              MI: Zondervan. 1:21–332.

Sammer, Jan
—   New Light on the Dark Age of Greece. varchive.org/nldag/index.htm

Sanders, Lita
2021   Neandertals Weren't 'Cave Men'. — Creation 43/2: 56.
              creation.com/neandertal-homes

Sanford, John C.
2014   Genetic Entropy. Fourth edition. Waterloo, NY: FMS Publications.

2018   What Is the Scientific Evidence for Adam and Eve? — The Harvest Handbook of Apologetics. Edited by Joseph M. Holden. Eugene, OR: Harvest House Publishers. 291–297.

Sarfati, Jonathan D.
2003   Biblical Chronogenealogies. — Journal of Creation 17/3: 14–18. creation.com/biblical-chronogenealogies
2011   Refuting Compromise. Updated and expanded edition. Powder Springs, GA: Creation Book Publishers.
2015   The Genesis Account: A Theological, Historical, and Scientific Commentary on Genesis 1–11. Powder Springs, GA: Creation Book Publishers.

Sarna, Nahum M.
1989   Genesis. The JPS Torah Commentary. Philadelphia, PA: The Jewish Publication Society.

Sasson, Jack M.
2014   Judges 1–12: A New Translation with Introduction and Commentary. The Anchor Yale Bible. Volume 6D. New Haven, CT: Yale University Press.
2015   From the Mari Archives: An Anthology of Old Babylonian Letters. Winona Lake, IN: Eisenbrauns.

Säve-Söderbergh, Torgny & Olsson, Ingrid U.
1970   C 14 Dating and Egyptian Chronology. — Radiocarbon Variations and Absolute Chronology: Proceedings of the Twelfth Nobel Symposium Held at the Institute of Physics at Uppsala University. Edited by Ingrid U. Olsson. Stockholm, Sweden: Almqvist & Wiksell. 35–53.

Scarre, Chris & Fagan, Brian M. & Golden, Charles
2021   Ancient Civilizations. Fifth edition. New York, NY: Routledge.

Schlegel, William
2016   Satellite Bible Atlas: Historical Geography of the Bible. Second edition. BiblePlaces.com.

Schmidt, Klaus
2011   Göbekli Tepe: A Neolithic Site in Southeastern Anatolia. — The Oxford Handbook of Ancient Anatolia, 10,000–323 BCE. Edited by Sharon R. Steadman & Gregory McMahon. Oxford, England: Oxford University Press. 917–933.
2012   Late Pleistocene and Early Holocene Hunters and Gatherers: Anatolia. — A Companion to the Archaeology of the Ancient Near East. 2 volumes. Edited by D. T. Potts. Chichester, England: Wiley-Blackwell. 1:144–160.

Schorr, Edwin M.
—   Applying the Revised Chronology: Mycenae. varchive.org/schorr/index.htm

Schrakamp, Ingo
2020   The Kingdom of Akkad: A View from Within. — The Oxford History of the
             Ancient Near East. Volume 1. Edited by Karen Radner et al. New York, NY:
             Oxford University Press. 612–685.

Schüle, Andreas
2009   Die Urgeschichte (Genesis 1–11). Zürcher Bibelkommentare. Zurich,
             Switzerland: Theologischer Verlag Zürich.

Scott, Emmet
2012   Hatshepsut, Queen of Sheba. New York, NY: Algora Publishing.

Scott, James C.
2017   Against the Grain: A Deep History of the Earliest States. New Haven, CT:
             Yale University Press.

Scurlock, Joann
2009   Nimrod. — The New Interpreter's Dictionary of the Bible. 5 volumes.
             Edited by Katharine Doob Sakenfeld et al. Nashville, TN: Abingdon Press.
             4:275.

Selz, Gebhard J.
2020   The Uruk Phenomenon. — The Oxford History of the Ancient Near East.
             Volume 1. Edited by Karen Radner et al. New York, NY: Oxford University
             Press. 163–244.

Seri, Andrea
2010   Adaptation of Cuneiform to Write Akkadian. — Visible Language:
             Inventions of Writing in the Ancient Middle East and Beyond. Edited by
             Christopher Woods, with Geoff Emberling & Emily Teeter. Chicago, IL: The
             Oriental Institute of the University of Chicago. 85–93.

Sexton, Jeremy
2015   Who Was Born When Enosh Was 90? A Semantic Reevaluation of William
             Henry Green's Chronological Gaps. — Westminster Theological Journal 77:
             193–218. biblearchaeology.org/images/articles/Sexton-WTJ-Article.pdf
2018   Evangelicalism's Search for Chronological Gaps in Genesis 5 and 11: A
             Historical, Hermeneutical, and Linguistic Critique. — Journal of the
             Evangelical Theological Society 61/1: 5–25.
             biblearchaeology.org/images/Genesis-5-and-
             11/Sexton_JETS_61.1_Evangelicalisms_Search_for_Chronological_Gaps.pdf

Sharon, Ilan
2014   Levantine Chronology. — The Oxford Handbook of the Archaeology of the
             Levant, c. 8000–332 BCE. Edited by Margreet L. Steiner & Ann E. Killebrew.
             Oxford, England: Oxford University Press. 44–65.

Shaw, Ian & Nicholson, Paul
2008   The Princeton Dictionary of Ancient Egypt. Princeton, NJ: Princeton
             University Press.

Shea, John J.
2013   Stone Tools in the Paleolithic and Neolithic Near East: A Guide. New York,
            NY: Cambridge University Press.

Simmons, Alan H.
2007   The Neolithic Revolution in the Near East: Transforming the Human
            Landscape. Tucson, AZ: University of Arizona Press.

Skinner, John
1910   A Critical and Exegetical Commentary on Genesis. The International Critical
            Commentary. New York, NY: Charles Scribner's Sons.

Snelling, Andrew A.
2014   Earth's Catastrophic Past. 2 volumes. Green Forest, AR: Master Books.

Solecki, Ralph S.
1971   Shanidar: The First Flower People. New York, NY: Alfred A. Knopf.

Speiser, Ephraim A.
2007   Genesis: A New Translation with Introduction and Commentary. The
            Anchor Yale Bible. Volume 1. New Haven, CT: Yale University Press.

St. Athanasius Academy of Orthodox Theology
2008   The Orthodox Study Bible: Ancient Christianity Speaks to Today's World.
            Nashville, TN: Thomas Nelson.

Stauder, Andréas
2010   The Earliest Egyptian Writing. — Visible Language: Inventions of Writing in
            the Ancient Middle East and Beyond. Edited by Christopher Woods, with
            Geoff Emberling & Emily Teeter. Chicago, IL: The Oriental Institute of the
            University of Chicago. 137–147.

Steinmann, Andrew E.
1999   The Oracles of God: The Old Testament Canon. St. Louis, MO: Concordia
            Publishing House.
2017   2 Samuel. Concordia Commentary. St. Louis, MO: Concordia Publishing
            House.
2019   Genesis: An Introduction and Commentary. Tyndale Old Testament
            Commentaries. Volume 1. Downers Grove, IL: IVP Academic.

Stern, Ephraim (ed.)
1993   The New Encyclopedia of Archaeological Excavations in the Holy Land. 4
            volumes. Jerusalem, Israel: Israel Exploration Society & Carta.
2008   The New Encyclopedia of Archaeological Excavations in the Holy Land.
            Supplementary Volume 5. Jerusalem, Israel: Israel Exploration Society;
            Washington, DC: Biblical Archaeology Society.

Stevenson, Alice
2013   Egypt and Mesopotamia. — The Sumerian World. Edited by Harriet
            Crawford. New York, NY: Routledge. 620–636.

Stiebing, William H., Jr. & Helft, Susan N.
2018   Ancient Near Eastern History and Culture. Third edition. New York, NY:
               Routledge.

Strommenger, Eva
1980   Habuba Kabira: Eine Stadt vor 5000 Jahren. Mainz, Germany: Philipp von
               Zabern.

Sweeney, Emmet
2006   Empire of Thebes, or Ages in Chaos Revisited. New York, NY: Algora
               Publishing.
2008   The Ramessides, Medes and Persians. New York, NY: Algora Publishing.
2009   Gods, Heroes and Tyrants: Greek Chronology in Chaos. New York, NY:
               Algora Publishing.

Swift, Dennis
2006   Secrets of the Ica Stones and Nazca Lines: Proofs that Dinosaurs and Man
               Lived Together. Portland, OR: Creation Science Ministries of Oregon.

Tadmor, Miriam
1986   Chalcolithic Period. — Treasures of the Holy Land: Ancient Art from the
               Israel Museum. Edited by John P. O'Neill & Kathleen Howard. New York,
               NY: The Metropolitan Museum of Art. 57–86.

Tal, Abraham (ed.)
2016   Biblia Hebraica Quinta: Genesis. Stuttgart, Germany: Deutsche
               Bibelgesellschaft.

Tallet, Pierre
2020   Egypt's Old Kingdom in Contact with the World. — The Oxford History of
               the Ancient Near East. Volume 1. Edited by Karen Radner et al. New York,
               NY: Oxford University Press. 397–458.

Taylor, Paul S.
1998   The Great Dinosaur Mystery and the Bible. Revised and updated edition.
               Colorado Springs, CO: Chariot Victor Publishing.

Thomas, Brian & Vance, Nelson
2015   Radiocarbon in Dinosaur and Other Fossils. — Creation Research Quarterly
               51/4: 299–311.

Thong, Chan Kei & Fu, Charlene L.
2009   Finding God in Ancient China: How the Ancient Chinese Worshiped the God
               of the Bible. Grand Rapids, MI: Zondervan.

Thuesen, Ingolf
1989   Diffusion of 'Ubaid Pottery into Western Syria. — Upon This Foundation:
               The 'Ubaid Reconsidered. Edited by Elizabeth F. Henrickson & Ingolf
               Thuesen. Copenhagen, Denmark: Museum Tusculanum Press. 419–437.

Tsumura, David Toshio
2019   The Second Book of Samuel. The New International Commentary on the
              Old Testament. Grand Rapids, MI: Eerdmans.

Tubb, Jonathan N.
1998   Canaanites. London, England: British Museum Press.

Unger, Merrill F. et al.
2006   The New Unger's Bible Dictionary. Full-color edition. Chicago, IL: Moody
              Publishers.

Ussher, James
2003   The Annals of the World. Edited by Larry Pierce & Marion Pierce. Green
              Forest, AR: Master Books.

Ussishkin, David
1971   The "Ghassulian" Temple in Ein Gedi and the Origin of the Hoard from
              Nahal   Mishmar.   —   The   Biblical   Archaeologist   34/1:   23–39.
              jstor.org/stable/3210951
2014   The Chalcolithic Temple in Ein Gedi: Fifty Years after Its Discovery. — Near
              East Archaeology 77: 15–26.

Vacca, Agnese & D'Andrea, Marta
2020   The Connections Between the Northern and Southern Levant During Early
              Bronze Age III: Reevaluations and New Vistas in the Light of New Data and
              Higher Chronologies. — New Horizons in the Study of the Early Bronze III
              and Early Bronze IV of the Levant. Edited by Suzanne Richard. University
              Park, PA: Eisenbrauns. 120–145.

Van De Mieroop, Marc
2005   King Hammurabi of Babylon: A Biography. Malden, MA: Blackwell.
2011   A History of Ancient Egypt. Chichester, England: Wiley-Blackwell.
2013   Democracy and the Rule of Law, the Assembly, and the First Law Code. —
              The Sumerian World. Edited by Harriet Crawford. New York, NY:
              Routledge. 277–289.
2016   A History of the Ancient Near East, ca. 3000–323 BC. Third edition.
              Chichester, England: Wiley-Blackwell.

VanDoodewaard, William
2015   The Quest for the Historical Adam: Genetics, Hermeneutics, and Human
              Origins. Grand Rapids, MI: Reformation Heritage Books.

VanGemeren, Willem A. et al. (eds.)
1997   New International Dictionary of Old Testament Theology and Exegesis. 5
              volumes. Grand Rapids, MI: Zondervan.

Velikovsky, Immanuel
—   Beth-Shan. varchive.org/ce/bethshan.htm
—   Hammurabi and the Revised Chronology. varchive.org/ce/hammurabi.html
—   The Assyrian Conquest. varchive.org/tac/index.htm

—   The Dark Age of Greece. varchive.org/dag/index.htm

1960   Oedipus and Akhnaton: Myth and History. Garden City, NY: Doubleday & Company.

2009   Ages in Chaos I: From the Exodus to King Akhnaton. New, unchanged edition. London, England: Paradigma. [Original edition (1952) by Doubleday & Company, Garden City, New York.]

2010   Ages in Chaos II: Ramses II and His Time. New, unchanged edition. London, England: Paradigma. [Original edition (1978) by Doubleday & Company, Garden City, New York.]

2011   Ages in Chaos III: Peoples of the Sea. New, unchanged edition. London, England: Paradigma. [Original edition (1977) by Doubleday & Company, Garden City, New York.]

Vogel, Helga
2019   The "Great Man of Uruk": The Art of Governance in the Late Fourth and Early Third Millennia BC. — Uruk: First City of the Ancient World. Edited by Nicola Crüsemann et al. Los Angeles, CA: J. Paul Getty Museum. 119–125.

von Fange, Erich A.
1990   Genesis and the Dinosaur. Syracuse, IN: Living Word Services.
1994   Noah to Abram: The Turbulent Years. Syracuse, IN: Living Word Services.
2006   In Search of the Genesis World: Debunking the Evolution Myth. St. Louis, MO: Concordia Publishing House.

von Rad, Gerhard
1981   Das erste Buch Mose/Genesis. Das Alte Testament Deutsch. Volume 2–4. Eleventh edition. Göttingen, Germany: Vandenhoeck & Ruprecht.

Wagensonner, Klaus
2022   The Middle East after the Fall of Ur: Isin and Larsa. — The Oxford History of the Ancient Near East. Volume 2. Edited by Karen Radner et al. New York, NY: Oxford University Press. 190–309.

Waltke, Bruce K. (with Cathi J. Fredricks)
2001   Genesis: A Commentary. Grand Rapids, MI: Zondervan.

Walton, John H.
2009   Genesis. — Zondervan Illustrated Bible Backgrounds Commentary: Old Testament. 5 volumes. Edited by John H. Walton. Grand Rapids, MI: Zondervan. 1:2–159.

Walton, John H. & Matthews, Victor H. & Chavalas, Mark W.
2000   The IVP Bible Background Commentary: Old Testament. Downers Grove, IL: IVP Academic.

Wang, Samuel & Nelson, Ethel R.
1998   God and the Ancient Chinese. Dunlap, TN: Read Books Publisher.

Watson, Patty Jo
1983   The Halafian Culture: A Review and Synthesis. — The Hilly Flanks and
            Beyond: Essays on the Prehistory of Southwestern Asia. Edited by T. Cuyler
            Young & Philip E. L. Smith & Peder Mortensen. Chicago, IL: The Oriental
            Institute of the University of Chicago. 231–250.

Webb, Barry G.
2012   The Book of Judges. The New International Commentary on the Old
            Testament. Grand Rapids, MI: Eerdmans.

Weiss, Harvey
2002   Akkadian: Akkadian Empire. — Encyclopedia of Prehistory. Volume 8:
            South and Southwest Asia. Edited by Peter N. Peregrine & Melvin Ember.
            New York, NY: Kluwer Academic/Plenum Publishers. 21–23.
2014   The Northern Levant during the Intermediate Bronze Age: Altered
            Trajectories. — The Oxford Handbook of the Archaeology of the Levant, c.
            8000–332 BCE. Edited by Margreet L. Steiner & Ann E. Killebrew. Oxford,
            England: Oxford University Press. 367–387.

Welch, Laura (ed.)
2016   Inside Noah's Ark: Why It Worked. Green Forest, AR: Master Books.

Welton, Lynn
2020   The 'Amuq in the Early Bronze Age III–IV from a Levantine Perspective. —
            New Horizons in the Study of the Early Bronze III and Early Bronze IV of the
            Levant. Edited by Suzanne Richard. University Park, PA: Eisenbrauns. 51–
            71.

Wenham, Gordon J.
1987   Genesis 1–15. Word Biblical Commentary. Volume 1. Waco, TX: Word
            Books Publisher.

Westermann, Claus
1994   Genesis 1–11. A Continental Commentary. Translated by John J. Scullion.
            Minneapolis, MN: Fortress Press.

Wevers, John William
1993   Notes on the Greek Text of Genesis. Atlanta, GA: Scholars Press.

White, William, Jr.
2009   Enuma Elish. — The Zondervan Encyclopedia of the Bible. Revised, full-
            color edition. 5 volumes. Edited by Merrill C. Tenney & Moisés Silva. Grand
            Rapids, MI: Zondervan. 2:340.

Wieland, Carl
2011   One Human Family: The Bible, Science, Race and Culture. Powder Springs,
            GA: Creation Book Publishers.
2013   Stones and Bones: Powerful Evidence against Evolution. Powder Springs,
            GA: Creation Book Publishers.

Wilkinson, Toby A. H.
2002   Uruk into Egypt: Imports and Imitations. — Artefacts of Complexity: Tracking the Uruk in the Near East. Edited by J. N. Postgate. London, England: British School of Archaeology in Iraq. 237–245.

Wilkinson, Tony J.
2013   Hydraulic Landscapes and Irrigation Systems of Sumer. — The Sumerian World. Edited by Harriet Crawford. New York, NY: Routledge. 33–54.

Willcox, George
2012   The Beginnings of Cereal Cultivation and Domestication in Southwest Asia. — A Companion to the Archaeology of the Ancient Near East. 2 volumes. Edited by D. T. Potts. Chichester, England: Wiley-Blackwell. 1:163–180.

Wiseman, Donald J.
1982   Chaldea, Chaldeans. — New Bible Dictionary. Second edition. Edited by J. D. Douglas et al. Leicester, England: Inter-Varsity Press. 182.
2009   Ur (city). — The Zondervan Encyclopedia of the Bible. Revised, full-color edition. 5 volumes. Edited by Merrill C. Tenney & Moisés Silva. Grand Rapids, MI: Zondervan. 5:969–971.

Woodmorappe, John
1997   Noah's Ark: A Feasibility Study. El Cajon, CA: Institute for Creation Research.
1999   The Mythology of Modern Dating Methods. El Cajon, CA: Institute for Creation Research.

Woods, Christopher
2010a   Introduction – Visible Language: The Earliest Writing Systems. — Visible Language: Inventions of Writing in the Ancient Middle East and Beyond. Edited by Christopher Woods, with Geoff Emberling & Emily Teeter. Chicago, IL: The Oriental Institute of the University of Chicago. 15–25.
2010b   The Earliest Mesopotamian Writing. — Visible Language: Inventions of Writing in the Ancient Middle East and Beyond. Edited by Christopher Woods, with Geoff Emberling & Emily Teeter. Chicago, IL: The Oriental Institute of the University of Chicago. 33–50.

Woudstra, Marten H.
1981   The Book of Joshua. The New International Commentary on the Old Testament. Grand Rapids, MI: Eerdmans.

Wright, Paul H.
2020   Holman Illustrated Guide to Biblical Geography: Reading the Land. Nashville, TN: B&H Publishing Group.

Wyatt, Mary Nell
—   The Tower of Babel.
2004   The Boat-Shaped Object on Doomsday Mountain: Is This the Remains of Noah's Ark? Cornersville, TN: Wyatt Archaeological Research.

2020   Battle for the Firstborn: The Exodus and the Death of Tutankhamun. Spring Hill, TN: Royal Hill Press.

Yasur-Landau, Assaf
2010   Wider Mediterranean: Levant. — The Oxford Handbook of the Bronze Age Aegean. Edited by Eric H. Cline. Oxford, England: Oxford University Press. 832–848.

Young, Edward J.
1959   The Relation of the First Verse of Genesis One to Verses Two and Three. — Westminster Theological Journal 21/2: 133–146.
1964a   An Introduction to the Old Testament. Grand Rapids, MI: Eerdmans.
1964b   Studies in Genesis One. Philadelphia, PA: The Presbyterian and Reformed Publishing Company.

Zettler, Richard L. & Horne, Lee (eds.)
1998   Treasures from the Royal Tombs of Ur. Philadelphia, PA: University of Pennsylvania Museum of Archaeology and Anthropology.

Zilhão, João
2014   The Neanderthals: Evolution, Palaeoecology, and Extinction. — The Oxford Handbook of the Archaeology and Anthropology of Hunter-Gatherers. Edited by Vicki Cummings & Peter Jordan & Marek Zvelebil. Oxford, England: Oxford University Press. 191–213.

Zuckerman, Sharon
2006   Where Is the Hazor Archive Buried? — Biblical Archaeology Review 32/2: 28, 30–37.

CHART 1: MESOPOTAMIA AND SURROUNDING AREAS AFTER THE DISPERSAL AT BABEL C. 2215 B.C.

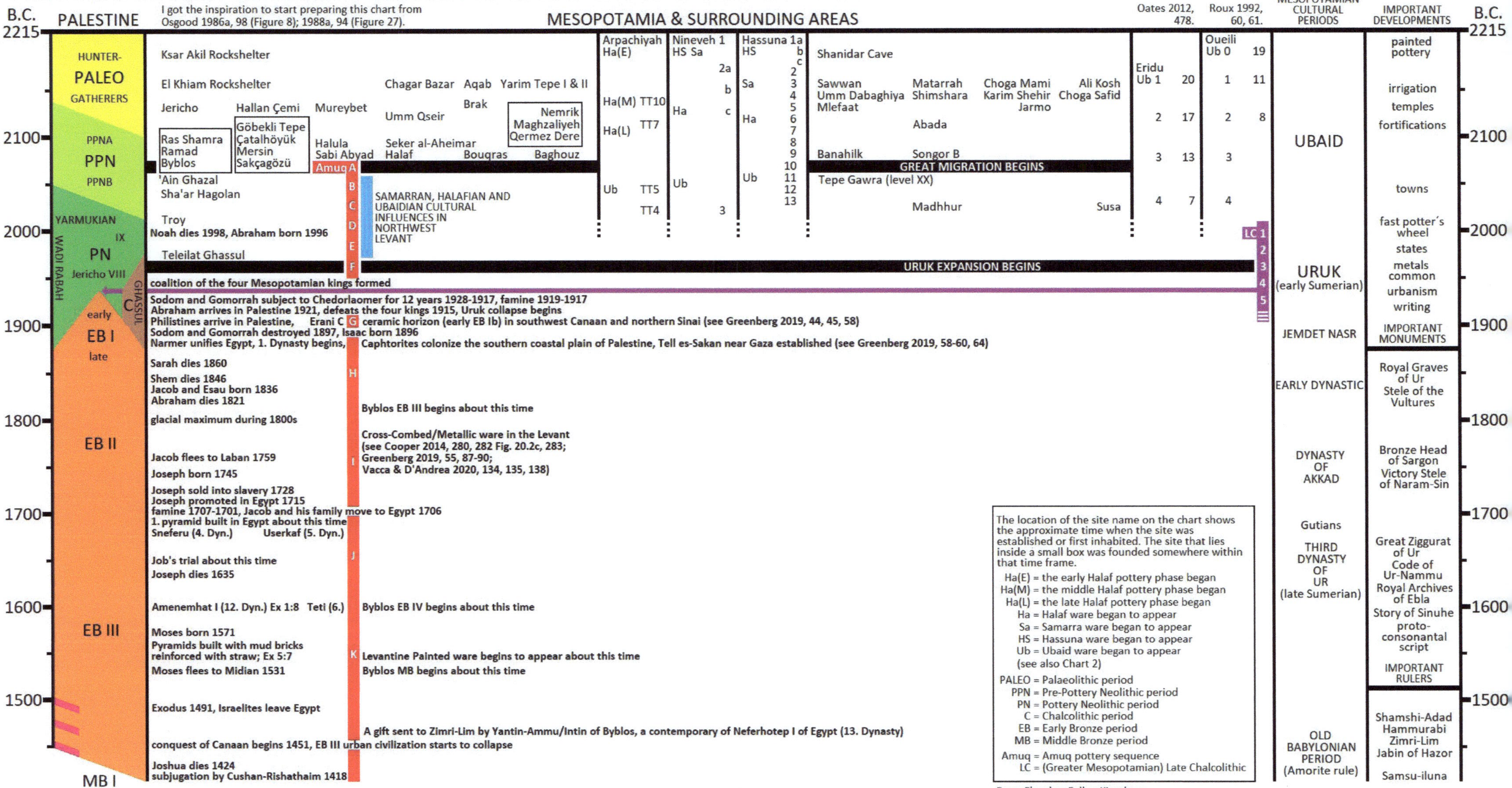

I got the inspiration to start preparing this chart from Osgood 1986a, 98 (Figure 8); 1988a, 94 (Figure 27).

MESOPOTAMIA & SURROUNDING AREAS

Oates 2012, 478. Roux 1992, 60, 61.

SOUTH MESOPOTAMIAN CULTURAL PERIODS

IMPORTANT DEVELOPMENTS

B.C. 2215 — **PALESTINE** — **B.C. 2215**

Palestine column (top to bottom)

- HUNTER-GATHERERS
- **PALEO**
- PPNA
- **PPN**
- PPNB
- YARMUKIAN — IX
- **PN** — Jericho VIII
- WADI RABAH
- GHASSUL — C
- early
- **EB I**
- late
- **EB II**
- **EB III**
- **MB I**

Palestine events

- Noah dies 1998, Abraham born 1996
- Teleilat Ghassul
- coalition of the four Mesopotamian kings formed
- Sodom and Gomorrah subject to Chedorlaomer for 12 years 1928-1917, famine 1919-1917
- Abraham arrives in Palestine 1921, defeats the four kings 1915, Uruk collapse begins
- Philistines arrive in Palestine, Erani C ceramic horizon (early EB Ib) in southwest Canaan and northern Sinai (see Greenberg 2019, 44, 45, 58)
- Sodom and Gomorrah destroyed 1897, Isaac born 1896
- Narmer unifies Egypt, 1. Dynasty begins, Caphtorites colonize the southern coastal plain of Palestine, Tell es-Sakan near Gaza established (see Greenberg 2019, 58-60, 64)
- Sarah dies 1860
- Shem dies 1846
- Jacob and Esau born 1836
- Abraham dies 1821
- glacial maximum during 1800s
- Jacob flees to Laban 1759
- Joseph born 1745
- Joseph sold into slavery 1728
- Joseph promoted in Egypt 1715
- famine 1707-1701, Jacob and his family move to Egypt 1706
- 1. pyramid built in Egypt about this time
- Sneferu (4. Dyn.)   Userkaf (5. Dyn.)
- Job's trial about this time
- Joseph dies 1635
- Amenemhat I (12. Dyn.) Ex 1:8 Teti (6.)
- Moses born 1571
- Pyramids built with mud bricks reinforced with straw; Ex 5:7
- Moses flees to Midian 1531
- Exodus 1491, Israelites leave Egypt
- conquest of Canaan begins 1451, EB III urban civilization starts to collapse
- Joshua dies 1424
- subjugation by Cushan-Rishathaim 1418

Mesopotamia & surrounding area site labels

- Ksar Akil Rockshelter
- El Khiam Rockshelter
- Jericho
- Ras Shamra / Ramad / Byblos
- 'Ain Ghazal
- Sha'ar Hagolan
- Troy
- Hallan Çemi
- Göbekli Tepe / Çatalhöyük / Mersin / Sakçagözü
- Mureybet
- Halula / Sabi Abyad
- Chagar Bazar
- Umm Qseir
- Brak
- Aqab
- Seker al-Aheimar
- Halaf
- Bouqras
- Yarim Tepe I & II
- Nemrik / Maghzaliyeh / Qermez Dere
- Baghouz
- Amuq A

SAMARRAN, HALAFIAN AND UBAIDIAN CULTURAL INFLUENCES IN NORTHWEST LEVANT

Amuq sequence letters: A B C D E F G H I J K

Columns: Arpachiyah Ha(E) / Nineveh 1 HS Sa / Hassuna 1a HS

Arpachiyah Ha(E)	Nineveh 1 HS Sa	Hassuna 1a HS
		a, b, c
	2a	2
	b	3
Ha(M) TT10		4
	c	5
Ha(L) TT7	Ha	6
		7
		8
		9
		10
Ub TT5	Ub	11 Ub
		12
TT4	3	13

Other sites

- Shanidar Cave
- Sawwan / Umm Dabaghiya / Mlefaat
- Matarrah / Shimshara
- Choga Mami / Karim Shehir / Jarmo
- Ali Kosh / Choga Safid
- Abada
- Banahilk
- Songor B
- **GREAT MIGRATION BEGINS**
- Tepe Gawra (level XX)
- Madhhur
- Susa

Oates 2012 / Roux 1992 columns

	Eridu	Oueili Ub 0	19
	Ub 1 20	1	11
	2 17	2	8
	3 13	3	
	4 7	4	

LC 1 2 3 4 5 (III)

URUK EXPANSION BEGINS

South Mesopotamian cultural periods

- UBAID
- URUK (early Sumerian)
- JEMDET NASR
- EARLY DYNASTIC
- DYNASTY OF AKKAD
- Gutians
- THIRD DYNASTY OF UR (late Sumerian)
- OLD BABYLONIAN PERIOD (Amorite rule)

Important developments

- painted pottery
- irrigation
- temples
- fortifications
- towns
- fast potter's wheel
- states
- metals common
- urbanism
- writing
- IMPORTANT MONUMENTS
- Royal Graves of Ur
- Stele of the Vultures
- Bronze Head of Sargon
- Victory Stele of Naram-Sin
- Great Ziggurat of Ur
- Code of Ur-Nammu
- Royal Archives of Ebla
- Story of Sinuhe
- proto-consonantal script
- IMPORTANT RULERS
- Shamshi-Adad
- Hammurabi
- Zimri-Lim
- Jabin of Hazor
- Samsu-iluna

Byblos / Levant notes (center column)

- Byblos EB III begins about this time
- Cross-Combed/Metallic ware in the Levant (see Cooper 2014, 280, 282 Fig. 20.2c, 283; Greenberg 2019, 55, 87-90; Vacca & D'Andrea 2020, 134, 135, 138)
- Byblos EB IV begins about this time
- Levantine Painted ware begins to appear about this time
- Byblos MB begins about this time
- A gift sent to Zimri-Lim by Yantin-Ammu/Intin of Byblos, a contemporary of Neferhotep I of Egypt (13. Dynasty)

Legend box

The location of the site name on the chart shows the approximate time when the site was established or first inhabited. The site that lies inside a small box was founded somewhere within that time frame.

Ha(E) = the early Halaf pottery phase began
Ha(M) = the middle Halaf pottery phase began
Ha(L) = the late Halaf pottery phase began
Ha = Halaf ware began to appear
Sa = Samarra ware began to appear
HS = Hassuna ware began to appear
Ub = Ubaid ware began to appear
(see also Chart 2)

PALEO = Palaeolithic period
PPN = Pre-Pottery Neolithic period
PN = Pottery Neolithic period
C = Chalcolithic period
EB = Early Bronze period
MB = Middle Bronze period
Amuq = Amuq pottery sequence
LC = (Greater Mesopotamian) Late Chalcolithic

From Flood to Fallen Kingdoms

CHART 2: COMPARATIVE STRATIGRAPHY OF TELL ARPACHIYAH, NINEVEH AND TELL HASSUNA

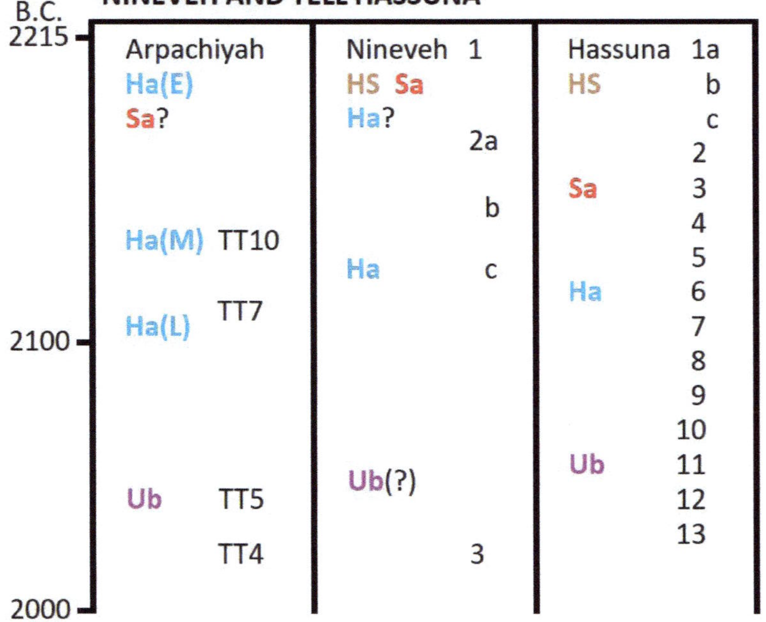

B.C.	Arpachiyah	Nineveh 1	Hassuna 1a
2215	Ha(E)	HS Sa	HS — b
	Sa?	Ha?	c
		2a	2
		b	Sa — 3
			4
	Ha(M) TT10	Ha — c	5
			Ha — 6
	Ha(L) TT7		7
2100			8
			9
			10
		Ub(?)	Ub — 11
	Ub TT5		12
			13
	TT4	3	
2000			

The stratigraphic correlations above are necessarily tentative but, in my opinion, close to the truth.

Ha(E) = the early Halaf pottery phase began

Ha(M) = the middle Halaf pottery phase began

Ha(L) = the late Halaf pottery phase began

Ha = Halaf ware began to appear

Sa = Samarra ware began to appear

HS = Hassuna ware began to appear

Ub = Ubaid ware began to appear

From Flood to Fallen Kingdoms

Commentary

Arpachiyah: The Halaf ware of Tell Arpachiyah is roughly divisible into three sequential phases — the early, the middle, and the late (see Perkins 1949, 16–21). The early Halaf pottery phase (Ha(E)) started at Arpachiyah soon after it was founded. The middle Halaf pottery phase (Ha(M)) began approximately in the level TT10 — a clear boundary between the early phase and the middle phase cannot be established (see Gut 1995, 194 note 479, 200–202). The level TT7 can be seen as a transition between the middle phase and the late phase (Ha(L)), some possible late Halaf ware already occurring there (see Perkins 1949, 38 note 243). The level TT5, in turn, shows a transition to the Ubaid cultural phase (Ub). Some pre-TT10 pottery types from Arpachiyah are comparable to certain Nineveh 1-ceramics (see Perkins 1949, 10; Gut 1995, 200). Some researchers have identified Samarran pottery (Sa) at Arpachiyah (e.g. Perkins 1949, 10). However, genuine/classic Samarra ware may not have been found really at all, and none of the alleged pieces were found in the earliest pre-TT10 levels. Further, the few possible Samarra-derived motifs on painted pottery at Arpachiyah may have begun to appear there only during the middle phase; see Gut 1995, 199, 200.

Nineveh: Samarran ware (Sa) occurred massively in the level 2b, but it appeared already in the levels 1 and 2a (Perkins 1949, 9; Gut 1995, 84, 89, 160). In the levels 1–2b were found also incised and painted wares that can be treated as Hassuna pottery (HS) (see Gut 1995, 79, 160). According to Renate Gut (1995, 203) real Hassuna pottery has not been found at Tell Arpachiyah. In the level 2c "Halaf pottery suddenly appears and from its beginning far outnumbers all other types" (Perkins 1949, 26; see also Gut 1995, 76). The majority of the Halaf ware (Ha) of Nineveh 2c is comparable to the early Halaf pottery of Arpachiyah, but there are also some pieces that show characteristics of the middle phase (see Perkins 1949, 26; Gut 1995, 202, 217). The disturbed context of the level 2c, however, makes the interpretation of its contents difficult. In terms of my view of the relative stratigraphy of Arpachiyah and Nineveh the "earliness" of the Halaf pottery of Nineveh 2c does not need to be seen as a problem. Early Halaf pottery forms could very well have lingered longer in Nineveh while at the same time pottery forms and decorative styles characteristic of the middle Halaf pottery phase already predominated at nearby Arpachiyah. It is totally possible to find "early" Halaf ware in later Halaf contexts, as the excavations at Banahilk and Tepe Gawra, for example, have demonstrated (see Watson 1983, 233, 234; see also Perkins 1949, 23; in support of the view that contemporary Halaf sites could sometimes have quite dissimilar pottery assemblages see the discussion of the great difficulties with the Halaf period ceramics in Gut 1995, 193 [in particular note 476], 194). Further, some sherds of Halaf ware were unearthed in Nineveh 1–2b (see Perkins 1949, 9; Gut 1995, 72, 73, 76, 202 note 503), which supports the view that the Halaf pottery tradition was as old as the Samarran and Hassunan traditions. Of course there is the possibility that those pieces were intrusive, that is to say, they belonged originally to the level 2c. Between the levels 2c and 3 — at the excavation spot on the mound of Küyünjik at Nineveh — there was a long occupation break (see Gut 1995, 52).

Hassuna: Classic Hassuna ware (HS) began to appear in the level 1b (Perkins 1949, 2; Gut 1995, 164). In the level 3 were unearthed a number of sherds of Samarran pottery (Sa) (Perkins 1949, 3; Gut 1995, 164), "distinctive in itself and clearly a luxury commodity imported from elsewhere, or copied locally" (Lloyd 1984, 77). The share of Samarra ware increased in the levels 4 and 5 and reached its maximum (nearly 15%) in the level 6 (Gut 1995, 164). Small percentages of Hassunan and Samarran potteries appeared still in the levels 7 and 8 and few pieces (intrusive?) even in the levels 10 and 11 (Gut 1995, 165). The Halaf ware (Ha) of Tell Hassuna, appearing there for the first time in the level 6 (Perkins 1949, 4; Gut 1995, 164, 165), corresponds to the middle and late Halaf pottery phases of Tell Arpachiyah (see Perkins 1949, 25, 26, 42, 43; Gut 1995, 203, 211). Ubaid ware (Ub) began to appear in the level 11. Ubaid cultural influence probably reached Hassuna before Nineveh and Arpachiyah. My view of the relative stratigraphy of Nineveh and Hassuna agrees well with that of Roger Matthews' (2000b, 69) for whom it seems that "levels 1–2a at Nineveh correlate with Hassuna levels Ia or Ib–II, and Nineveh 2b–2c correlate with Hassuna III–V". Ann Perkins (1949, 14) suggests with caution that "Ninevite 1 and 2a correspond to Hassunah Ib–III, while Ninevite 2b corresponds to Hassunah IV–V". She also seems to position Nineveh 2c, Hassuna 6 and Arpachiyah TT10–TT8 relatively close to each other (see Table 1 in Perkins 1949).

CHART 3: PALESTINE FROM THE CONQUEST OF THE LAND BY THE ISRAELITES UNTIL ALEXANDER THE GREAT

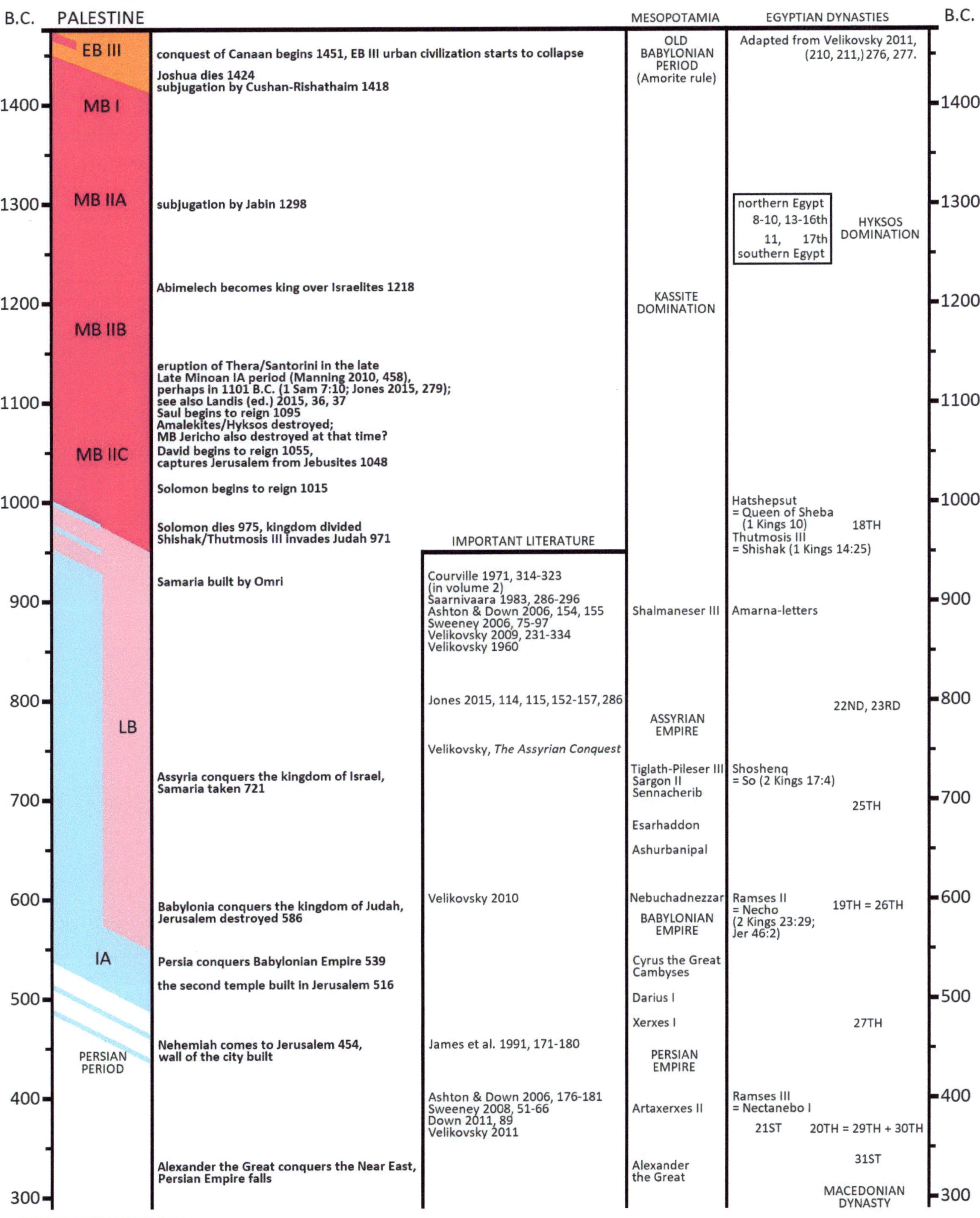

CHART 4: KINGS OF ISIN, LARSA AND BABYLON C. 1600-1480 B.C.

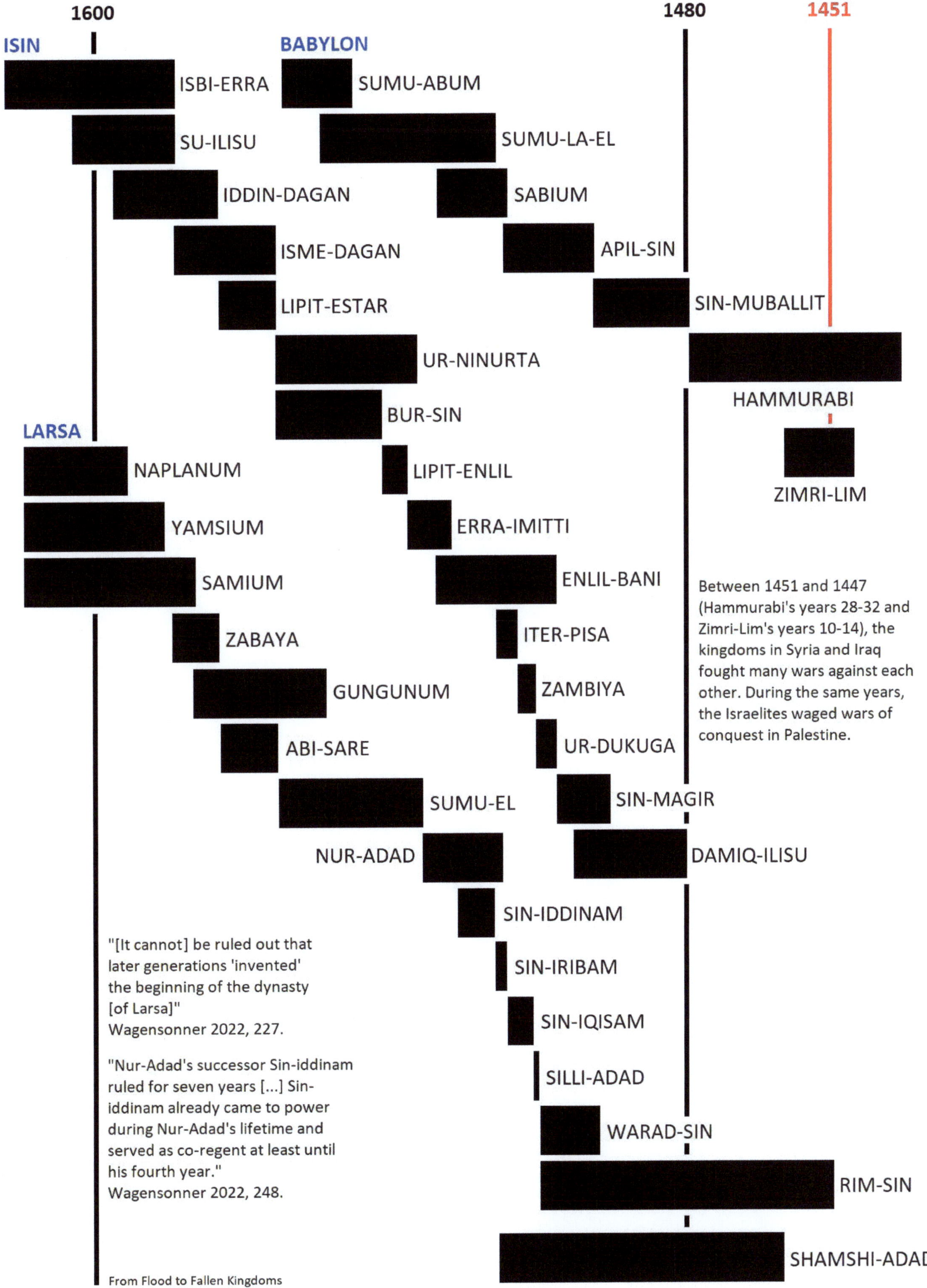